JUDGE DREDD

HEAVY METAL DREDD

JUDGE DREDD CREATED BY JOHN WAGNER & CARLOS EZQUERRA

JUDGE DREDD

HEAVY METAL DREDD

JOHN WAGNER ★ ALAN GRANT ★ JOHN SMITH ★ JIM ALEXANDER ★ DAVID BISHOP
Writers

SIMON BISLEY ★ JOHN HICKLENTON ★ DEAM ORMSTON ★ BRENDAN McCARTHY ★ COLIN MACNEIL
Artists

JOHN HICKLENTON ★ CLINT LANGLEY
Cover Artists

Creative Director and CEO: Jason Kingsley
Chief Technical Officer: Chris Kingsley
2000 AD Editor in Chief: Matt Smith
Graphic Novels Editor: Keith Richardson
Graphic Design: Simon Parr & Sam Gretton
Reprographics: Kathryn Symes
PR: Michael Molcher
Publishing Manager: Ben Smith
Original Commissioning Editors: David Bishop and John Tomlinson

Published by Rebellion, Riverside House, Osney Mead, Oxford OX2 0ES, UK.
www.rebellion.co.uk

ISBN: 978-1-905437-96-2
Printed in Malta by Gutenberg Press
Manufactured in the EU by LPPS Ltd., Wellingborough, NN8 3PJ, UK.
Second Printing: March 2014
10 9 8 7 6 5 4 3 2

Printed on FSC Accredited Paper

A CIP catalogue record for this book is available from the British Library.

For information on other *2000 AD* graphic novels, or if you have any comments on this book, please email books@2000ADonline.com

To find out more about *2000 AD*, visit www.2000ADonline.com

THE BIG HIT
Script: John Smith
Art: John Hicklenton
Colour: Keith Page
Letters: Tom Frame

Originally published in *Judge Dredd Megazine* 2.24

GRACELAND
Script: David Bishop
Art: John Hicklenton
Colour: Keith Page
Letters: Tom Frame

Originally published in *Judge Dredd Megazine* 2.25

MONKEY BEAT
Script: John Smith
Art: John Hicklenton
Colour: Keith Page
Letters: Tom Frame

Originally published in *Judge Dredd Megazine* 2.34-2.35

KISS OF DEATH
Script: Jim Alexander
Art: John Hicklenton
Colour: Keith Page
Letters: Tom Frame

Originally published in *Judge Dredd Megazine* 2.36

IRONFIST
Script: John Wagner and Alan Grant
Art: Simon Bisley
Letters: Tom Frame

Originally published in *Judge Dredd Megazine* 2.61

NIGHT BEFORE CHRISTMAS
Script: John Wagner and Alan Grant
Art: Simon Bisley
Letters: Tom Frame

Originally published in *Judge Dredd Megazine* 2.62

THE GREAT ARSOLI
Script: John Wagner and Alan Grant
Art: Simon Bisley
Letters: Tom Frame

Originally published in *Judge Dredd Megazine* 3.15

BIMBA
Script: John Wagner and Alan Grant
Art: Simon Bisley
Letters: Tom Frame

Originally published in *Judge Dredd Megazine* 3.17

THE BALLAD OF TOAD MACFARLANE
Script: John Wagner and Alan Grant
Art: Brendan McCarthy
Letters: Tom Frame

Originally published in *Judge Dredd Megazine* 3.35

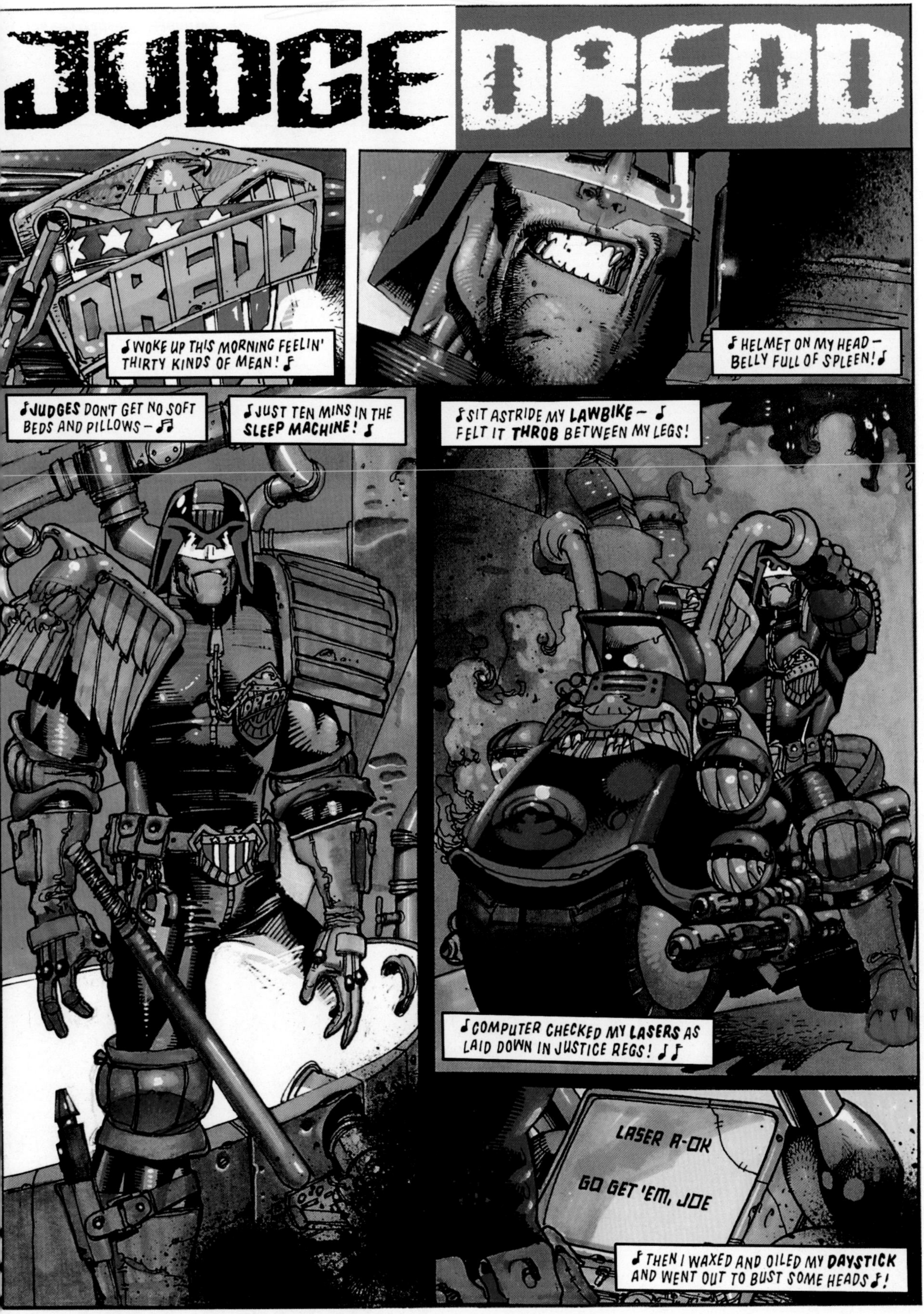
JUDGE DREDD
DREDD
WOKE UP THIS MORNING FEELIN' THIRTY KINDS OF MEAN!
HELMET ON MY HEAD — BELLY FULL OF SPLEEN!
JUDGES DON'T GET NO SOFT BEDS AND PILLOWS —
JUST TEN MINS IN THE SLEEP MACHINE!
DREDD
SIT ASTRIDE MY LAWBIKE — FELT IT THROB BETWEEN MY LEGS!
COMPUTER CHECKED MY LASERS AS LAID DOWN IN JUSTICE REGS!
LASER A-OK
GO GET 'EM, JOE
THEN I WAXED AND OILED MY DAYSTICK AND WENT OUT TO BUST SOME HEADS!

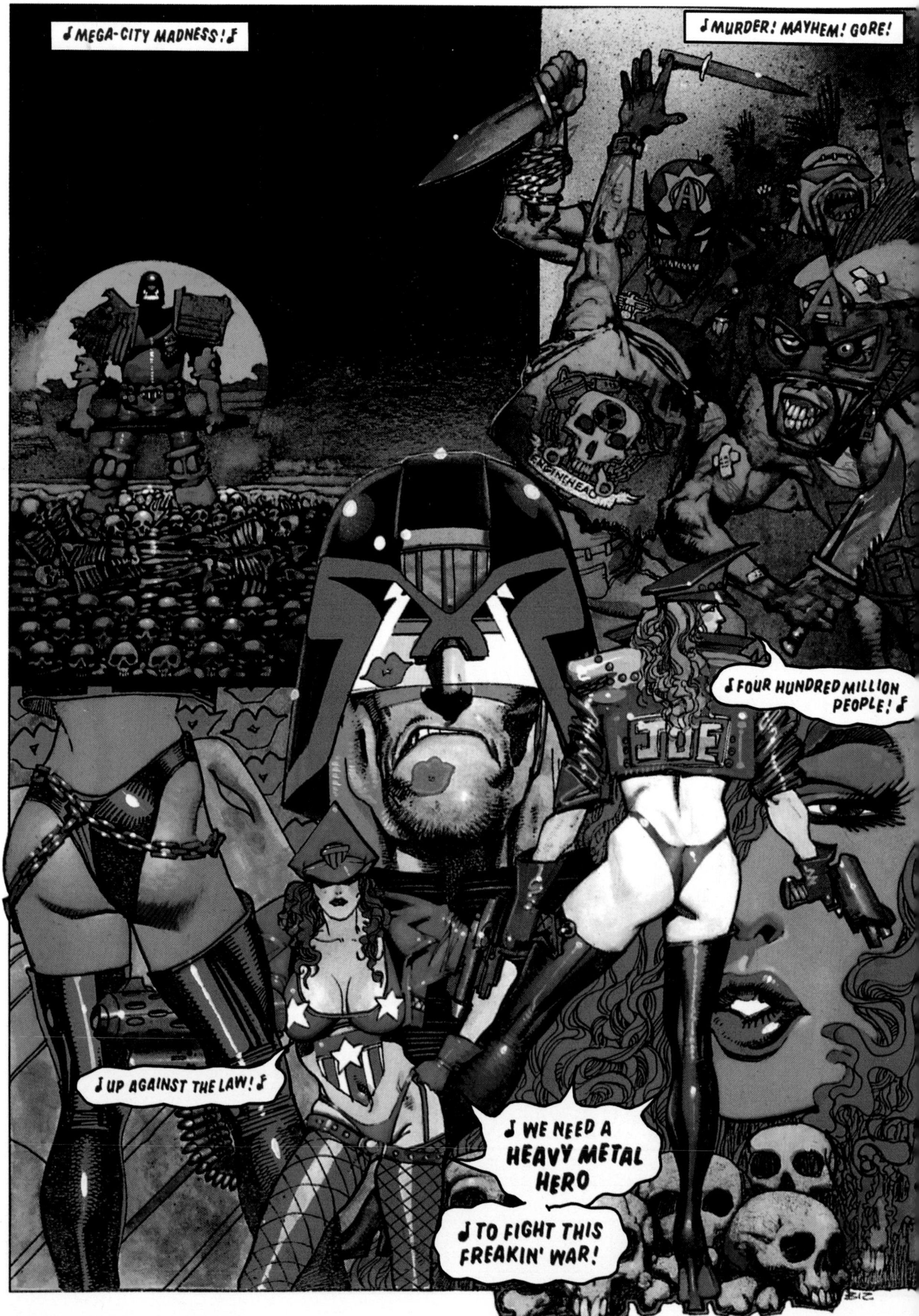
♪ MEGA-CITY MADNESS! ♪
♪ MURDER! MAYHEM! GORE!
♪ FOUR HUNDRED MILLION PEOPLE! ♪
♪ UP AGAINST THE LAW! ♪
♪ WE NEED A HEAVY METAL HERO
♪ TO FIGHT THIS FREAKIN' WAR!

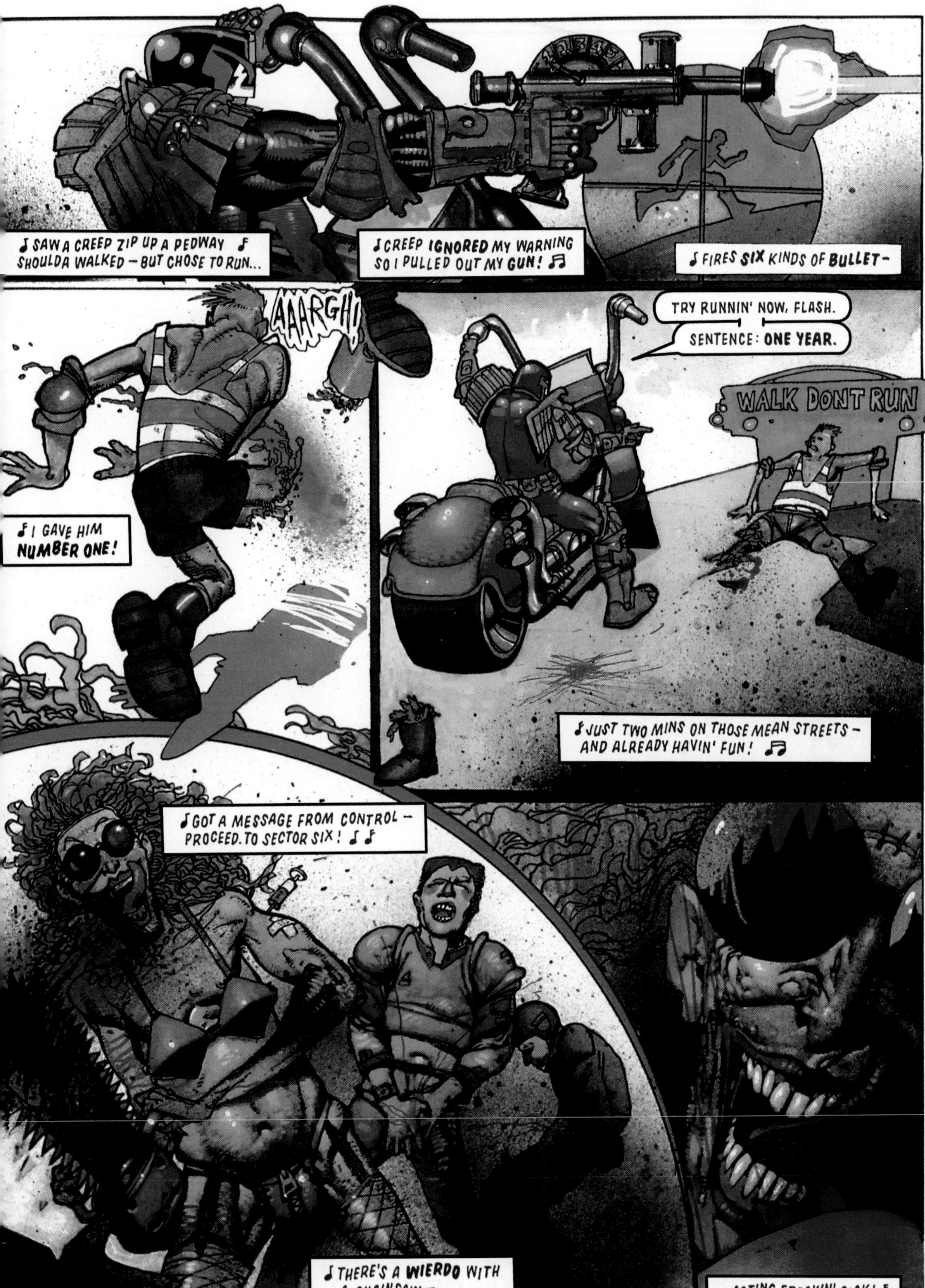
SAW A CREEP ZIP UP A PEDWAY SHOULDA WALKED — BUT CHOSE TO RUN...
CREEP IGNORED MY WARNING SO I PULLED OUT MY GUN!
FIRES SIX KINDS OF BULLET—
AAARGH!
I GAVE HIM NUMBER ONE!
TRY RUNNIN' NOW, FLASH.
SENTENCE: ONE YEAR.
WALK DONT RUN
JUST TWO MINS ON THOSE MEAN STREETS — AND ALREADY HAVIN' FUN!
GOT A MESSAGE FROM CONTROL — PROCEED TO SECTOR SIX!
THERE'S A WIERDO WITH A CHAINSAW—
—ACTING FREAKIN' SICK!

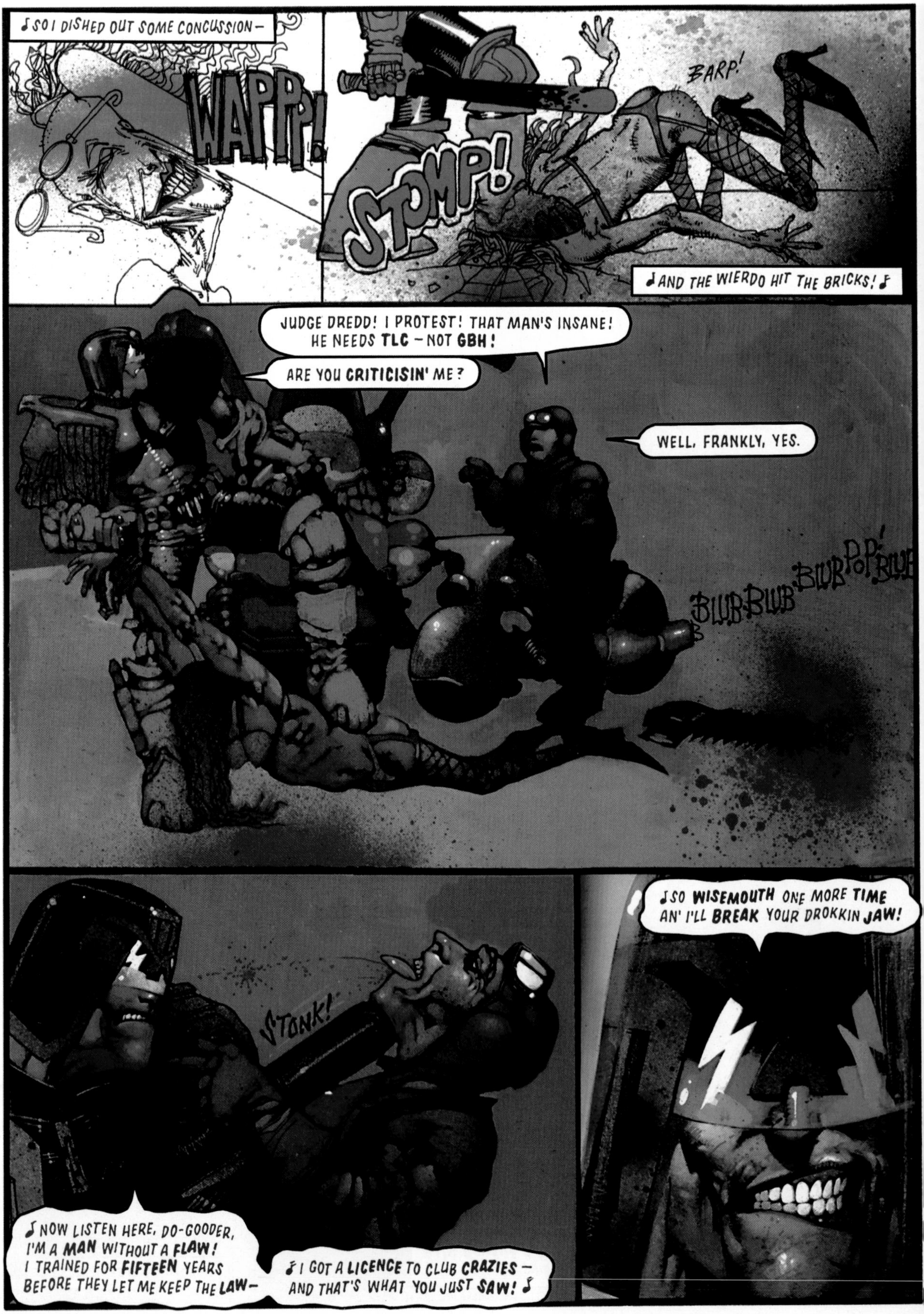
♪SO I DISHED OUT SOME CONCUSSION—
WAPPP!
STOMP!
BARP!
♪AND THE WIERDO HIT THE BRICKS!♪
JUDGE DREDD! I PROTEST! THAT MAN'S INSANE! HE NEEDS TLC — NOT GBH!
ARE YOU CRITICISIN' ME?
WELL, FRANKLY, YES.
BLUB BLUB BLUB POP! BLUB
STONK!
♪NOW LISTEN HERE, DO-GOODER, I'M A MAN WITHOUT A FLAW! I TRAINED FOR FIFTEEN YEARS BEFORE THEY LET ME KEEP THE LAW—
♪I GOT A LICENCE TO CLUB CRAZIES — AND THAT'S WHAT YOU JUST SAW!♪
♪SO WISEMOUTH ONE MORE TIME AN' I'LL BREAK YOUR DROKKIN JAW!

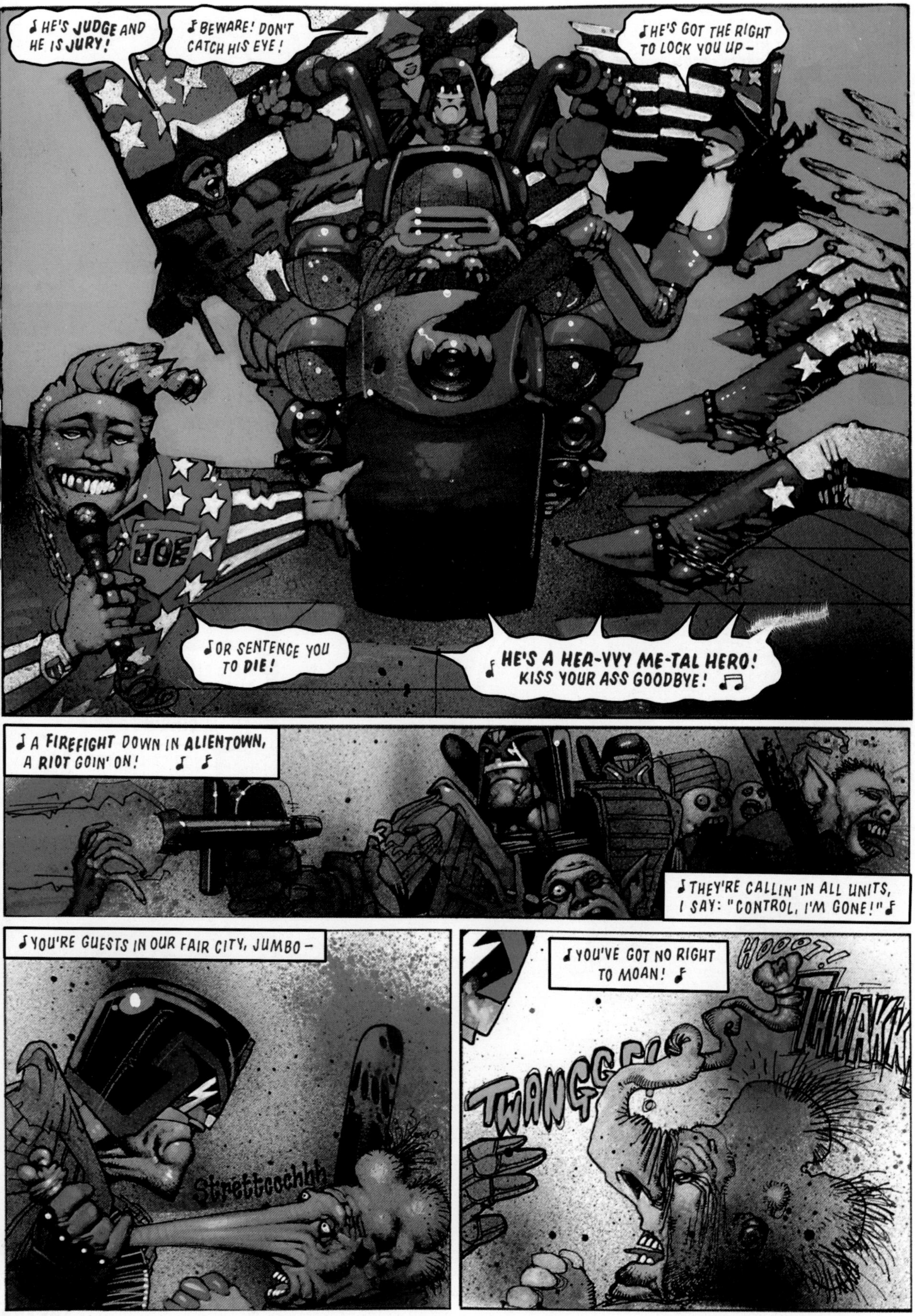
HE'S JUDGE AND HE IS JURY!
BEWARE! DON'T CATCH HIS EYE!
HE'S GOT THE RIGHT TO LOCK YOU UP –
JOE
OR SENTENCE YOU TO DIE!
HE'S A HEA-VVY ME-TAL HERO! KISS YOUR ASS GOODBYE!
A FIREFIGHT DOWN IN ALIENTOWN, A RIOT GOIN' ON!
THEY'RE CALLIN' IN ALL UNITS, I SAY: "CONTROL, I'M GONE!"
YOU'RE GUESTS IN OUR FAIR CITY, JUMBO –
Strettcchhh
YOU'VE GOT NO RIGHT TO MOAN!
HOOOT!
THWAKK
TWANGG

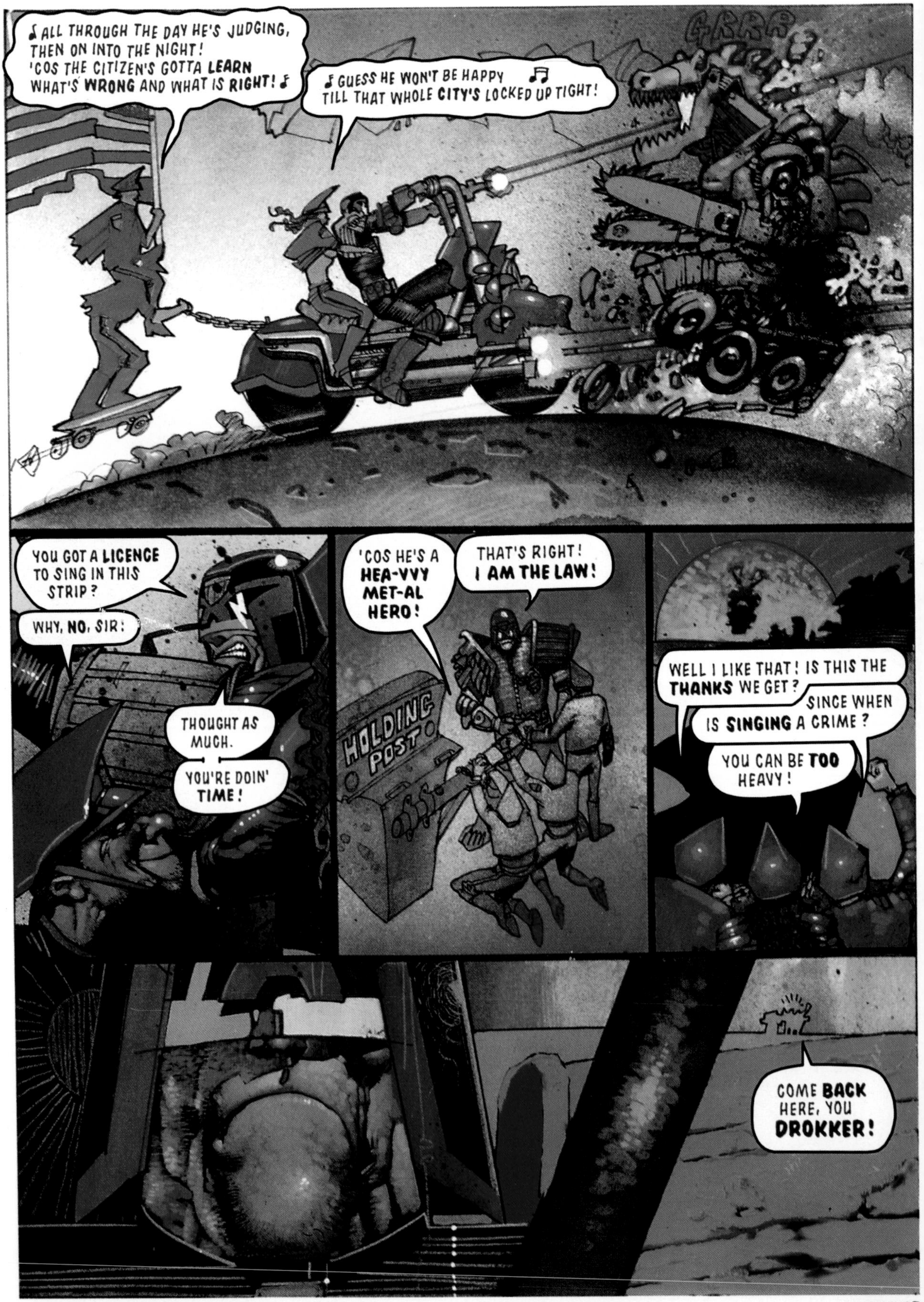
ALL THROUGH THE DAY HE'S JUDGING, THEN ON INTO THE NIGHT! 'COS THE CITIZEN'S GOTTA LEARN WHAT'S WRONG AND WHAT IS RIGHT!
GUESS HE WON'T BE HAPPY TILL THAT WHOLE CITY'S LOCKED UP TIGHT!
GRRR
YOU GOT A LICENCE TO SING IN THIS STRIP?
WHY, NO, SIR:
THOUGHT AS MUCH.
YOU'RE DOIN' TIME!
'COS HE'S A HEA-VVY MET-AL HERO!
THAT'S RIGHT! I AM THE LAW!
HOLDING POST
WELL I LIKE THAT! IS THIS THE THANKS WE GET?
SINCE WHEN IS SINGING A CRIME?
YOU CAN BE TOO HEAVY!
COME BACK HERE, YOU DROKKER!

THE END

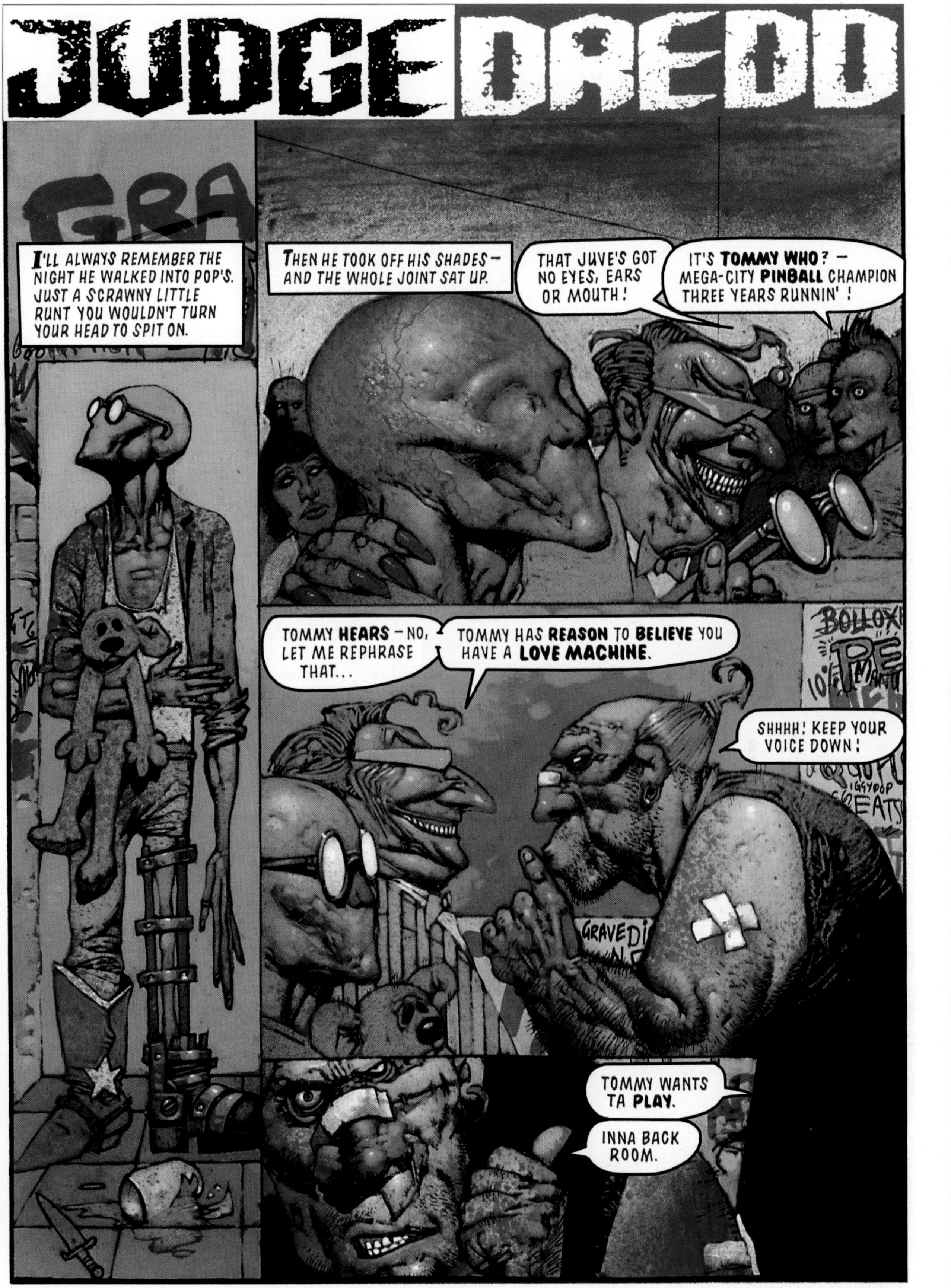
JUDGE DREDD
I'LL ALWAYS REMEMBER THE NIGHT HE WALKED INTO POP'S. JUST A SCRAWNY LITTLE RUNT YOU WOULDN'T TURN YOUR HEAD TO SPIT ON.
THEN HE TOOK OFF HIS SHADES — AND THE WHOLE JOINT SAT UP.
THAT JUVE'S GOT NO EYES, EARS OR MOUTH!
IT'S TOMMY WHO? — MEGA-CITY PINBALL CHAMPION THREE YEARS RUNNIN'!
TOMMY HEARS — NO, LET ME REPHRASE THAT...
TOMMY HAS REASON TO BELIEVE YOU HAVE A LOVE MACHINE.
SHHHH! KEEP YOUR VOICE DOWN!
TOMMY WANTS TA PLAY.
INNA BACK ROOM.

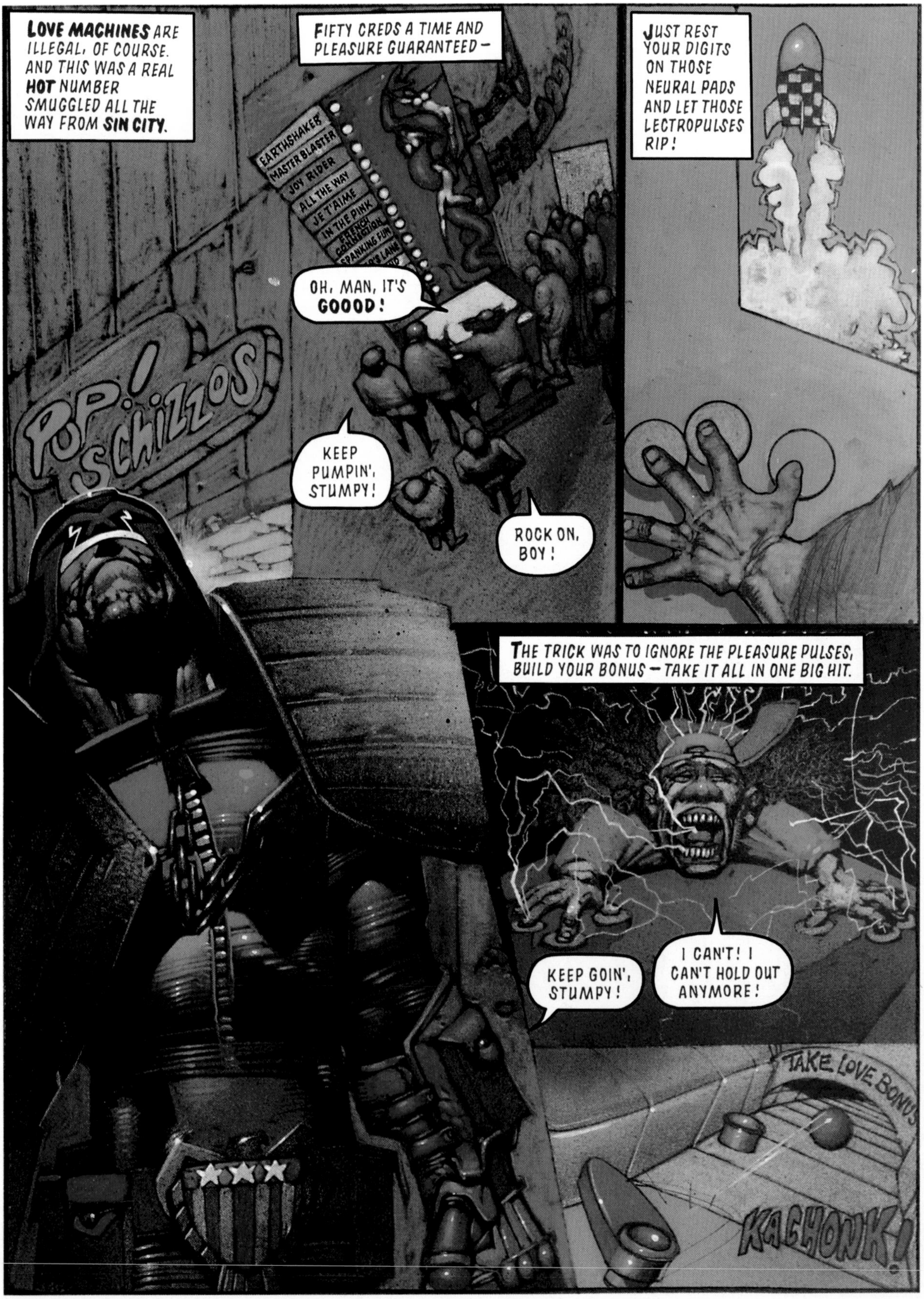
LOVE MACHINES ARE ILLEGAL, OF COURSE. AND THIS WAS A REAL HOT NUMBER SMUGGLED ALL THE WAY FROM SIN CITY.
POP! SCHIZZOS
FIFTY CREDS A TIME AND PLEASURE GUARANTEED—
EARTHSHAKER
MASTER BLASTER
JOY RIDER
ALL THE WAY
JE T'AIME
IN THE PINK
FRENCH CONNECTION
SPANKING FUN
OH, MAN, IT'S GOOOD!
KEEP PUMPIN', STUMPY!
ROCK ON, BOY!
JUST REST YOUR DIGITS ON THOSE NEURAL PADS AND LET THOSE LECTROPULSES RIP!
THE TRICK WAS TO IGNORE THE PLEASURE PULSES, BUILD YOUR BONUS—TAKE IT ALL IN ONE BIG HIT.
KEEP GOIN', STUMPY!
I CAN'T! I CAN'T HOLD OUT ANYMORE!
TAKE LOVE BONUS
KACHONK!

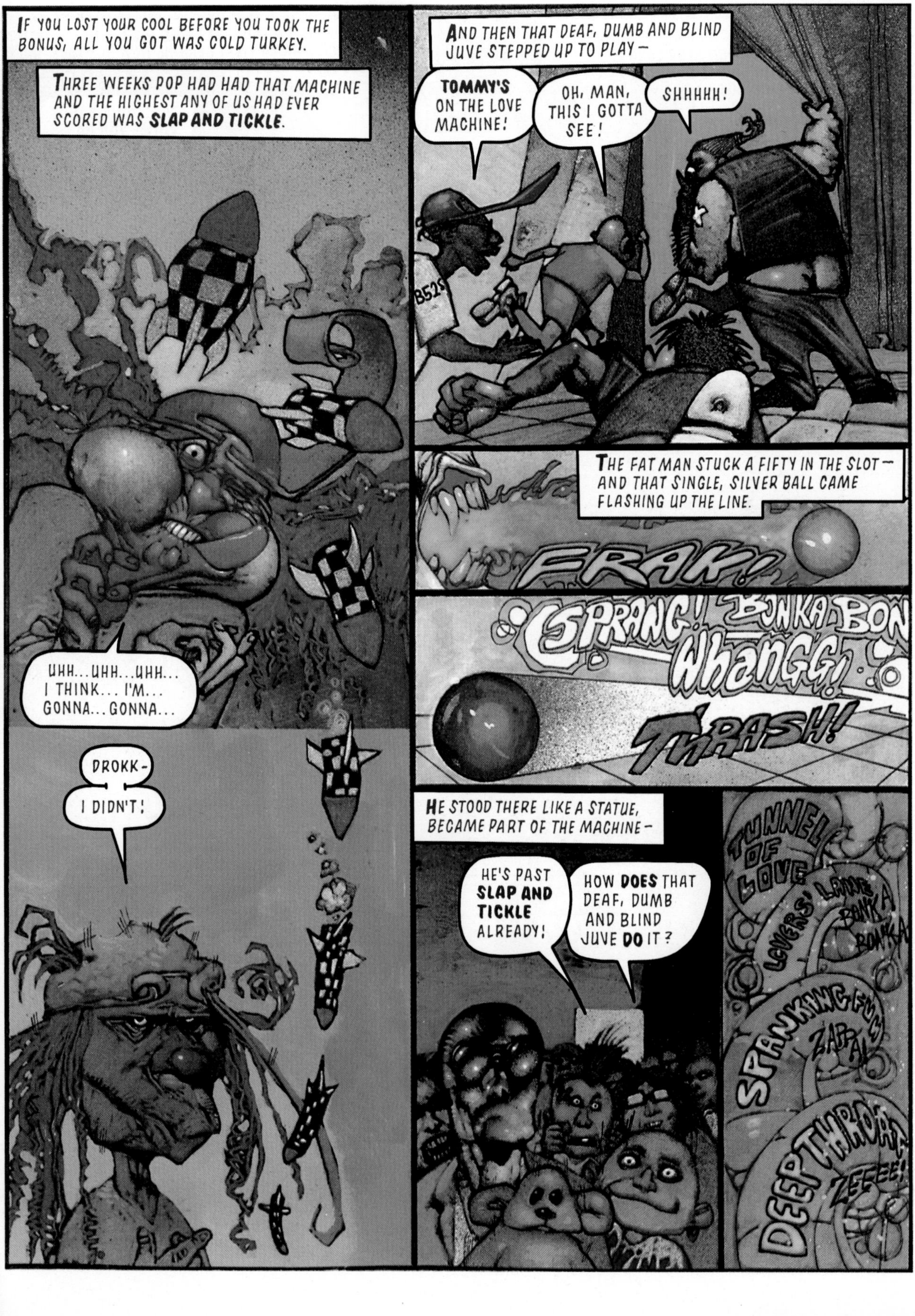
IF YOU LOST YOUR COOL BEFORE YOU TOOK THE BONUS, ALL YOU GOT WAS COLD TURKEY.
THREE WEEKS POP HAD HAD THAT MACHINE AND THE HIGHEST ANY OF US HAD EVER SCORED WAS **SLAP AND TICKLE**.
UHH... UHH... UHH... I THINK... I'M... GONNA... GONNA...
DROKK-
I DIDN'T!
AND THEN THAT DEAF, DUMB AND BLIND JUVE STEPPED UP TO PLAY—
TOMMY'S ON THE LOVE MACHINE!
OH, MAN, THIS I GOTTA SEE!
SHHHHH!
B52S
THE FAT MAN STUCK A FIFTY IN THE SLOT— AND THAT SINGLE, SILVER BALL CAME FLASHING UP THE LINE.
FRAK!
SPRANG! BONKA BON
WHANGG!
THRASH!
HE STOOD THERE LIKE A STATUE, BECAME PART OF THE MACHINE—
HE'S PAST **SLAP AND TICKLE** ALREADY!
HOW **DOES** THAT DEAF, DUMB AND BLIND JUVE **DO** IT?
TUNNEL OF LOVE
LOVERS' LANE
BONK A BONKA
ZAP A!
ZEEEE!

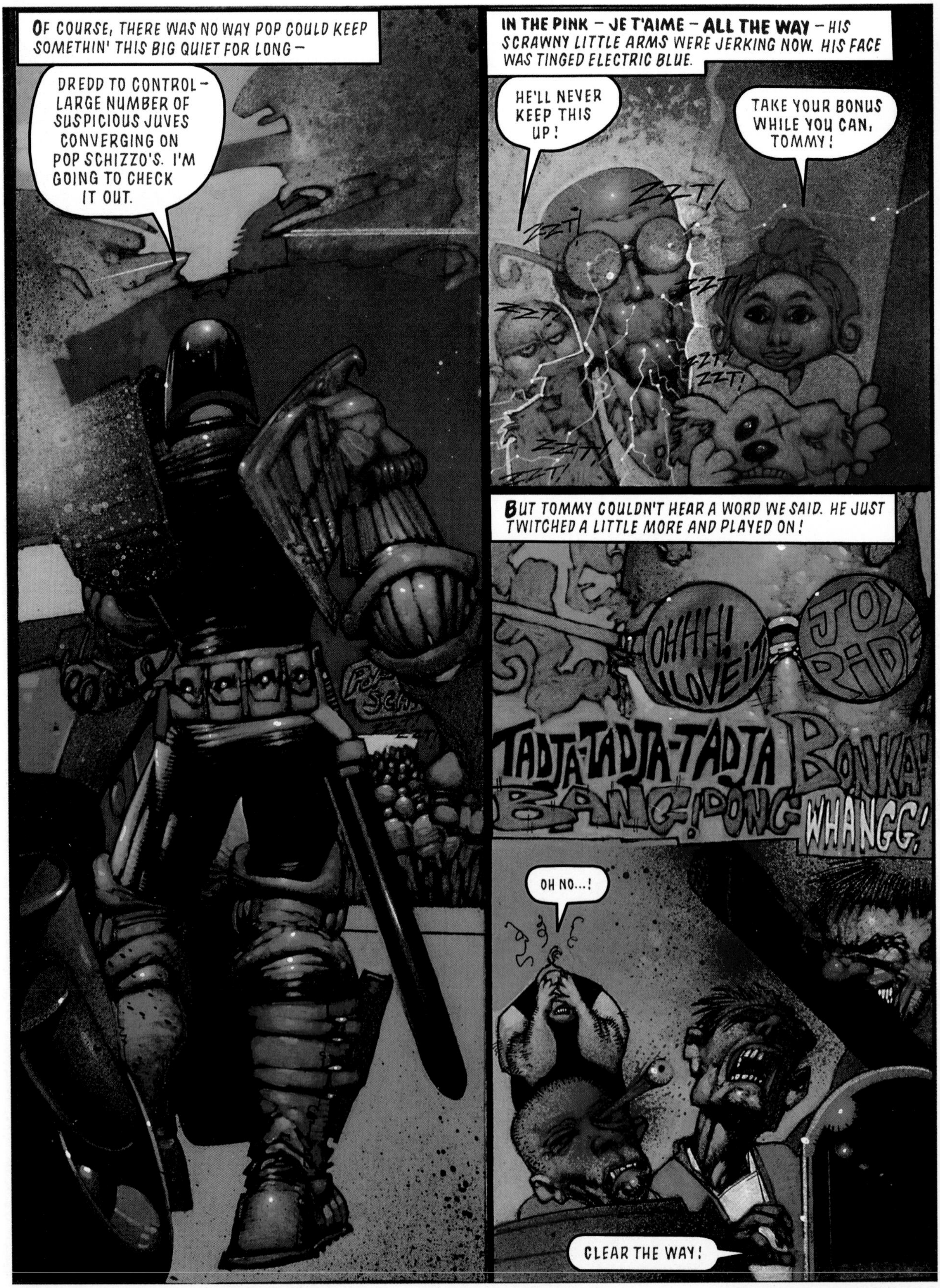
OF COURSE, THERE WAS NO WAY POP COULD KEEP SOMETHIN' THIS BIG QUIET FOR LONG –
DREDD TO CONTROL – LARGE NUMBER OF SUSPICIOUS JUVES CONVERGING ON POP SCHIZZO'S. I'M GOING TO CHECK IT OUT.
IN THE PINK – JE T'AIME – ALL THE WAY – HIS SCRAWNY LITTLE ARMS WERE JERKING NOW. HIS FACE WAS TINGED ELECTRIC BLUE.
HE'LL NEVER KEEP THIS UP!
TAKE YOUR BONUS WHILE YOU CAN, TOMMY!
ZZZT!
BUT TOMMY COULDN'T HEAR A WORD WE SAID. HE JUST TWITCHED A LITTLE MORE AND PLAYED ON!
OHHH! I LOVE IT!
JOY RIDE
TADJA-TADJA-TADJA BONKA!
BANG! DONG WHANGG!
OH NO...!
CLEAR THE WAY!

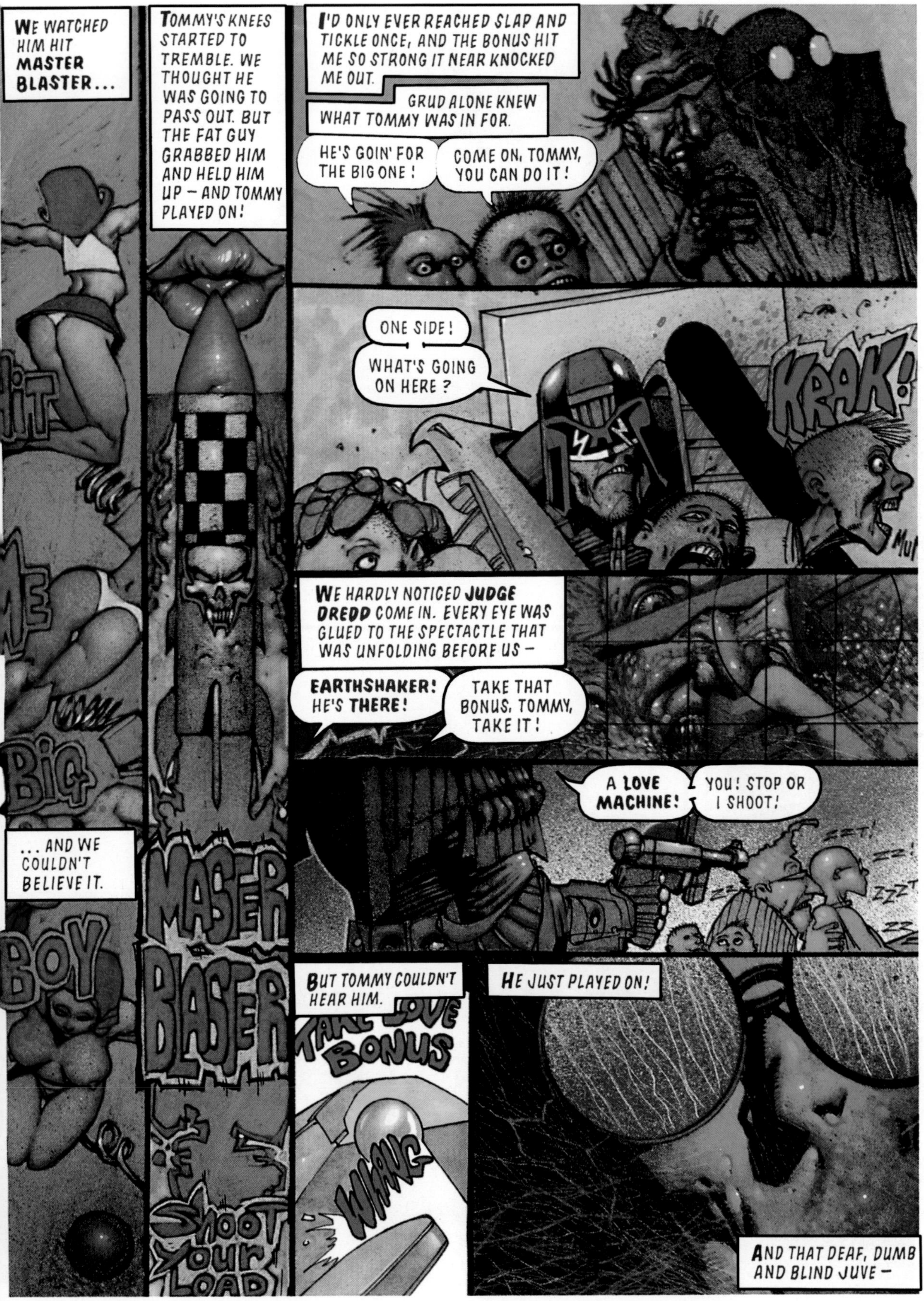
WE WATCHED HIM HIT MASTER BLASTER...
TOMMY'S KNEES STARTED TO TREMBLE. WE THOUGHT HE WAS GOING TO PASS OUT. BUT THE FAT GUY GRABBED HIM AND HELD HIM UP — AND TOMMY PLAYED ON!
I'D ONLY EVER REACHED SLAP AND TICKLE ONCE, AND THE BONUS HIT ME SO STRONG IT NEAR KNOCKED ME OUT.
GRUD ALONE KNEW WHAT TOMMY WAS IN FOR.
HE'S GOIN' FOR THE BIG ONE!
COME ON, TOMMY, YOU CAN DO IT!
ONE SIDE!
WHAT'S GOING ON HERE?
KRAK!
WE HARDLY NOTICED JUDGE DREDD COME IN. EVERY EYE WAS GLUED TO THE SPECTACLE THAT WAS UNFOLDING BEFORE US —
EARTHSHAKER! HE'S THERE!
TAKE THAT BONUS, TOMMY, TAKE IT!
A LOVE MACHINE!
YOU! STOP OR I SHOOT!
... AND WE COULDN'T BELIEVE IT.
BUT TOMMY COULDN'T HEAR HIM.
TAKE LOVE BONUS
WHANG
HE JUST PLAYED ON!
AND THAT DEAF, DUMB AND BLIND JUVE —

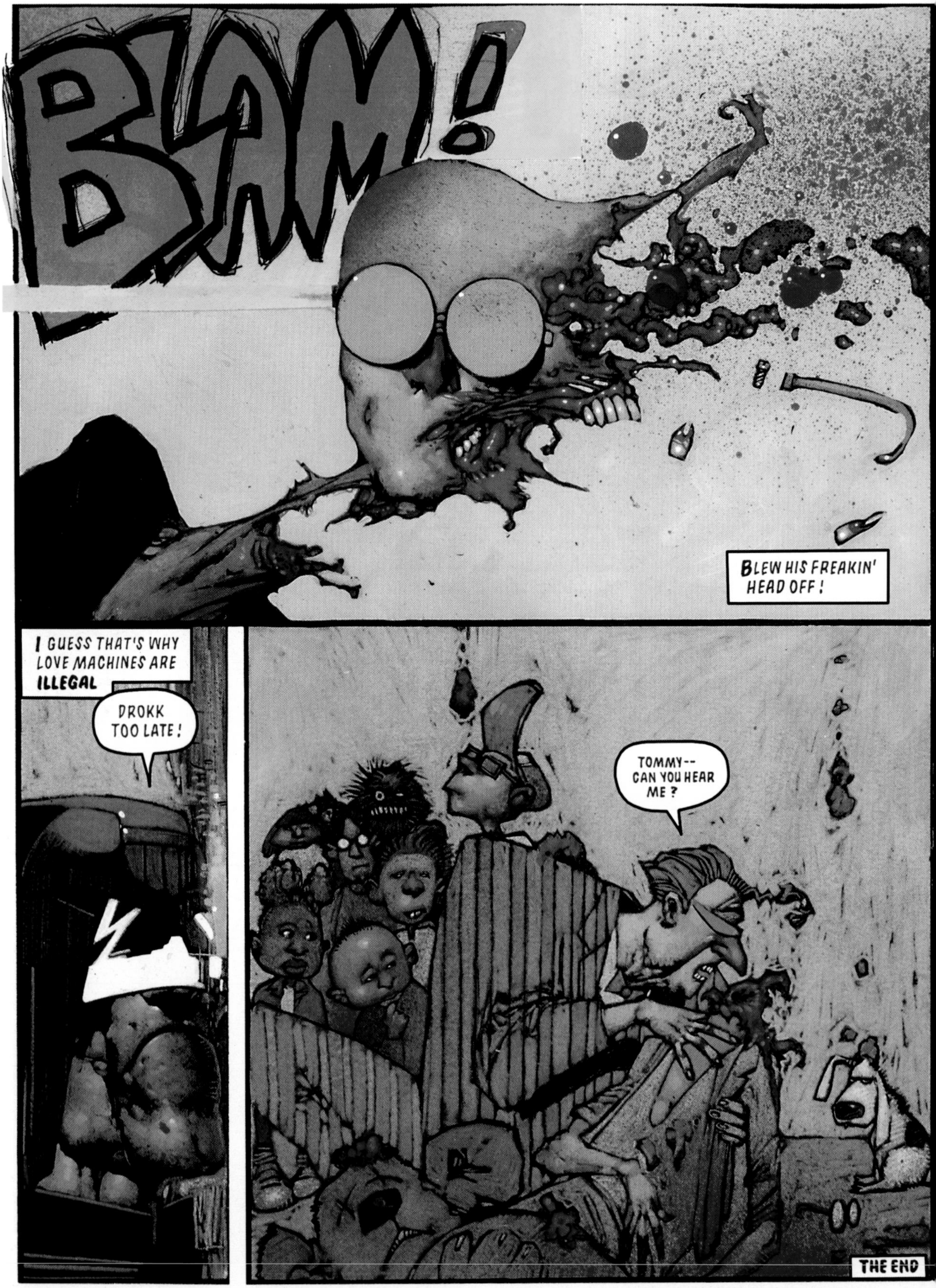
BLAM!
BLEW HIS FREAKIN' HEAD OFF!
I GUESS THAT'S WHY LOVE MACHINES ARE ILLEGAL
DROKK TOO LATE!
TOMMY-- CAN YOU HEAR ME?
THE END

JUDGE DREDD

THE GUYS IN THE GANG WERE BORED THAT DAY — AND WHEN THE GUYS ARE BORED IT USUALLY MEANS TROUBLE.

'COS WHEN THE GUYS ARE BORED THERE'S NOTHIN' THEY LIKE BETTER THAN BLANKIN' OUT THEIR COLOURS, GUNNIN' UP THEIR HOVERHAWGS —

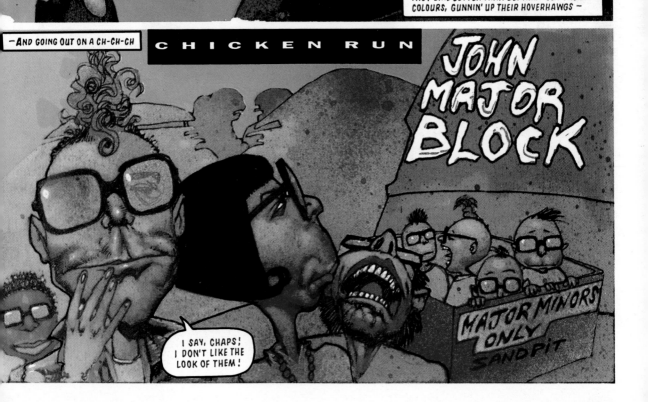

— AND GOING OUT ON A CH-CH-CH   CHICKEN RUN

JOHN MAJOR BLOCK

MAJOR MINORS ONLY SANDPIT

I SAY, CHAPS! I DON'T LIKE THE LOOK OF THEM!

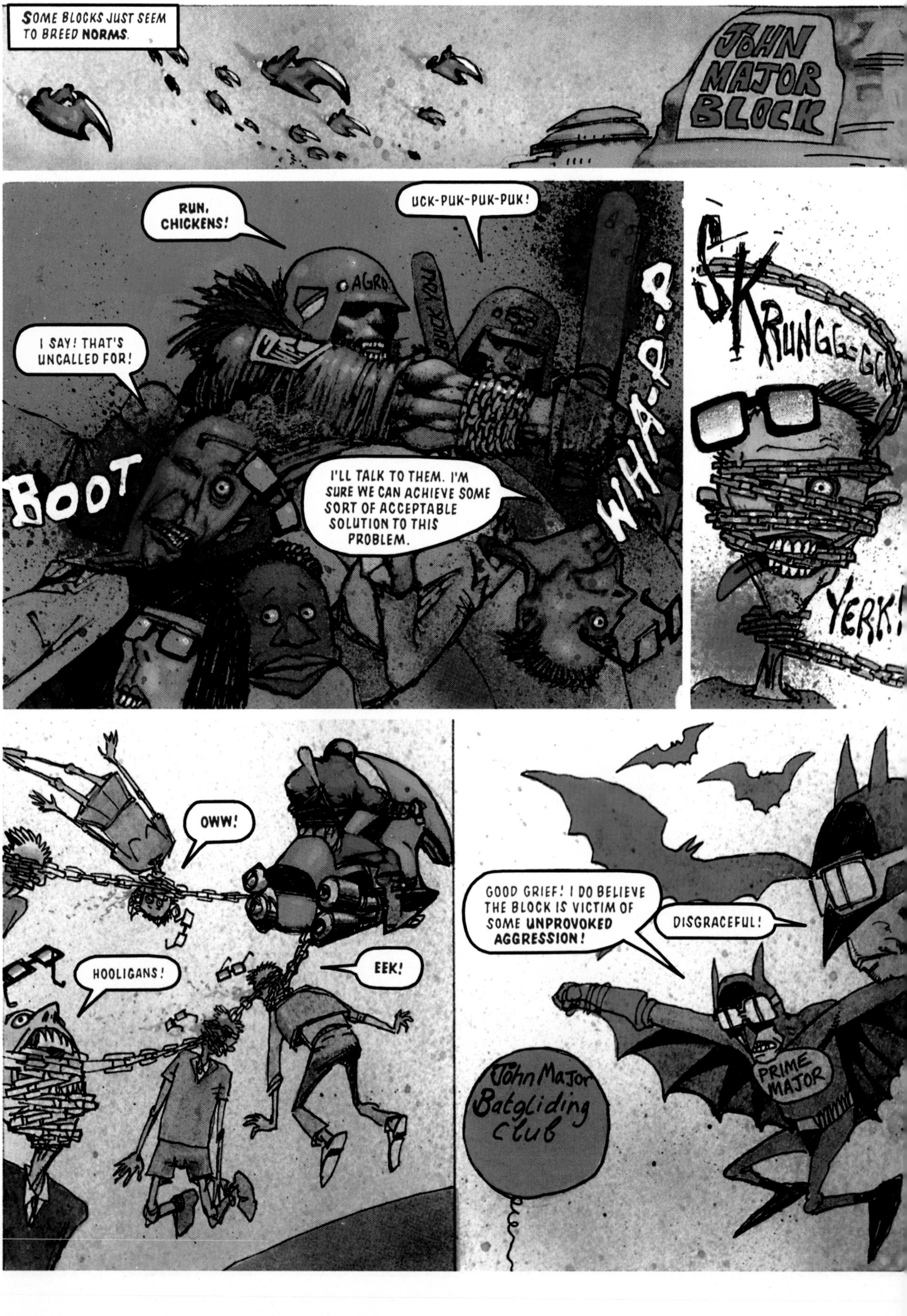
SOME BLOCKS JUST SEEM TO BREED **NORMS**.
JOHN MAJOR BLOCK
RUN, CHICKENS!
UCK-PUK-PUK-PUK!
I SAY! THAT'S UNCALLED FOR!
BOOT
I'LL TALK TO THEM. I'M SURE WE CAN ACHIEVE SOME SORT OF ACCEPTABLE SOLUTION TO THIS PROBLEM.
SKRUNGG-GG
YERK!
OWW!
HOOLIGANS!
EEK!
GOOD GRIEF! I DO BELIEVE THE BLOCK IS VICTIM OF SOME **UNPROVOKED AGGRESSION**!
DISGRACEFUL!
John Major Batgliding Club
PRIME MAJOR

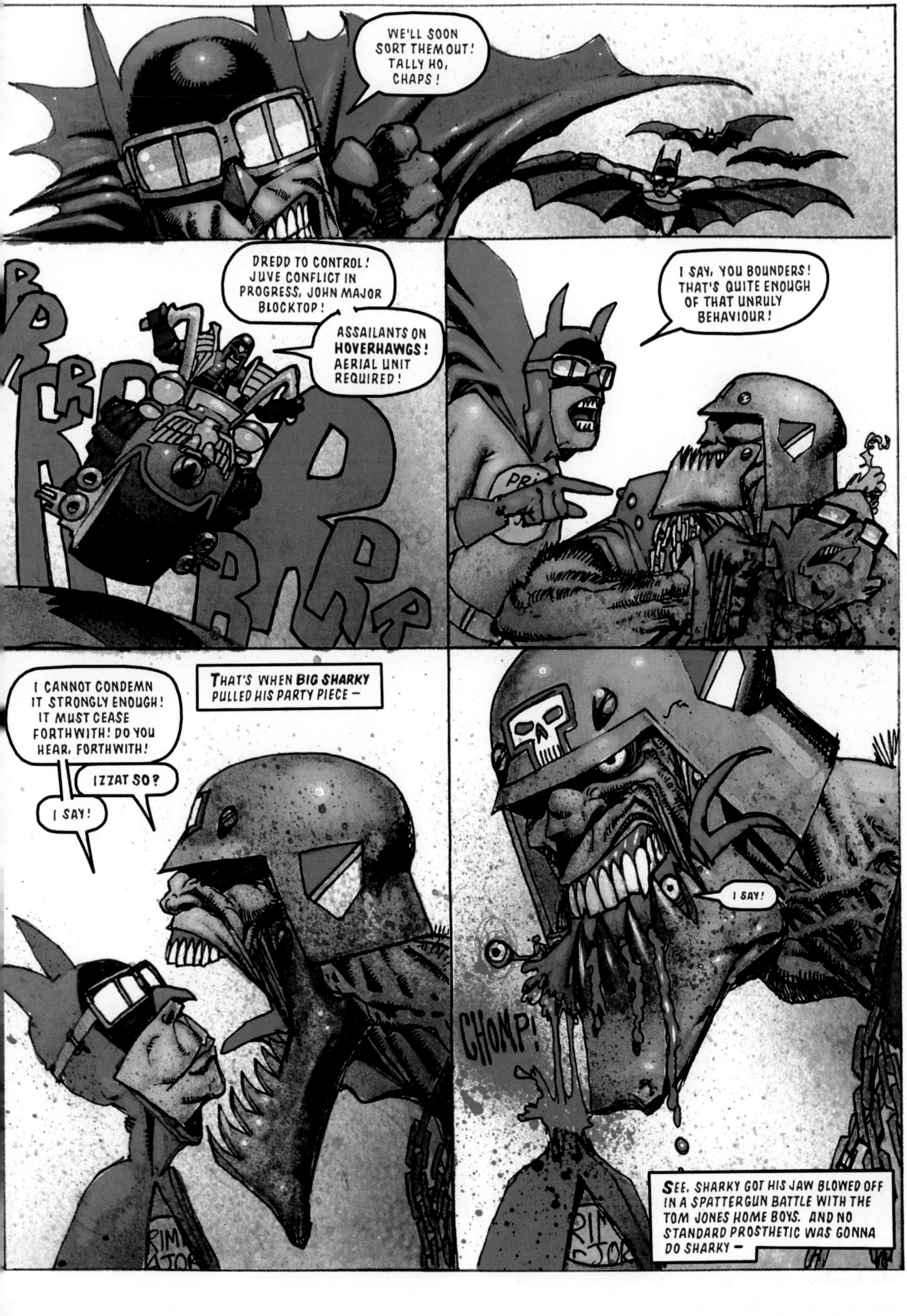

WE'LL SOON SORT THEM OUT! TALLY HO, CHAPS!
DREDD TO CONTROL! JUVE CONFLICT IN PROGRESS, JOHN MAJOR BLOCKTOP!
ASSAILANTS ON HOVERHAWGS! AERIAL UNIT REQUIRED!
RRRRRRRR
I SAY, YOU BOUNDERS! THAT'S QUITE ENOUGH OF THAT UNRULY BEHAVIOUR!
I CANNOT CONDEMN IT STRONGLY ENOUGH! IT MUST CEASE FORTHWITH! DO YOU HEAR, FORTHWITH!
THAT'S WHEN BIG SHARKY PULLED HIS PARTY PIECE —
IZZAT SO?
I SAY!
I SAY!
CHOMP!
SEE, SHARKY GOT HIS JAW BLOWED OFF IN A SPATTERGUN BATTLE WITH THE TOM JONES HOME BOYS. AND NO STANDARD PROSTHETIC WAS GONNA DO SHARKY —

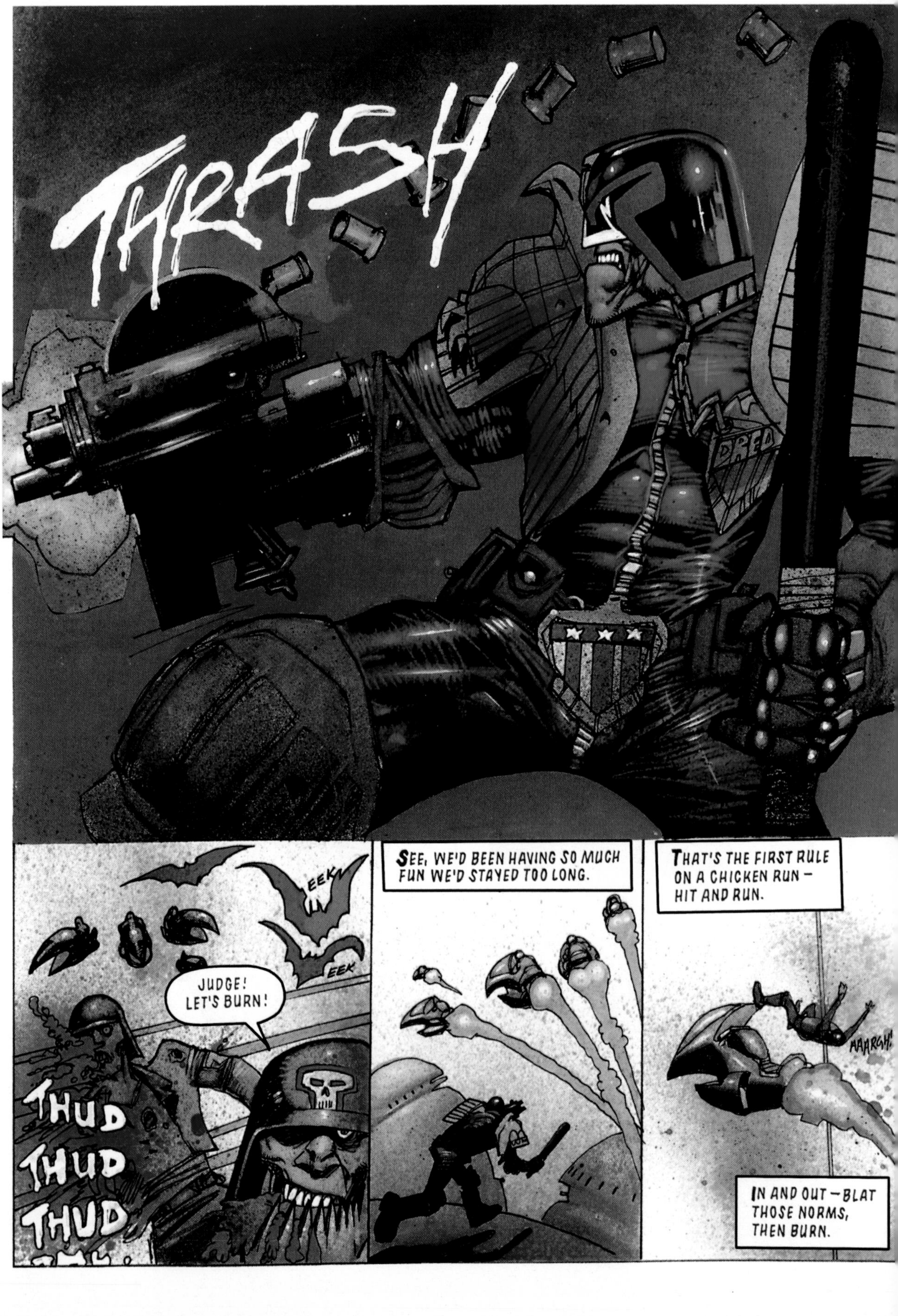
THRASH
EEK
EEK
JUDGE! LET'S BURN!
THUD
THUD
THUD
SEE, WE'D BEEN HAVING SO MUCH FUN WE'D STAYED TOO LONG.
THAT'S THE FIRST RULE ON A CHICKEN RUN — HIT AND RUN.
IN AND OUT — BLAT THOSE NORMS, THEN BURN.

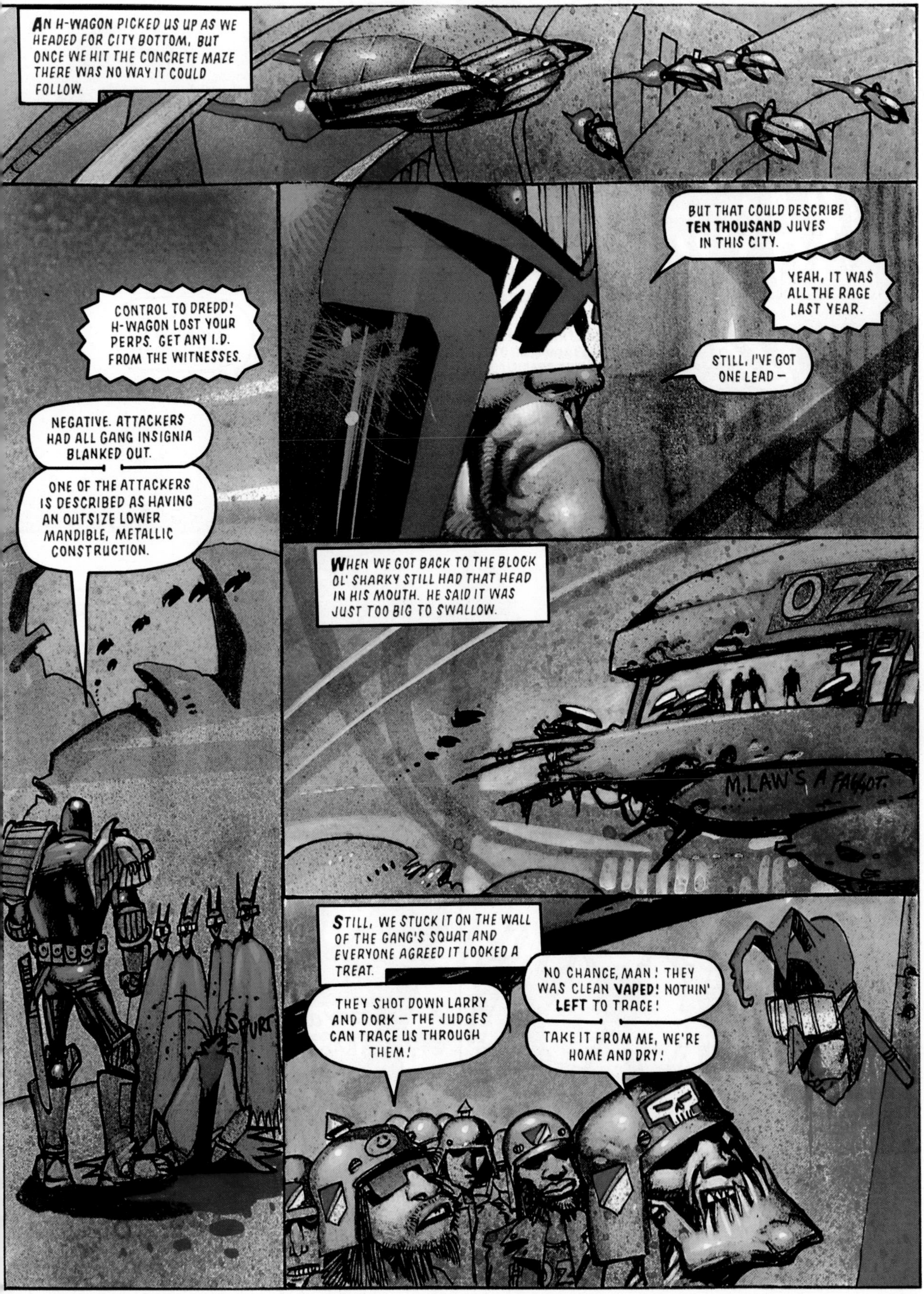
AN H-WAGON PICKED US UP AS WE HEADED FOR CITY BOTTOM, BUT ONCE WE HIT THE CONCRETE MAZE THERE WAS NO WAY IT COULD FOLLOW.
CONTROL TO DREDD! H-WAGON LOST YOUR PERPS. GET ANY I.D. FROM THE WITNESSES.
NEGATIVE. ATTACKERS HAD ALL GANG INSIGNIA BLANKED OUT.
ONE OF THE ATTACKERS IS DESCRIBED AS HAVING AN OUTSIZE LOWER MANDIBLE, METALLIC CONSTRUCTION.
SPURT
BUT THAT COULD DESCRIBE TEN THOUSAND JUVES IN THIS CITY.
YEAH, IT WAS ALL THE RAGE LAST YEAR.
STILL, I'VE GOT ONE LEAD —
WHEN WE GOT BACK TO THE BLOCK OL' SHARKY STILL HAD THAT HEAD IN HIS MOUTH. HE SAID IT WAS JUST TOO BIG TO SWALLOW.
OZZ
M.LAW'S A FAGGOT.
STILL, WE STUCK IT ON THE WALL OF THE GANG'S SQUAT AND EVERYONE AGREED IT LOOKED A TREAT.
THEY SHOT DOWN LARRY AND DORK — THE JUDGES CAN TRACE US THROUGH THEM!
NO CHANCE, MAN! THEY WAS CLEAN VAPED! NOTHIN' LEFT TO TRACE!
TAKE IT FROM ME, WE'RE HOME AND DRY!

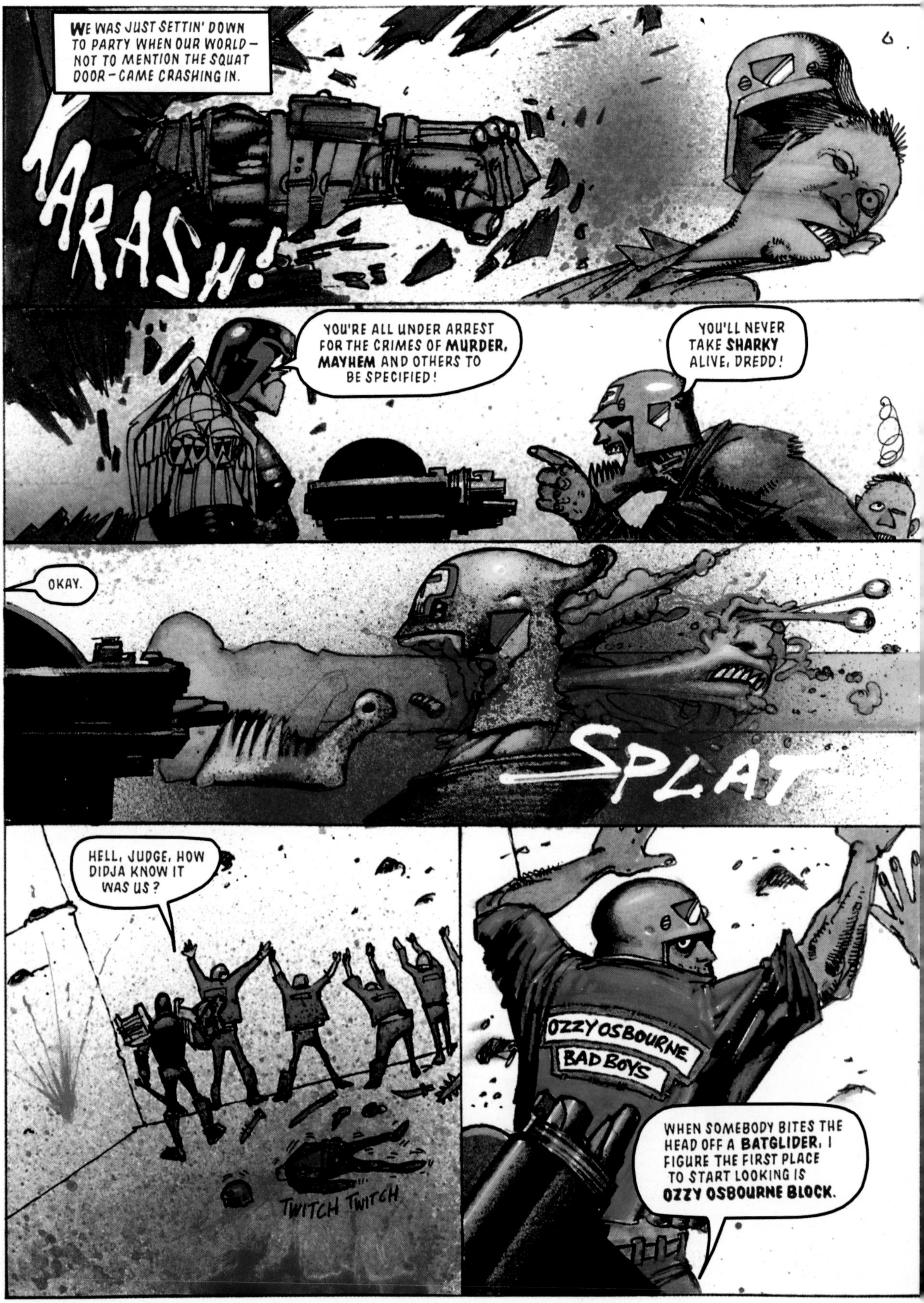
WE WAS JUST SETTIN' DOWN TO PARTY WHEN OUR WORLD — NOT TO MENTION THE SQUAT DOOR — CAME CRASHING IN.
KARASH!
YOU'RE ALL UNDER ARREST FOR THE CRIMES OF MURDER, MAYHEM AND OTHERS TO BE SPECIFIED!
YOU'LL NEVER TAKE SHARKY ALIVE, DREDD!
OKAY.
SPLAT
HELL, JUDGE, HOW DIDJA KNOW IT WAS US?
TWITCH TWITCH
OZZY OSBOURNE
BAD BOYS
WHEN SOMEBODY BITES THE HEAD OFF A BATGLIDER, I FIGURE THE FIRST PLACE TO START LOOKING IS OZZY OSBOURNE BLOCK.

THE END

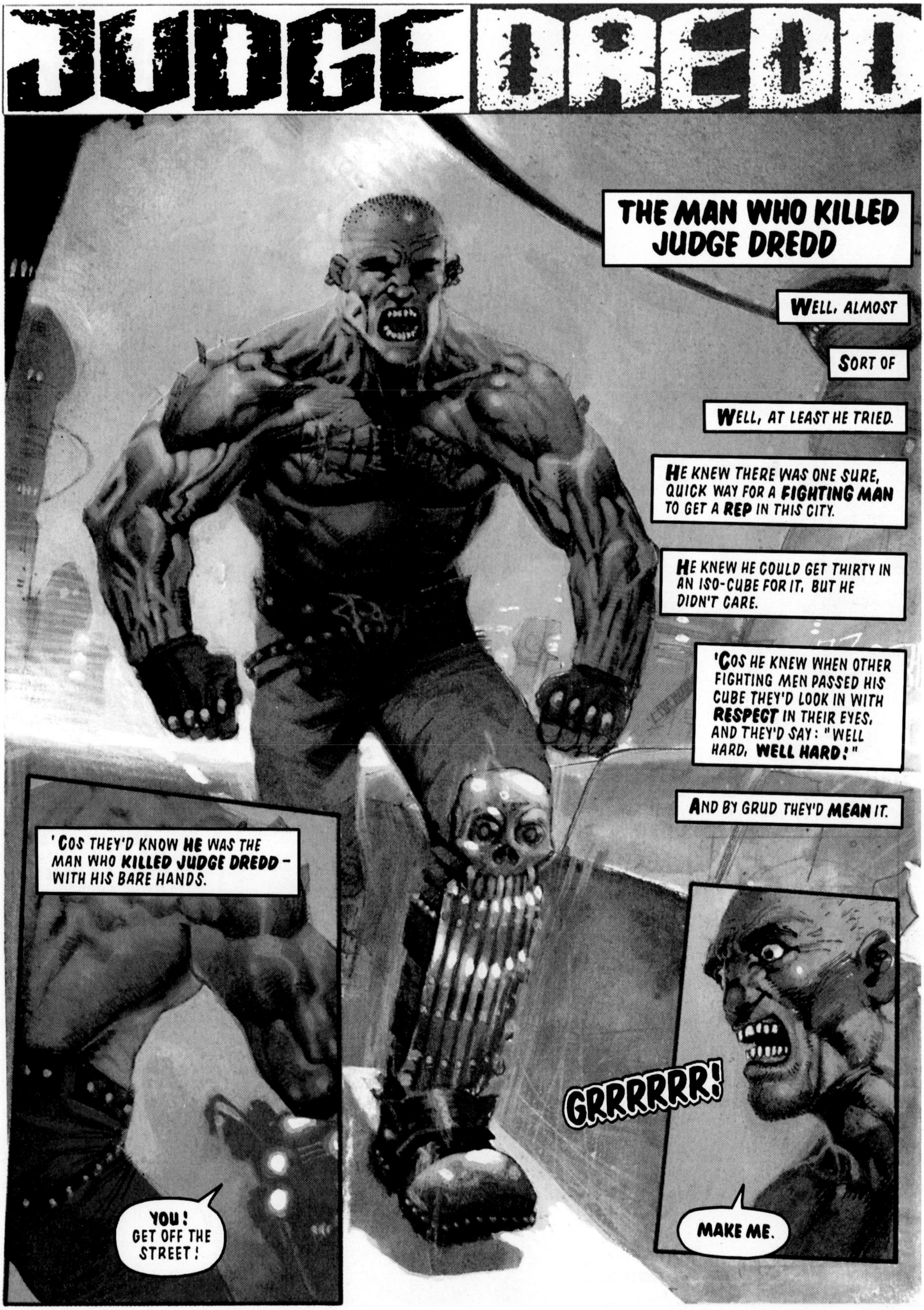
JUDGE DREDD
THE MAN WHO KILLED JUDGE DREDD
WELL, ALMOST
SORT OF
WELL, AT LEAST HE TRIED.
HE KNEW THERE WAS ONE SURE, QUICK WAY FOR A FIGHTING MAN TO GET A REP IN THIS CITY.
HE KNEW HE COULD GET THIRTY IN AN ISO-CUBE FOR IT, BUT HE DIDN'T CARE.
'COS HE KNEW WHEN OTHER FIGHTING MEN PASSED HIS CUBE THEY'D LOOK IN WITH RESPECT IN THEIR EYES, AND THEY'D SAY: "WELL HARD, WELL HARD!"
AND BY GRUD THEY'D MEAN IT.
'COS THEY'D KNOW HE WAS THE MAN WHO KILLED JUDGE DREDD – WITH HIS BARE HANDS.
YOU! GET OFF THE STREET!
GRRRRRR!
MAKE ME.

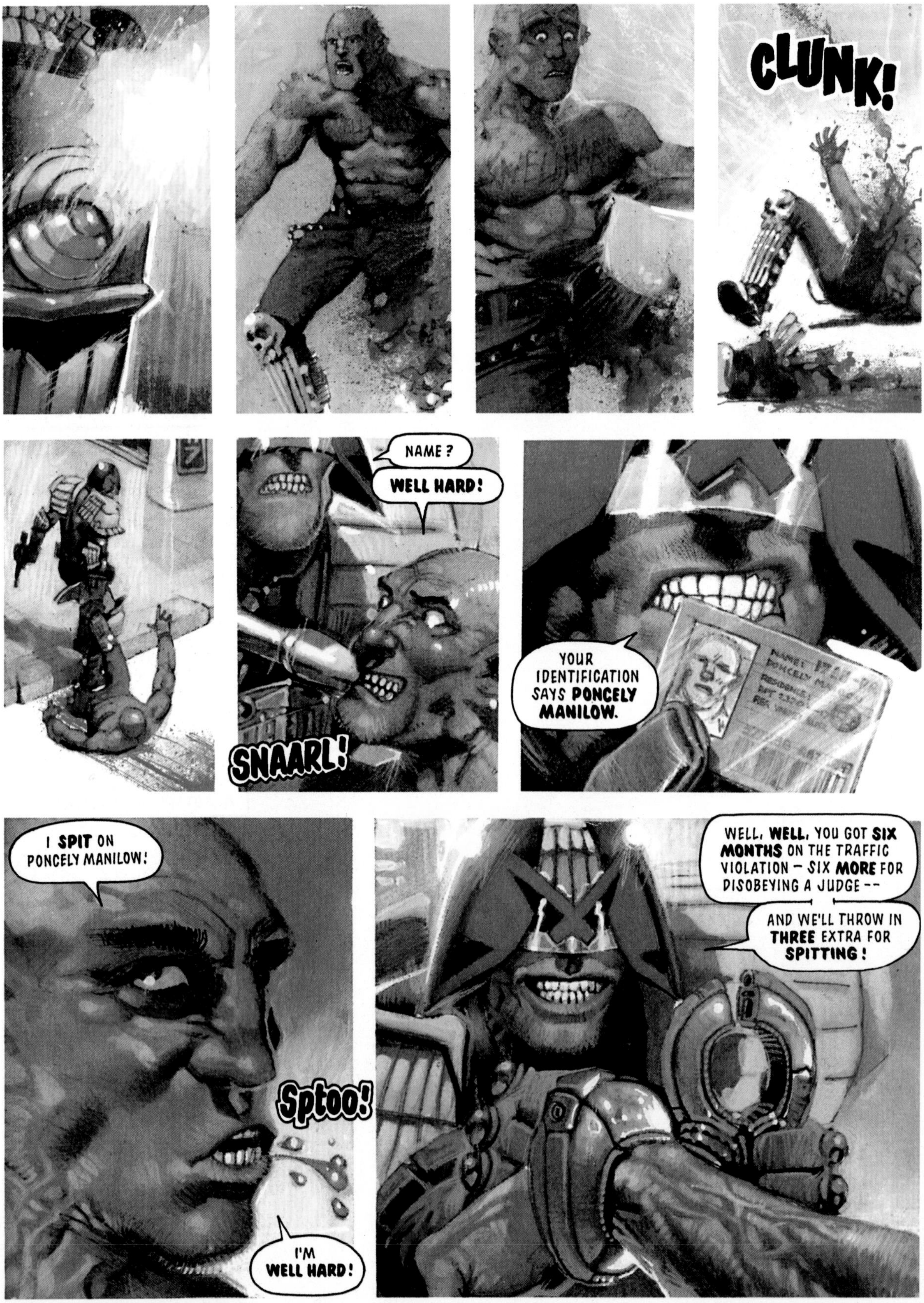
CLUNK!
NAME?
WELL HARD!
SNAARL!
YOUR IDENTIFICATION SAYS PONCELY MANILOW.
I SPIT ON PONCELY MANILOW!
Sptoo!
I'M WELL HARD!
WELL, WELL, YOU GOT SIX MONTHS ON THE TRAFFIC VIOLATION — SIX MORE FOR DISOBEYING A JUDGE --
AND WE'LL THROW IN THREE EXTRA FOR SPITTING!

WELL. ALMOST

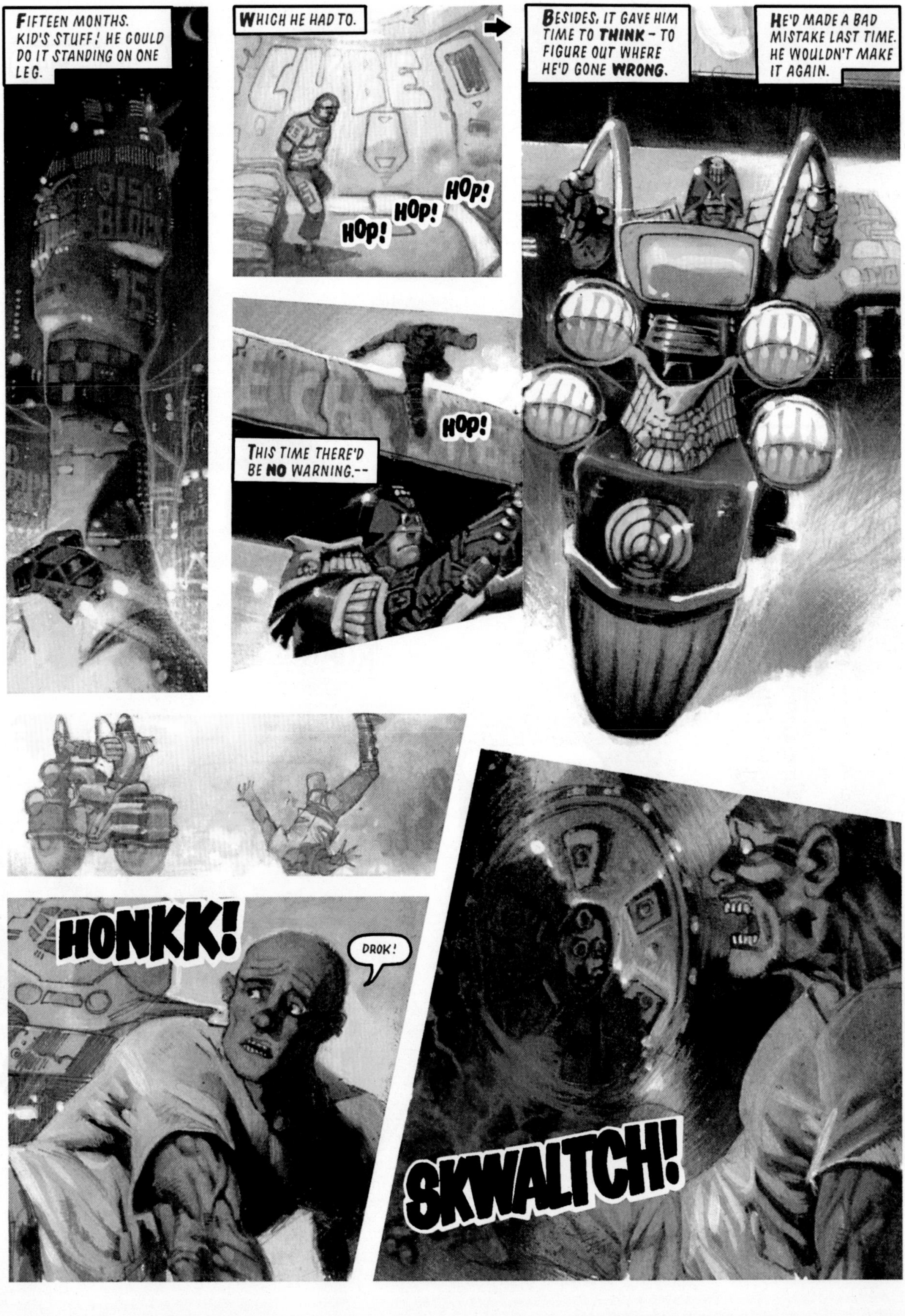
FIFTEEN MONTHS. KID'S STUFF! HE COULD DO IT STANDING ON ONE LEG.
WHICH HE HAD TO.
HOP!
HOP!
HOP!
HOP!
THIS TIME THERE'D BE NO WARNING.--
BESIDES, IT GAVE HIM TIME TO THINK - TO FIGURE OUT WHERE HE'D GONE WRONG.
HE'D MADE A BAD MISTAKE LAST TIME. HE WOULDN'T MAKE IT AGAIN.
HONKK!
DROK!
SKWALTCH!

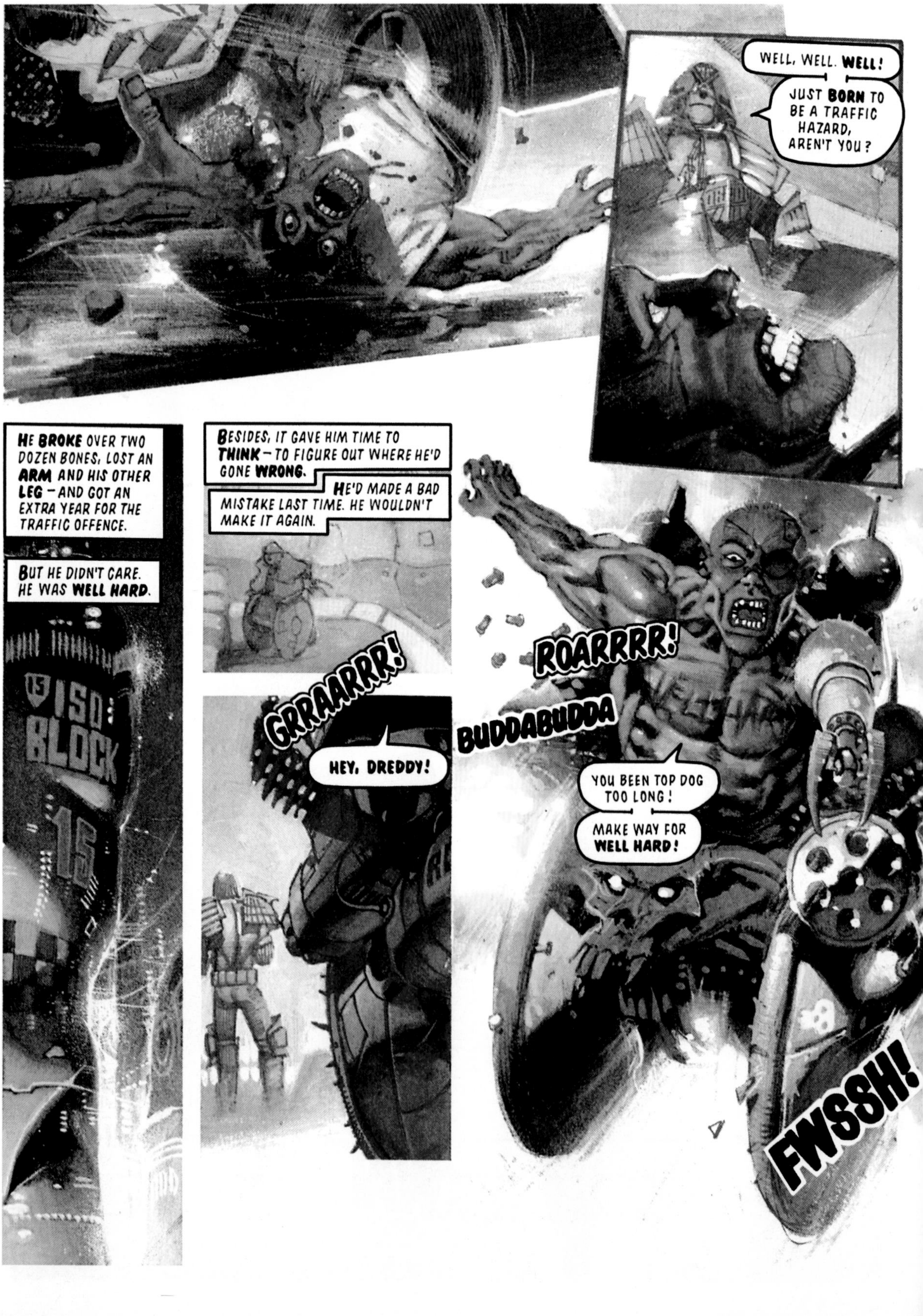

WELL, WELL. WELL!
JUST BORN TO BE A TRAFFIC HAZARD, AREN'T YOU?
HE BROKE OVER TWO DOZEN BONES, LOST AN ARM AND HIS OTHER LEG – AND GOT AN EXTRA YEAR FOR THE TRAFFIC OFFENCE.
BUT HE DIDN'T CARE. HE WAS WELL HARD.
15
ISO BLOCK
15
BESIDES, IT GAVE HIM TIME TO THINK – TO FIGURE OUT WHERE HE'D GONE WRONG.
HE'D MADE A BAD MISTAKE LAST TIME. HE WOULDN'T MAKE IT AGAIN.
GRRAARRR!
HEY, DREDDY!
BUDDABUDDA
ROARRRR!
YOU BEEN TOP DOG TOO LONG!
MAKE WAY FOR WELL HARD!
FWSSH!

SORT OF

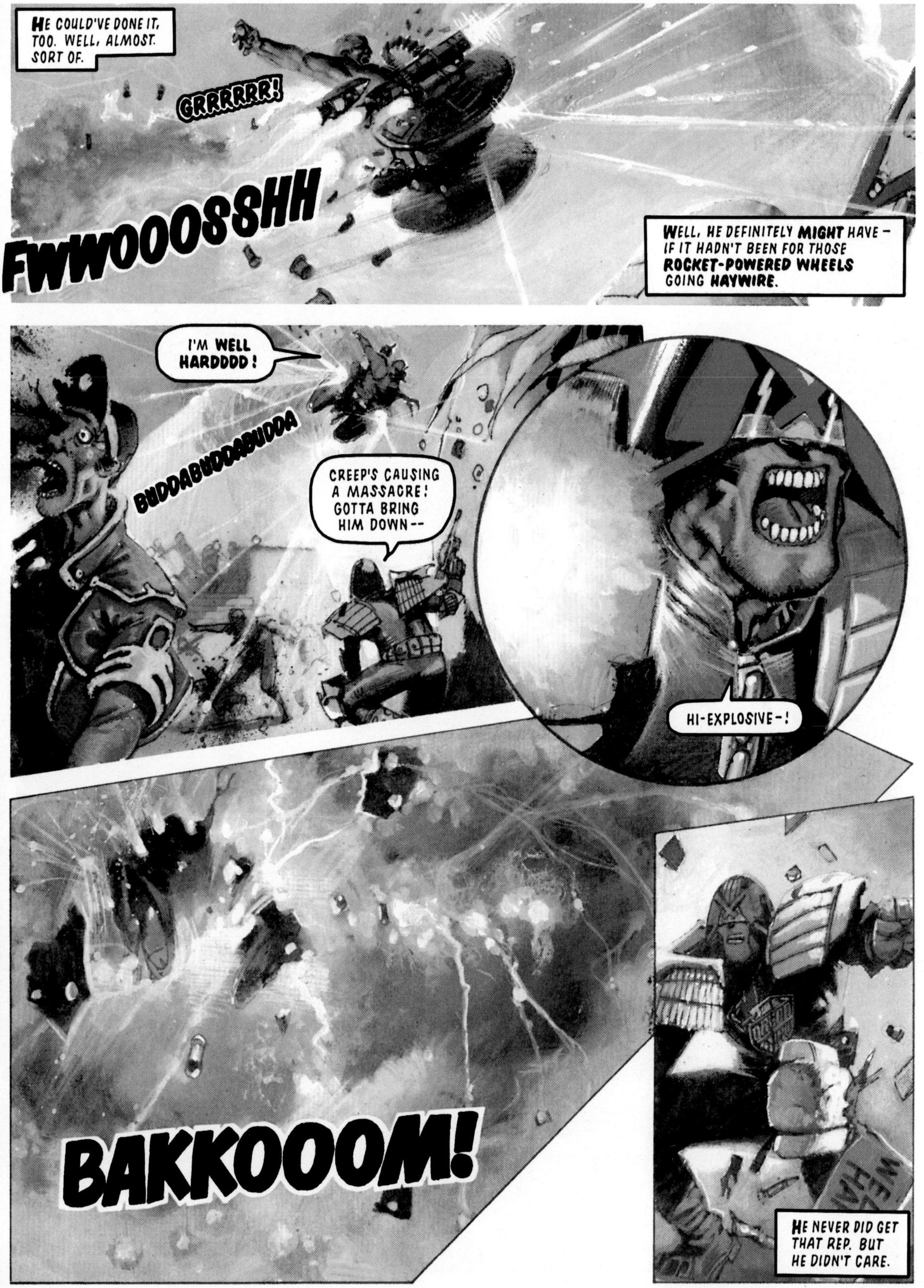
HE COULD'VE DONE IT, TOO. WELL, ALMOST. SORT OF.
GRRRRRR!
FWWOOOSSHH
WELL, HE DEFINITELY MIGHT HAVE – IF IT HADN'T BEEN FOR THOSE ROCKET-POWERED WHEELS GOING HAYWIRE.
I'M WELL HARDDDD!
BUDDABUDDABUDDA
CREEP'S CAUSING A MASSACRE! GOTTA BRING HIM DOWN--
HI-EXPLOSIVE-!
BAKKOOOM!
HE NEVER DID GET THAT REP. BUT HE DIDN'T CARE.

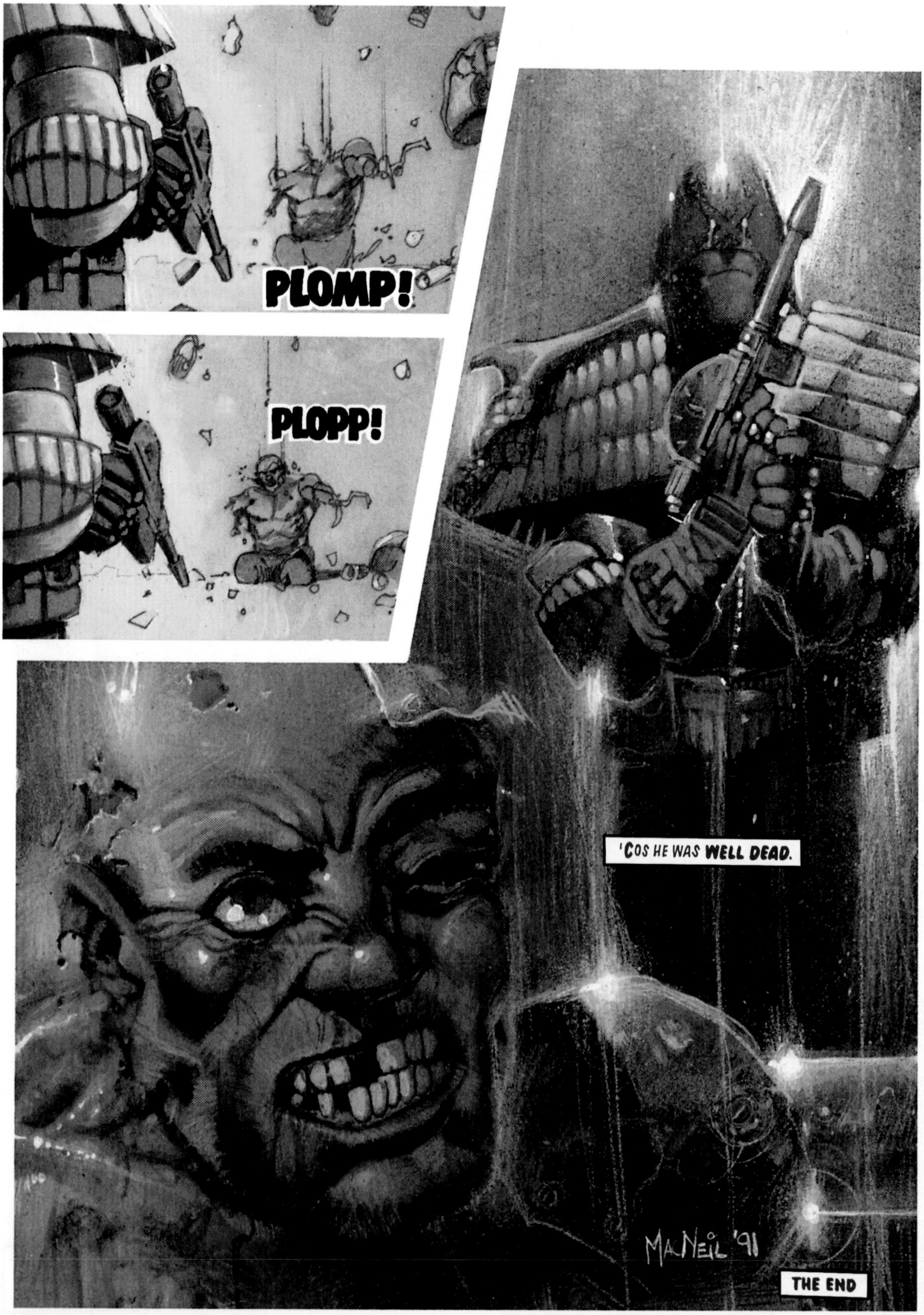
PLOMP!
PLOPP!
'COS HE WAS WELL DEAD.
MacNEIL '91
THE END

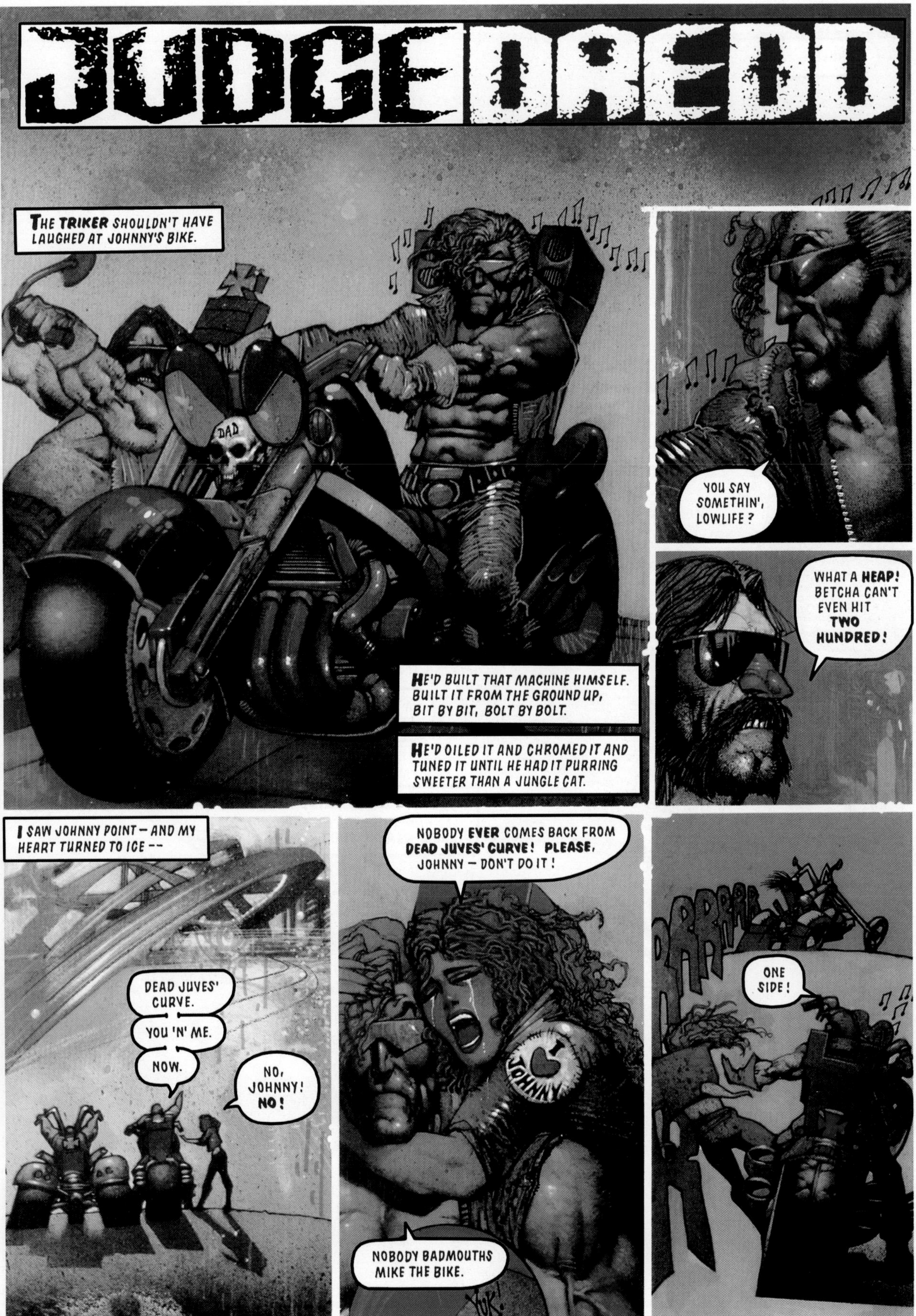
JUDGE DREDD
THE TRIKER SHOULDN'T HAVE LAUGHED AT JOHNNY'S BIKE.
DAD
HE'D BUILT THAT MACHINE HIMSELF. BUILT IT FROM THE GROUND UP, BIT BY BIT, BOLT BY BOLT.
HE'D OILED IT AND CHROMED IT AND TUNED IT UNTIL HE HAD IT PURRING SWEETER THAN A JUNGLE CAT.
YOU SAY SOMETHIN', LOWLIFE?
WHAT A HEAP! BETCHA CAN'T EVEN HIT TWO HUNDRED!
I SAW JOHNNY POINT — AND MY HEART TURNED TO ICE --
DEAD JUVES' CURVE.
YOU 'N' ME.
NOW.
NO, JOHNNY! NO!
NOBODY EVER COMES BACK FROM DEAD JUVES' CURVE! PLEASE, JOHNNY — DON'T DO IT!
I ♥ JOHNNY
NOBODY BADMOUTHS MIKE THE BIKE.
ONE SIDE!

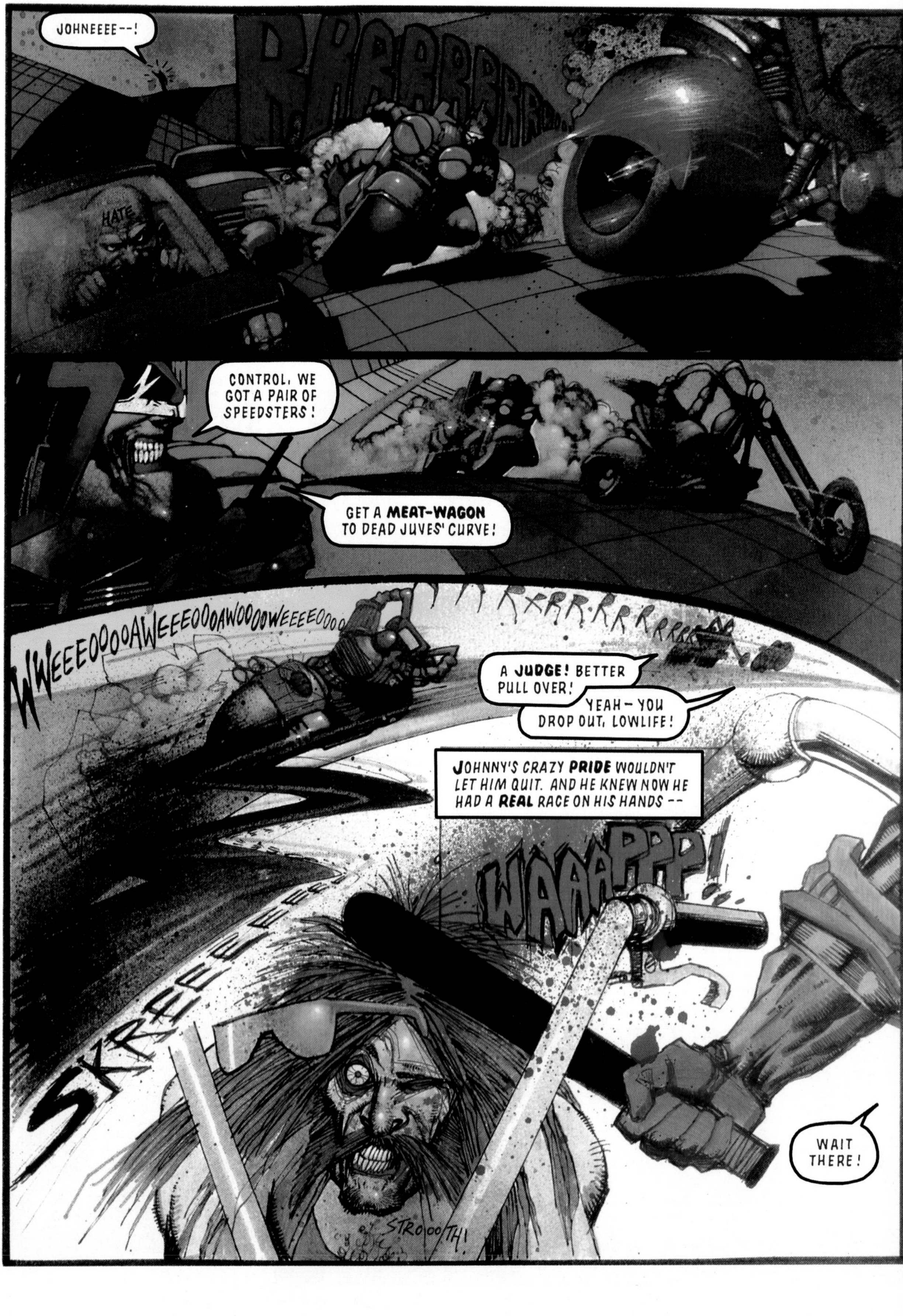
JOHNEEEE--!
RRARRRRRR
CONTROL, WE GOT A PAIR OF SPEEDSTERS!
GET A MEAT-WAGON TO DEAD JUVES' CURVE!
WWEEEOOOOAWEEEOOOAWOOOOWEEEEOOOO
RRRR.RRRRRRR
A JUDGE! BETTER PULL OVER!
YEAH – YOU DROP OUT, LOWLIFE!
JOHNNY'S CRAZY PRIDE WOULDN'T LET HIM QUIT. AND HE KNEW NOW HE HAD A REAL RACE ON HIS HANDS --
WAAAPPP!
SKREEEEEE
WAIT THERE!
STROOOTH!

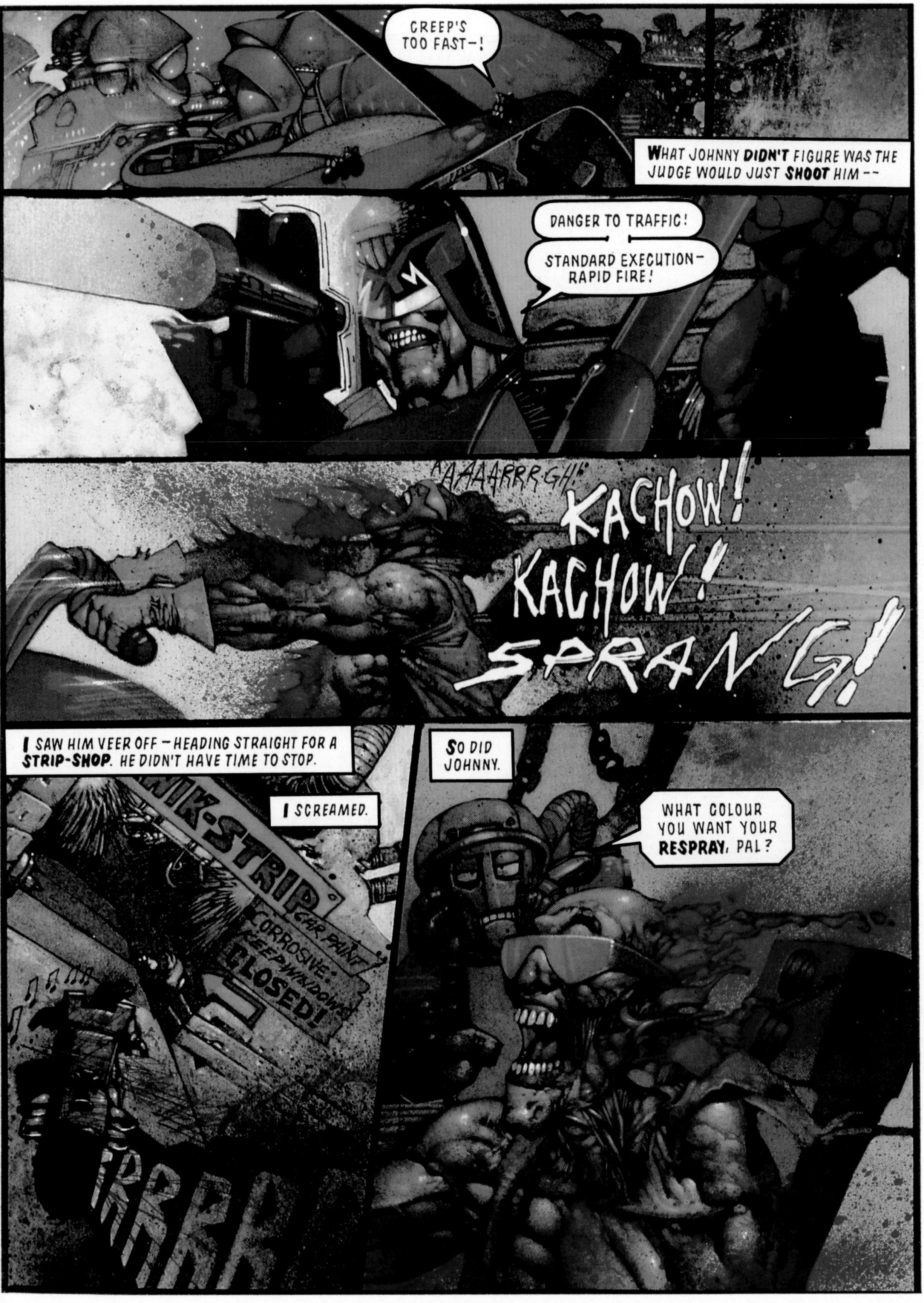
CREEP'S TOO FAST—!
WHAT JOHNNY DIDN'T FIGURE WAS THE JUDGE WOULD JUST SHOOT HIM--
DANGER TO TRAFFIC!
STANDARD EXECUTION—RAPID FIRE!
AAAAARRRGH!
KACHOW!
KACHOW!
SPRANG!
I SAW HIM VEER OFF — HEADING STRAIGHT FOR A STRIP-SHOP. HE DIDN'T HAVE TIME TO STOP.
I SCREAMED.
CAR PAINT
CORROSIVE: KEEP WINDOWS CLOSED!
SO DID JOHNNY.
WHAT COLOUR YOU WANT YOUR RESPRAY, PAL?

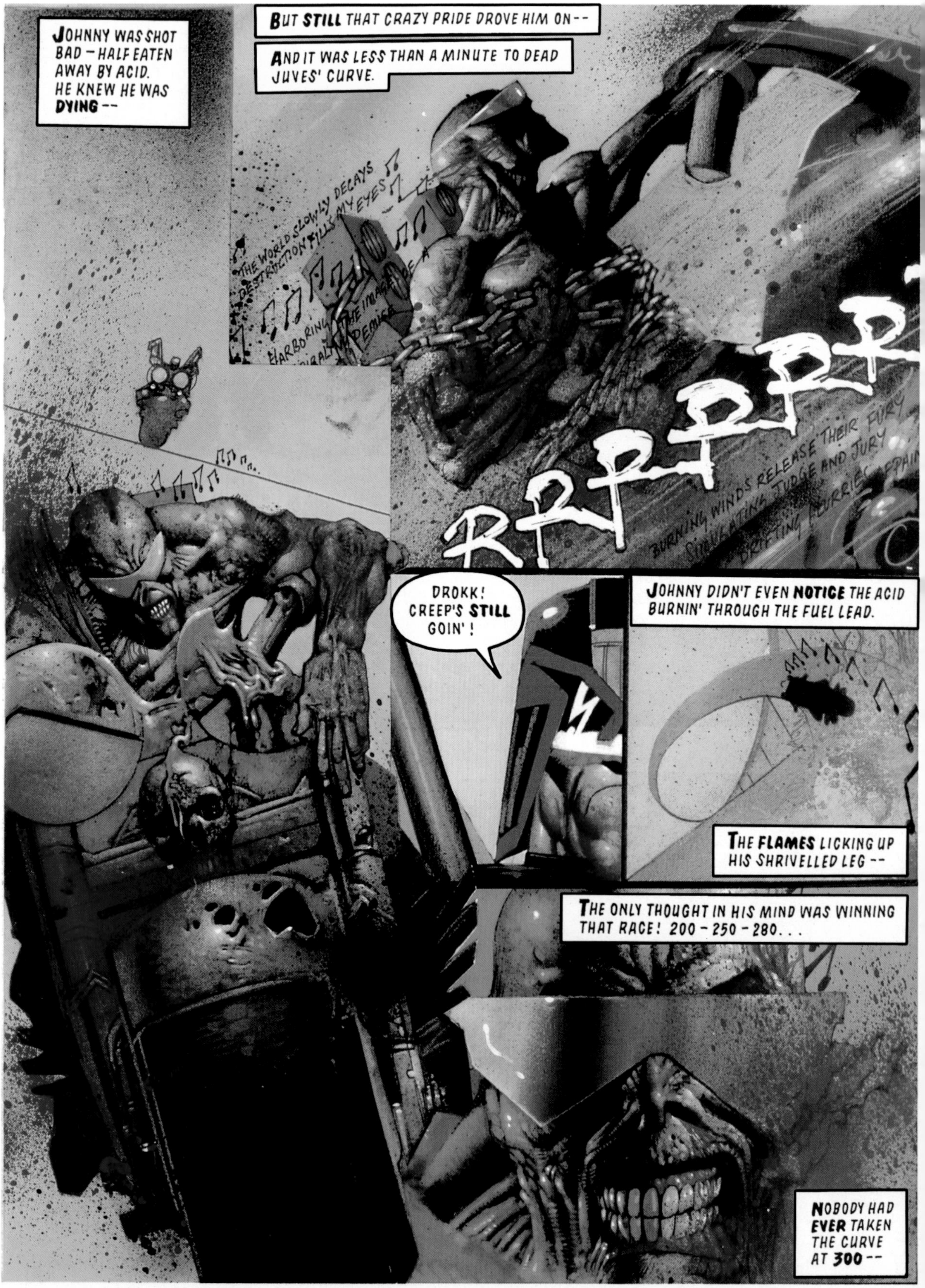
JOHNNY WAS SHOT BAD — HALF EATEN AWAY BY ACID. HE KNEW HE WAS DYING --
BUT STILL THAT CRAZY PRIDE DROVE HIM ON --
AND IT WAS LESS THAN A MINUTE TO DEAD JUVES' CURVE.
THE WORLD SLOWLY DECAYS
DESTRUCTION FILLS MY EYES
RRRRRRR
BURNING WINDS RELEASE THEIR FURY
SUBJUGATING JUDGE AND JURY
DROKK! CREEP'S STILL GOIN'!
JOHNNY DIDN'T EVEN NOTICE THE ACID BURNIN' THROUGH THE FUEL LEAD.
THE FLAMES LICKING UP HIS SHRIVELLED LEG --
THE ONLY THOUGHT IN HIS MIND WAS WINNING THAT RACE! 200 - 250 - 280...
NOBODY HAD EVER TAKEN THE CURVE AT 300 --

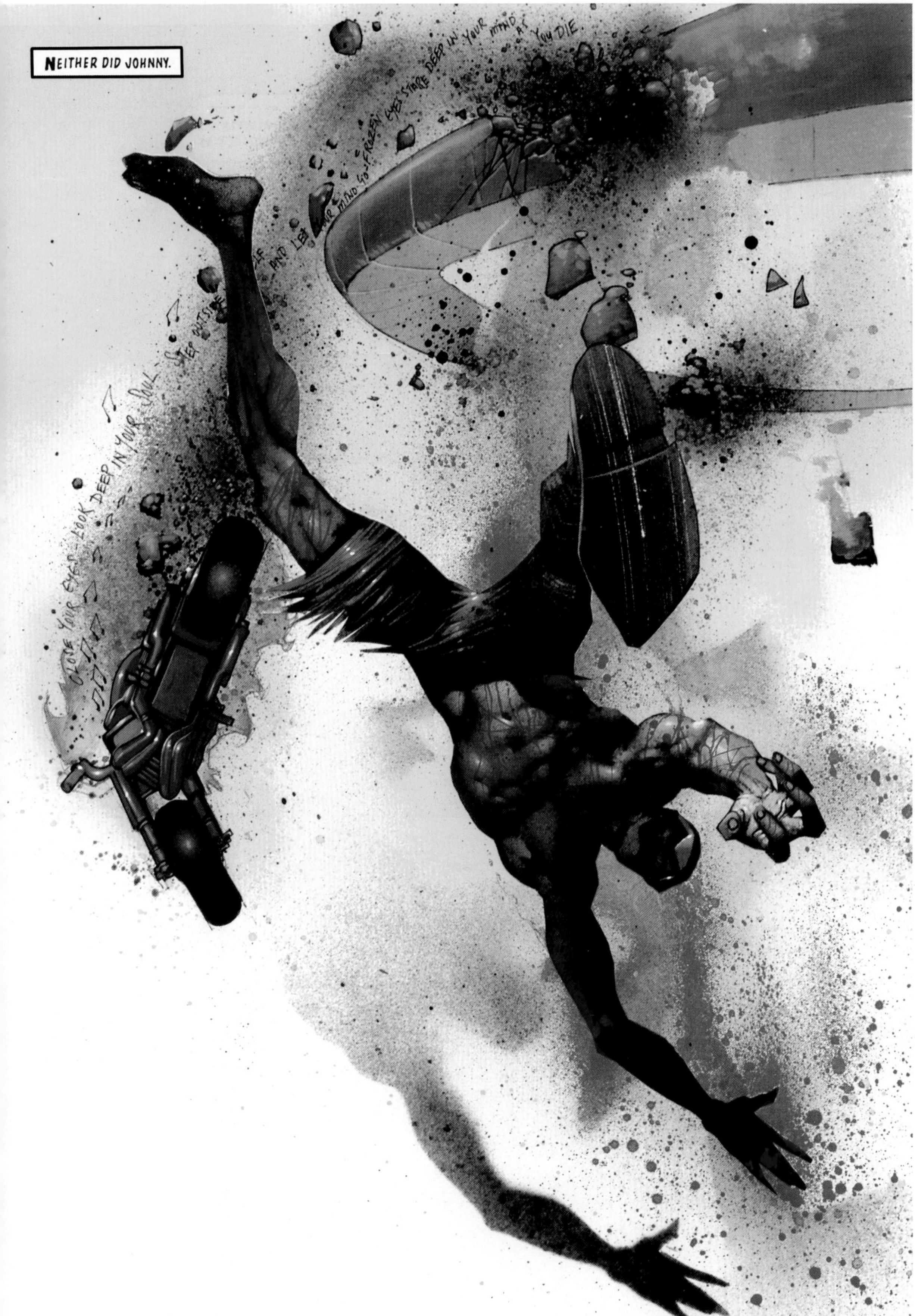
NEITHER DID JOHNNY.
CLOSE YOUR EYES – LOOK DEEP IN YOUR SOUL – STEP OUTSIDE
AND LET
MIND GO – FROZEN EYES STARE DEEP IN YOUR MIND AS YOU DIE

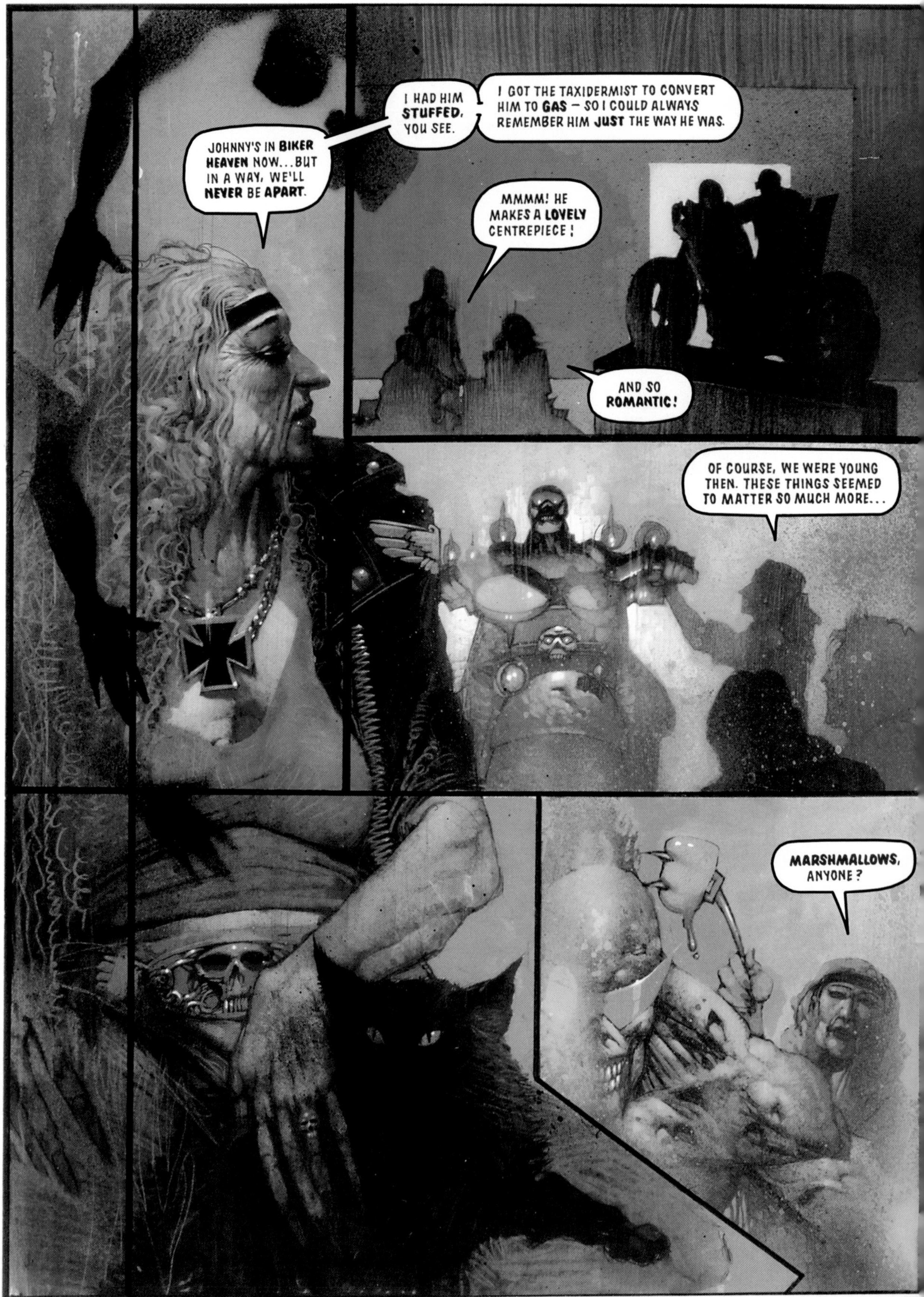
JOHNNY'S IN BIKER HEAVEN NOW...BUT IN A WAY, WE'LL NEVER BE APART.
I HAD HIM STUFFED, YOU SEE.
I GOT THE TAXIDERMIST TO CONVERT HIM TO GAS – SO I COULD ALWAYS REMEMBER HIM JUST THE WAY HE WAS.
MMMM! HE MAKES A LOVELY CENTREPIECE!
AND SO ROMANTIC!
OF COURSE, WE WERE YOUNG THEN. THESE THINGS SEEMED TO MATTER SO MUCH MORE...
MARSHMALLOWS, ANYONE?

THE EN

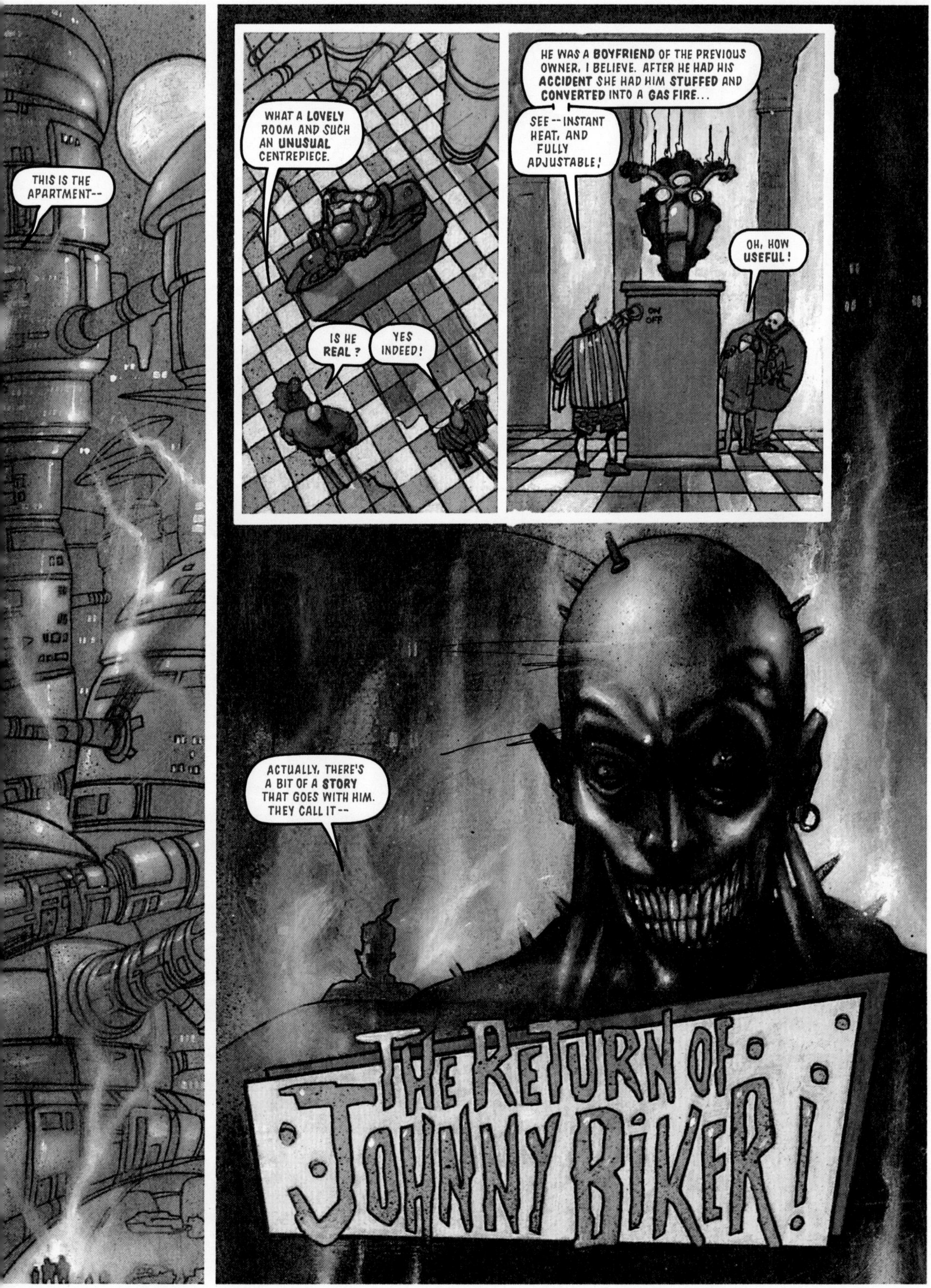
THIS IS THE APARTMENT--
WHAT A LOVELY ROOM AND SUCH AN UNUSUAL CENTREPIECE.
IS HE REAL?
YES INDEED!
HE WAS A BOYFRIEND OF THE PREVIOUS OWNER, I BELIEVE. AFTER HE HAD HIS ACCIDENT SHE HAD HIM STUFFED AND CONVERTED INTO A GAS FIRE...
SEE--INSTANT HEAT, AND FULLY ADJUSTABLE!
ON OFF
OH, HOW USEFUL!
ACTUALLY, THERE'S A BIT OF A STORY THAT GOES WITH HIM. THEY CALL IT--
THE RETURN OF JOHNNY RIKER!

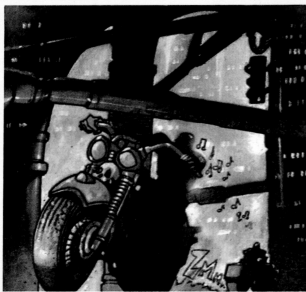

SOMETHING FAMILIAR ABOUT THAT CREEP --

DREDD TO CONTROL! DIG OUT THE FILE ON JOHNNY BIKER!

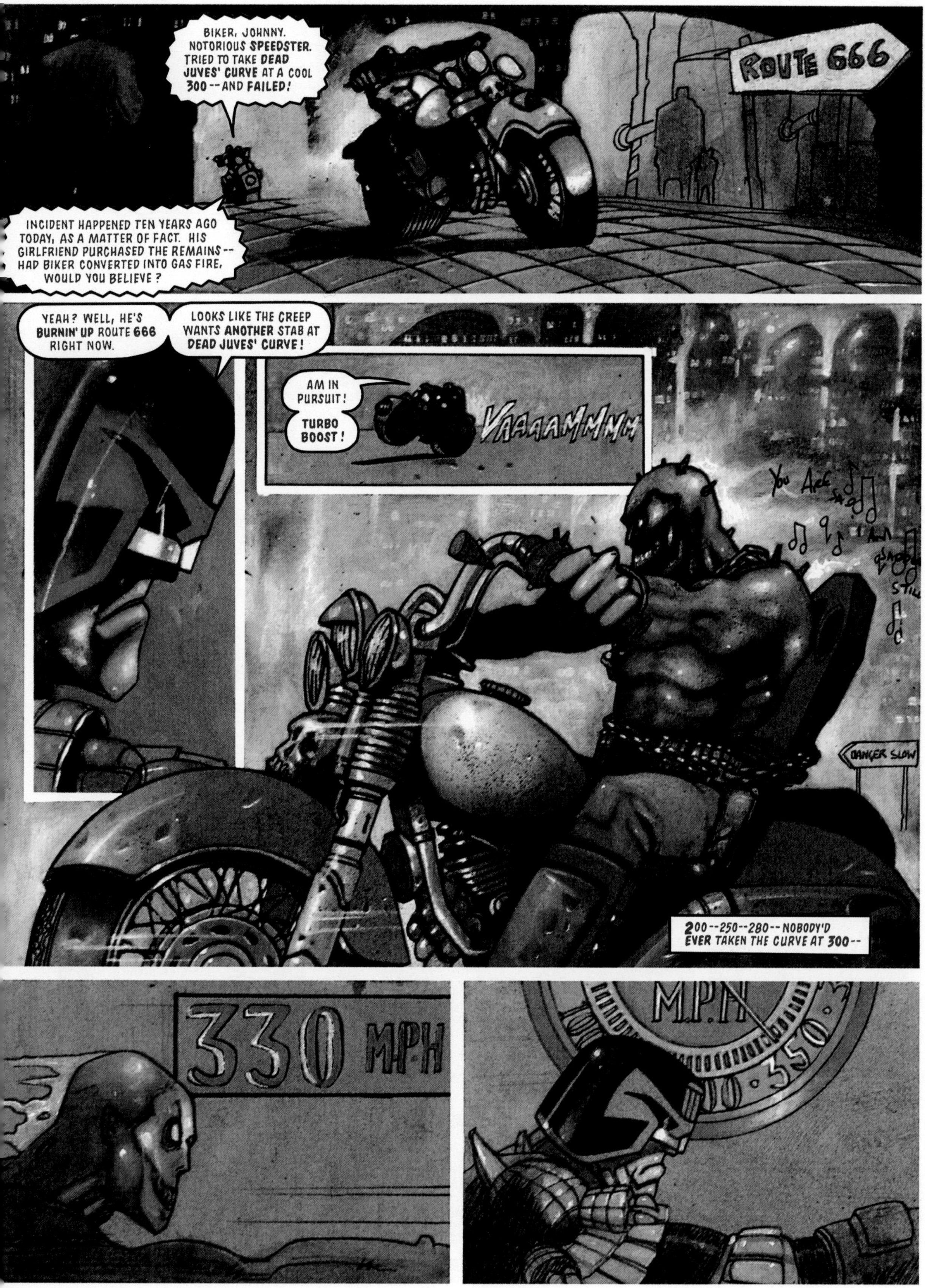
BIKER, JOHNNY. NOTORIOUS SPEEDSTER. TRIED TO TAKE DEAD JUVES' CURVE AT A COOL 300 -- AND FAILED!
ROUTE 666
INCIDENT HAPPENED TEN YEARS AGO TODAY, AS A MATTER OF FACT. HIS GIRLFRIEND PURCHASED THE REMAINS -- HAD BIKER CONVERTED INTO GAS FIRE, WOULD YOU BELIEVE?
YEAH? WELL, HE'S BURNIN' UP ROUTE 666 RIGHT NOW.
LOOKS LIKE THE CREEP WANTS ANOTHER STAB AT DEAD JUVES' CURVE!
AM IN PURSUIT!
TURBO BOOST!
VAAAAMMMM
DANGER SLOW
200--250--280--NOBODY'D EVER TAKEN THE CURVE AT 300--
330 MPH
M.P.H

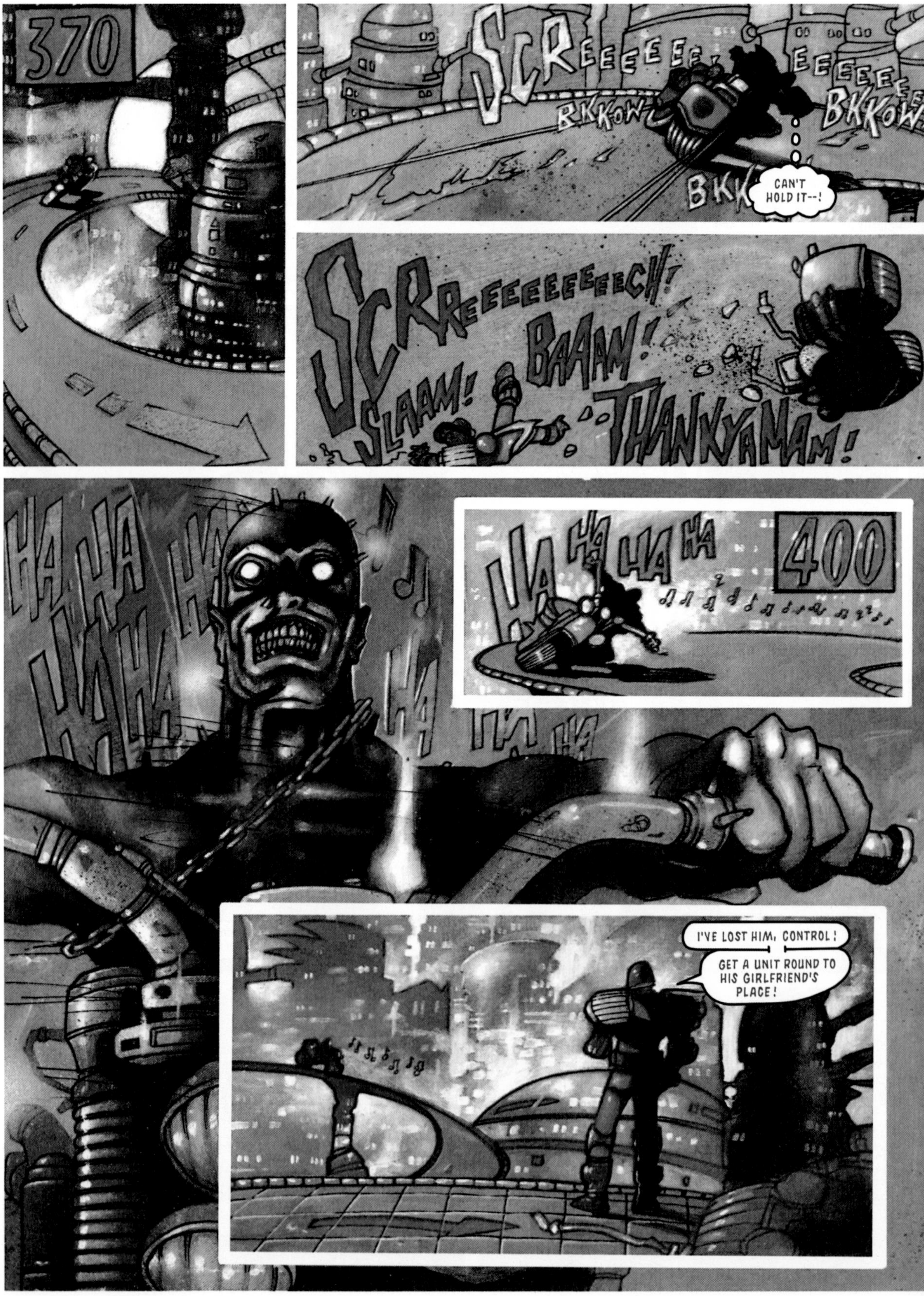
370
SCREEEEEEEEEEEE
BKKOW!
BKKOW!
BKK
CAN'T HOLD IT--!
SCRREEEEEEEEECH!
SLAAM!
BAAAM!
THANKYAMAM!
HA HA HA HA HA HA HA HA HA HA HA
HA HA HA HA HA
400
I'VE LOST HIM, CONTROL!
GET A UNIT ROUND TO HIS GIRLFRIEND'S PLACE!

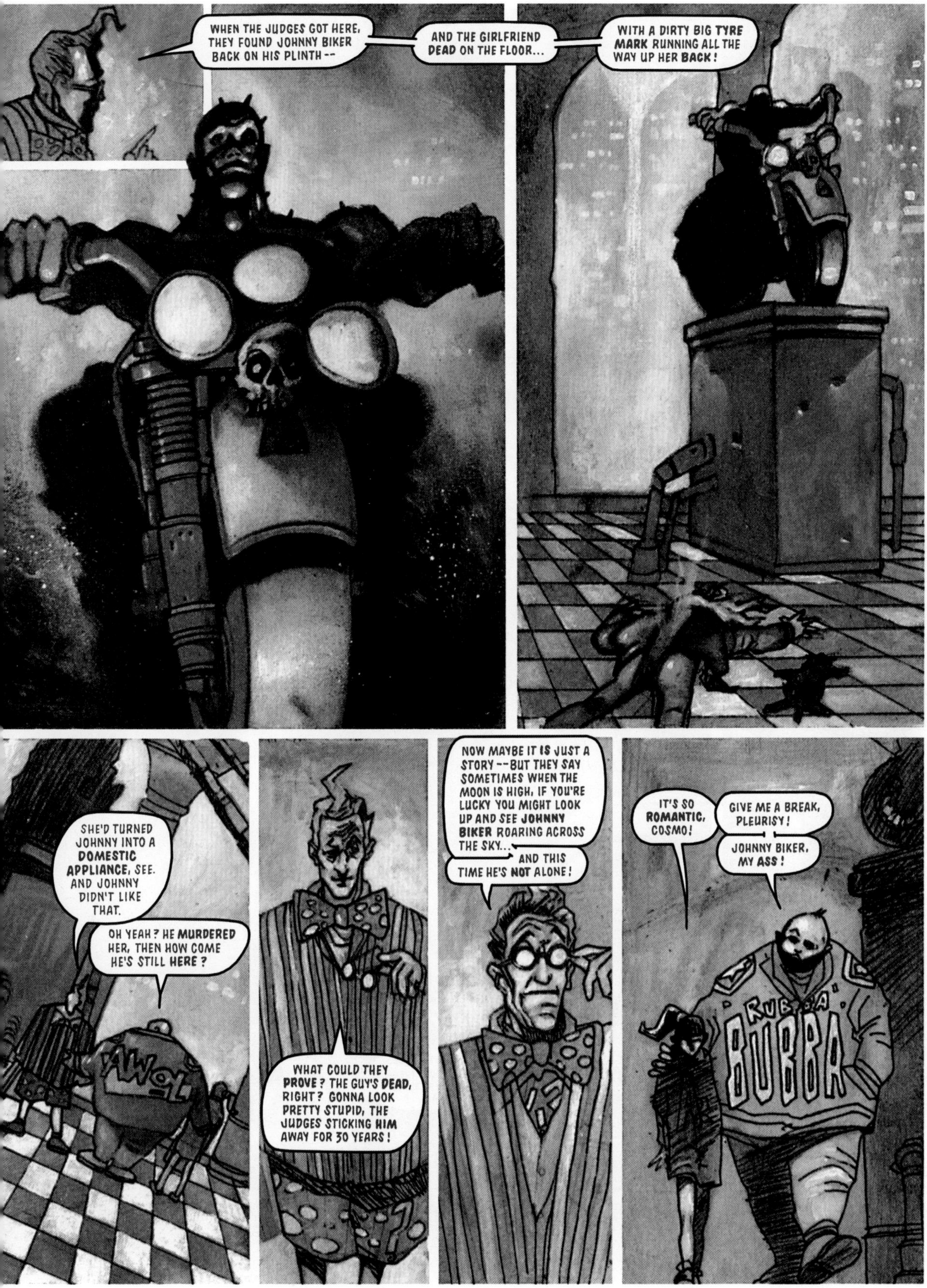

WHEN THE JUDGES GOT HERE, THEY FOUND JOHNNY BIKER BACK ON HIS PLINTH --
AND THE GIRLFRIEND DEAD ON THE FLOOR...
WITH A DIRTY BIG TYRE MARK RUNNING ALL THE WAY UP HER BACK!
SHE'D TURNED JOHNNY INTO A DOMESTIC APPLIANCE, SEE. AND JOHNNY DIDN'T LIKE THAT.
OH YEAH? HE MURDERED HER, THEN HOW COME HE'S STILL HERE?
AWOL
WHAT COULD THEY PROVE? THE GUY'S DEAD, RIGHT? GONNA LOOK PRETTY STUPID, THE JUDGES STICKING HIM AWAY FOR 30 YEARS!
NOW MAYBE IT IS JUST A STORY -- BUT THEY SAY SOMETIMES WHEN THE MOON IS HIGH, IF YOU'RE LUCKY YOU MIGHT LOOK UP AND SEE JOHNNY BIKER ROARING ACROSS THE SKY...
AND THIS TIME HE'S NOT ALONE!
IT'S SO ROMANTIC, COSMO!
GIVE ME A BREAK, PLEURISY!
JOHNNY BIKER, MY ASS!
BUBBA

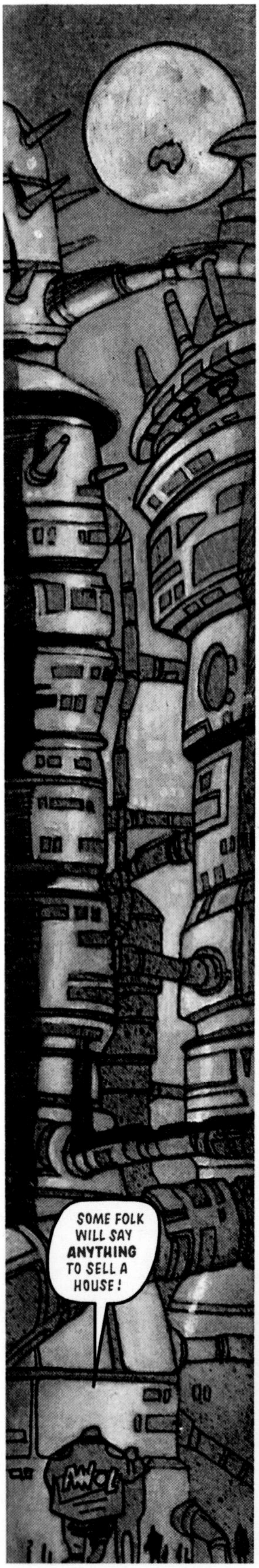
SOME FOLK WILL SAY ANYTHING TO SELL A HOUSE!

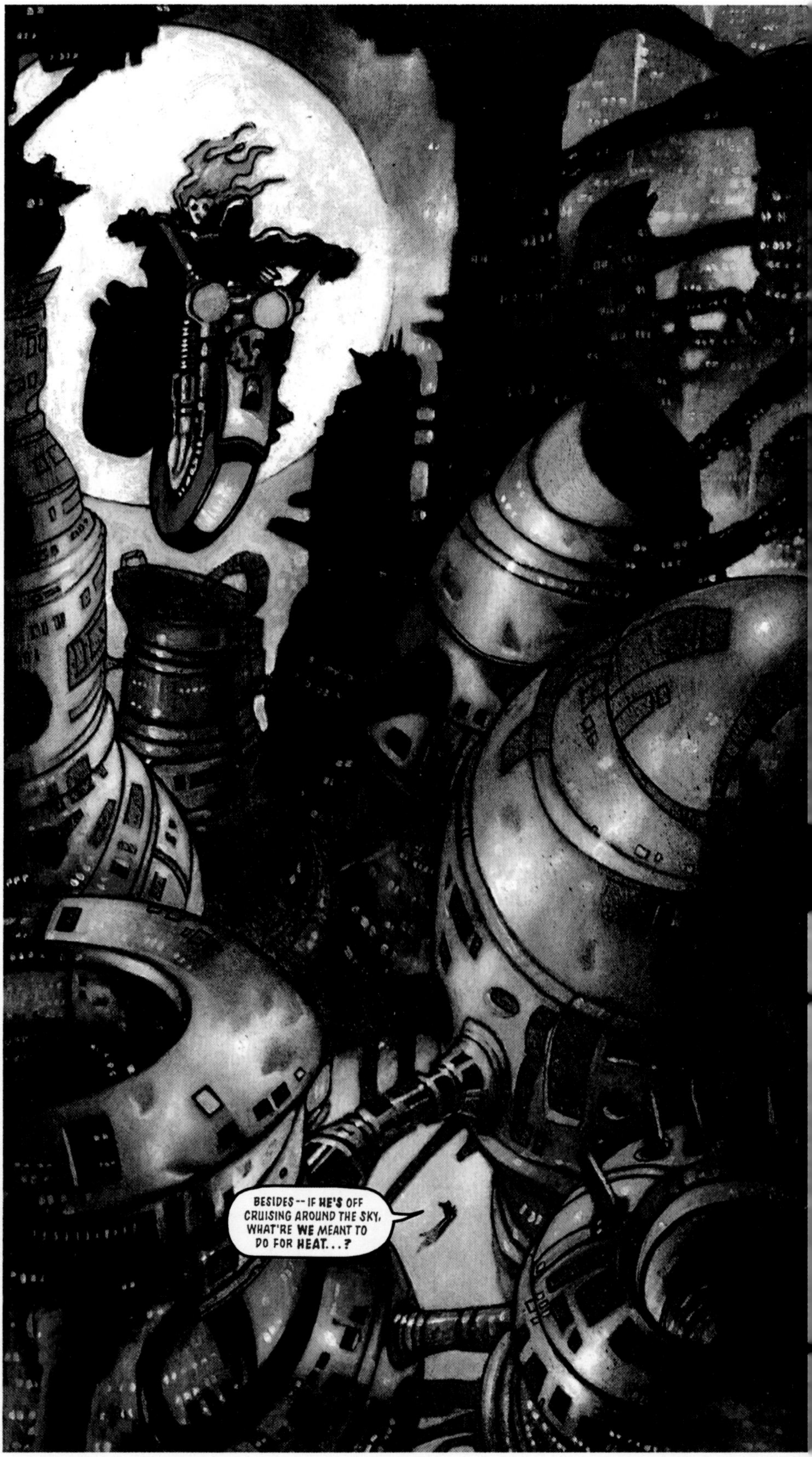
BESIDES -- IF HE'S OFF CRUISING AROUND THE SKY, WHAT'RE WE MEANT TO DO FOR HEAT...?

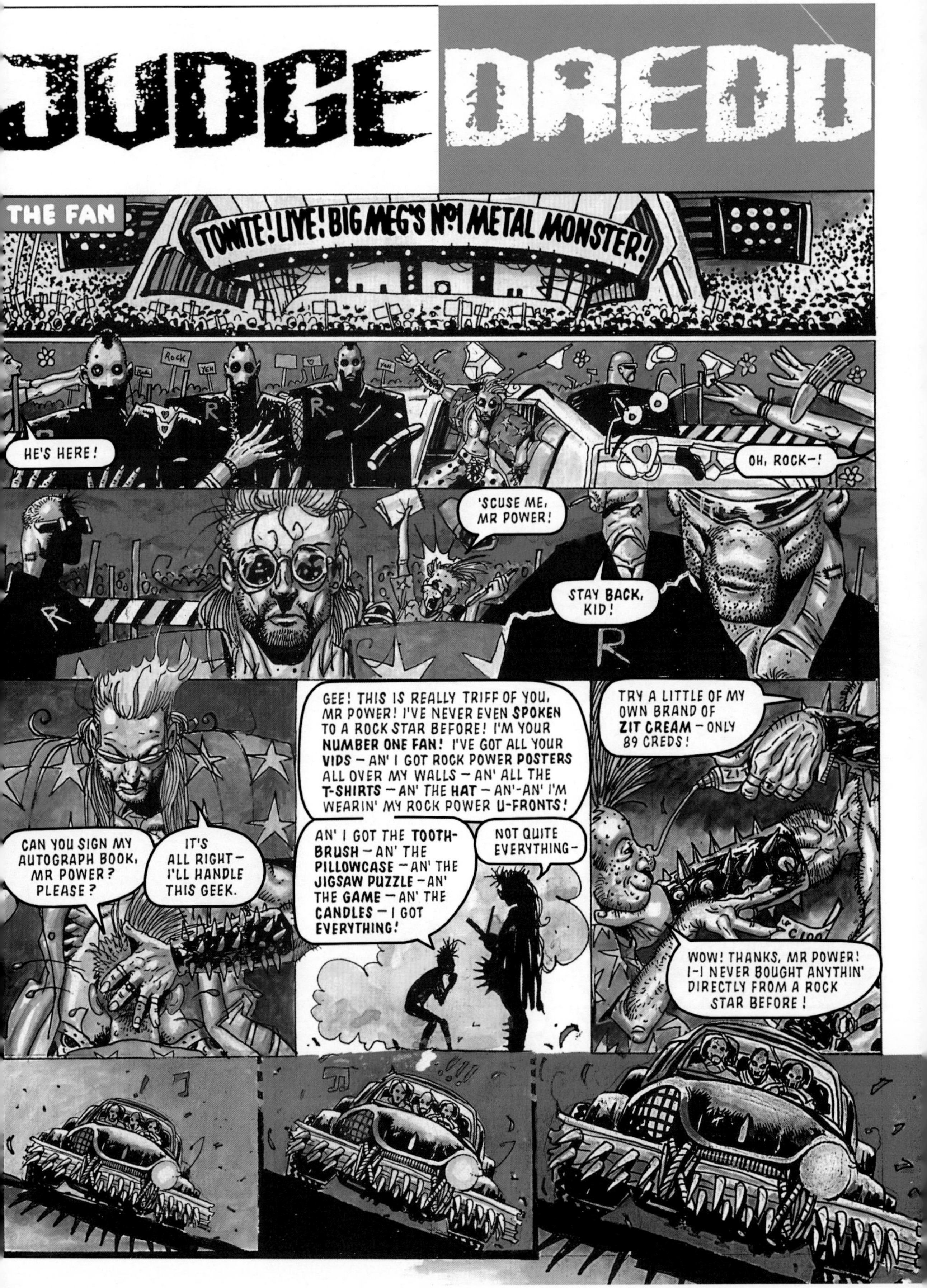
JUDGE DREDD
THE FAN
TONITE! LIVE! BIG MEG'S No1 METAL MONSTER!
HE'S HERE!
OH, ROCK–!
'SCUSE ME, MR POWER!
STAY BACK, KID!
CAN YOU SIGN MY AUTOGRAPH BOOK, MR POWER? PLEASE?
IT'S ALL RIGHT– I'LL HANDLE THIS GEEK.
GEE! THIS IS REALLY TRIFF OF YOU, MR POWER! I'VE NEVER EVEN SPOKEN TO A ROCK STAR BEFORE! I'M YOUR NUMBER ONE FAN! I'VE GOT ALL YOUR VIDS – AN' I GOT ROCK POWER POSTERS ALL OVER MY WALLS – AN' ALL THE T-SHIRTS – AN' THE HAT – AN'-AN' I'M WEARIN' MY ROCK POWER U-FRONTS!
AN' I GOT THE TOOTH-BRUSH – AN' THE PILLOWCASE – AN' THE JIGSAW PUZZLE – AN' THE GAME – AN' THE CANDLES – I GOT EVERYTHING!
NOT QUITE EVERYTHING–
TRY A LITTLE OF MY OWN BRAND OF ZIT CREAM – ONLY 89 CREDS!
WOW! THANKS, MR POWER! I-I NEVER BOUGHT ANYTHIN' DIRECTLY FROM A ROCK STAR BEFORE!

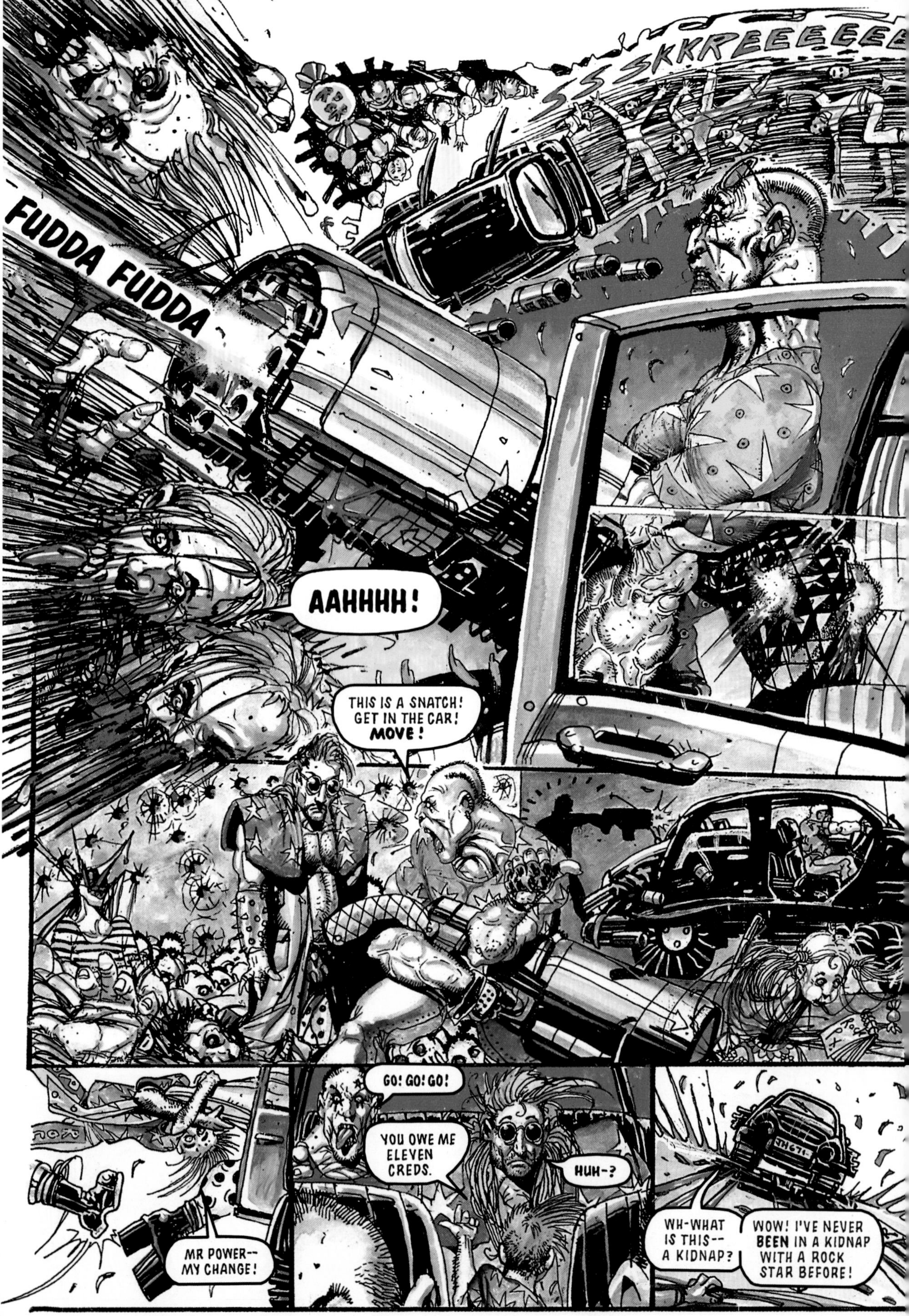
SSSKKREEEEEE
FUDDA FUDDA FUDDA
AAHHHH!
THIS IS A SNATCH! GET IN THE CAR! MOVE!
MR POWER-- MY CHANGE!
GO! GO! GO!
YOU OWE ME ELEVEN CREDS.
HUH-?
WH-WHAT IS THIS-- A KIDNAP?
WOW! I'VE NEVER BEEN IN A KIDNAP WITH A ROCK STAR BEFORE!

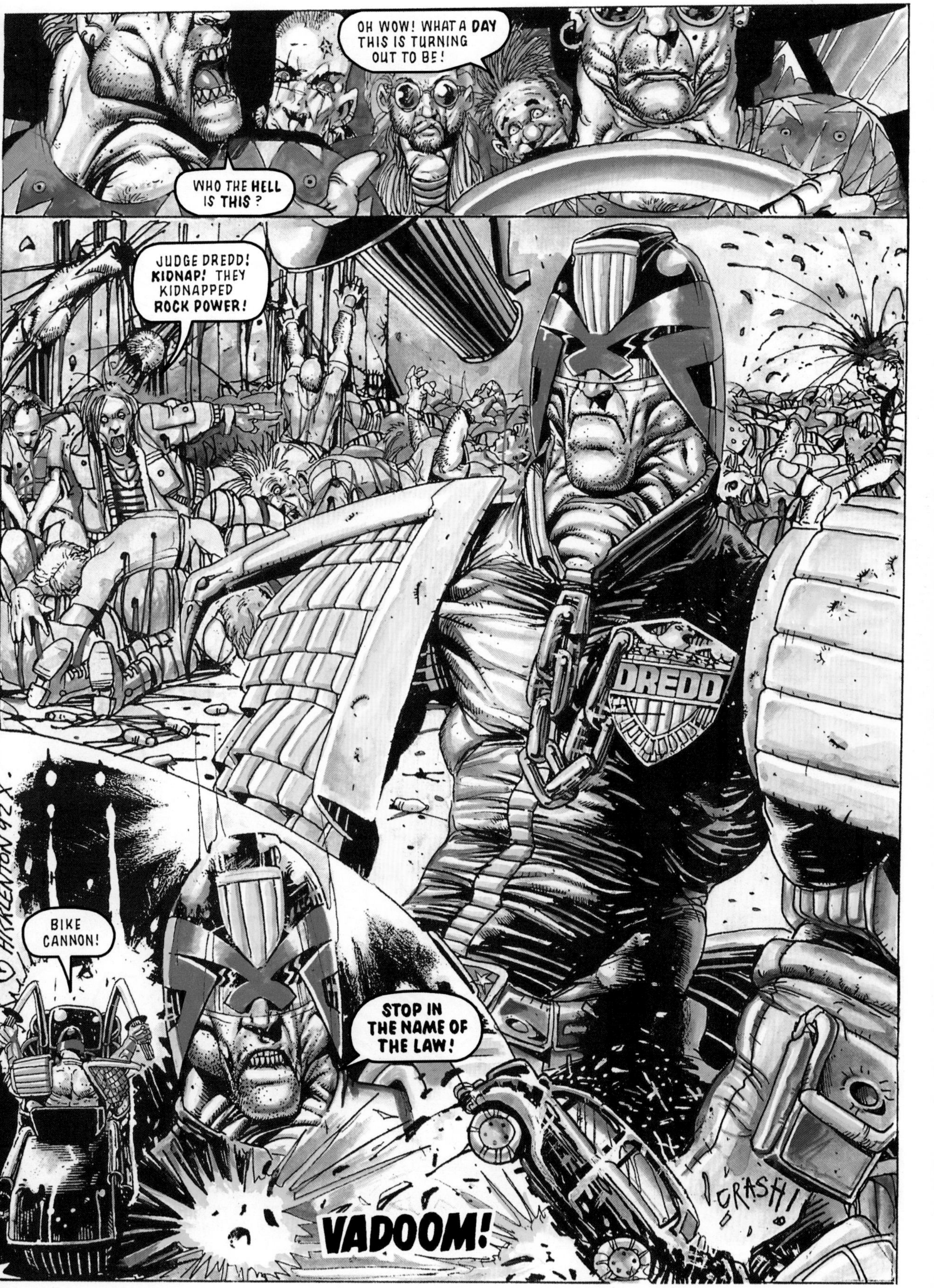
OH WOW! WHAT A DAY THIS IS TURNING OUT TO BE!
WHO THE HELL IS THIS?
JUDGE DREDD! KIDNAP! THEY KIDNAPPED ROCK POWER!
DREDD
BIKE CANNON!
STOP IN THE NAME OF THE LAW!
VADOOM!
CRASH!
HICKLENTON 92 X

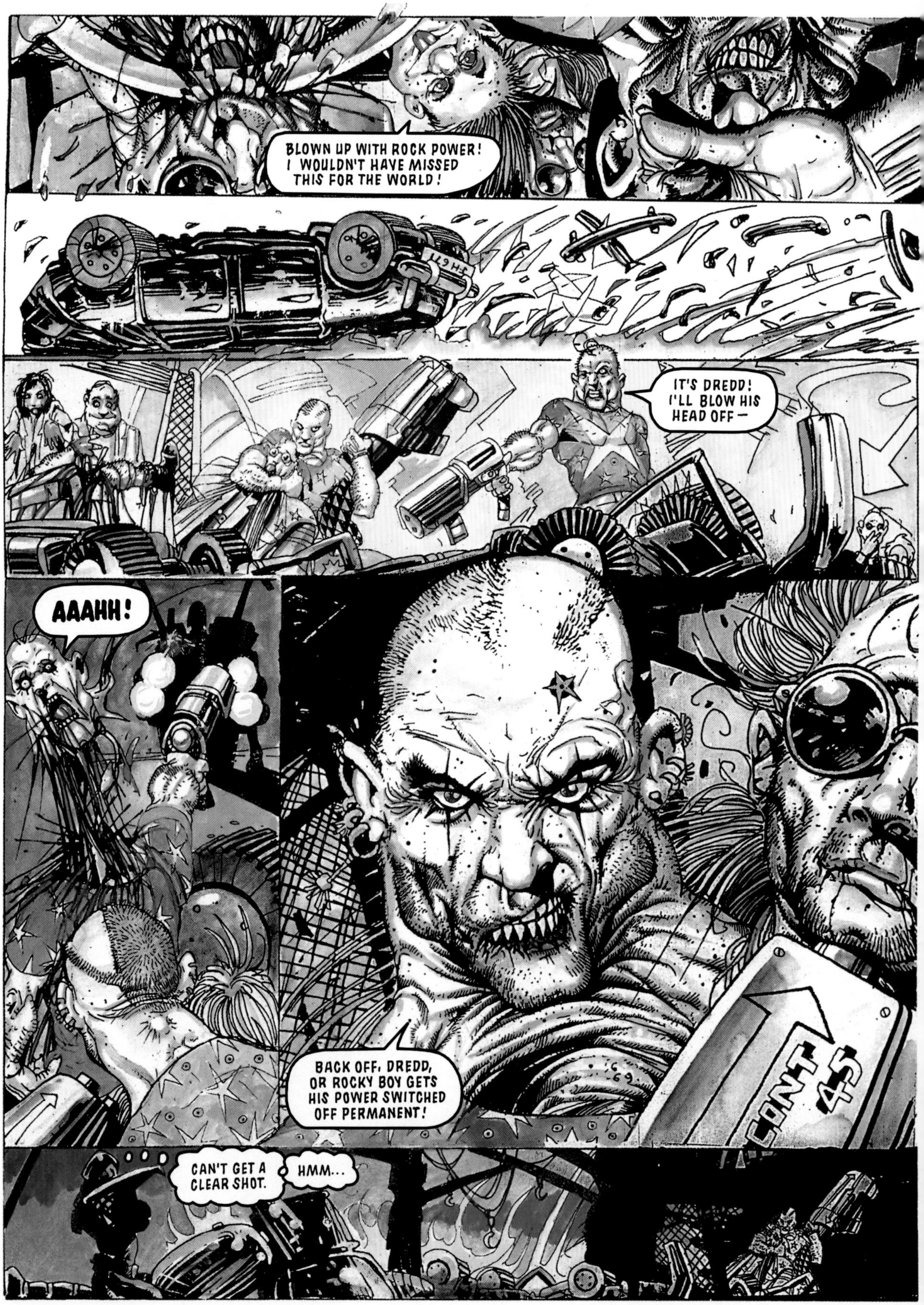

BLOWN UP WITH ROCK POWER! I WOULDN'T HAVE MISSED THIS FOR THE WORLD!
IT'S DREDD! I'LL BLOW HIS HEAD OFF —
AAAHH!
BACK OFF, DREDD, OR ROCKY BOY GETS HIS POWER SWITCHED OFF PERMANENT!
CAN'T GET A CLEAR SHOT.
HMM...

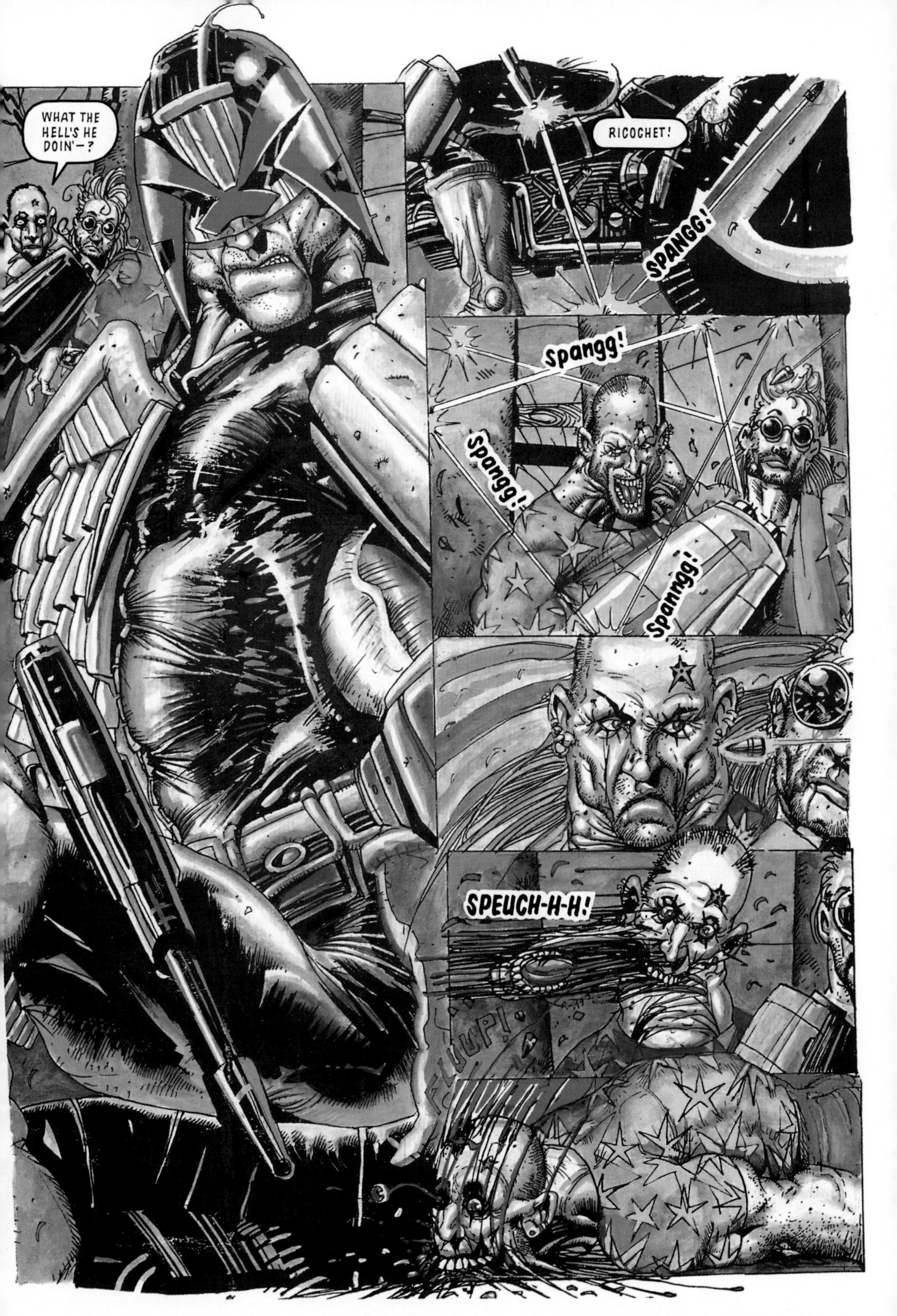
WHAT THE HELL'S HE DOIN'–?
RICOCHET!
SPANGG!
Spangg!
Spangg!
Spanngg!
SPEUCH-H-H!
FLUUP!

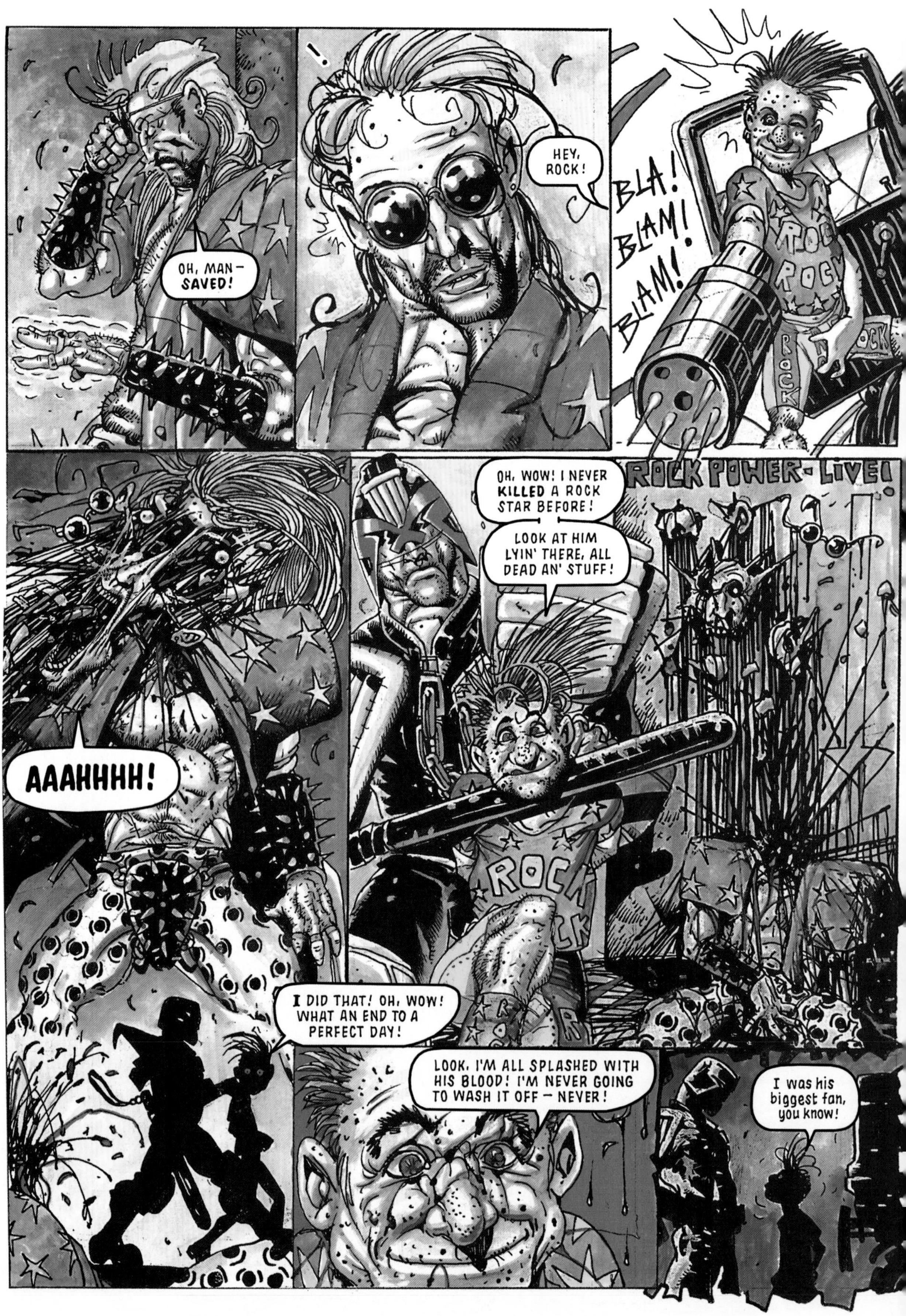
OH, MAN— SAVED!
!
HEY, ROCK!
BLA! BLAM! BLAM!
ROCK ROCK
ROCK
OH, WOW! I NEVER KILLED A ROCK STAR BEFORE!
LOOK AT HIM LYIN' THERE, ALL DEAD AN' STUFF!
ROCK POWER-LIVE!
AAAHHHH!
ROCK
I DID THAT! OH, WOW! WHAT AN END TO A PERFECT DAY!
LOOK, I'M ALL SPLASHED WITH HIS BLOOD! I'M NEVER GOING TO WASH IT OFF — NEVER!
I was his biggest fan, you know!

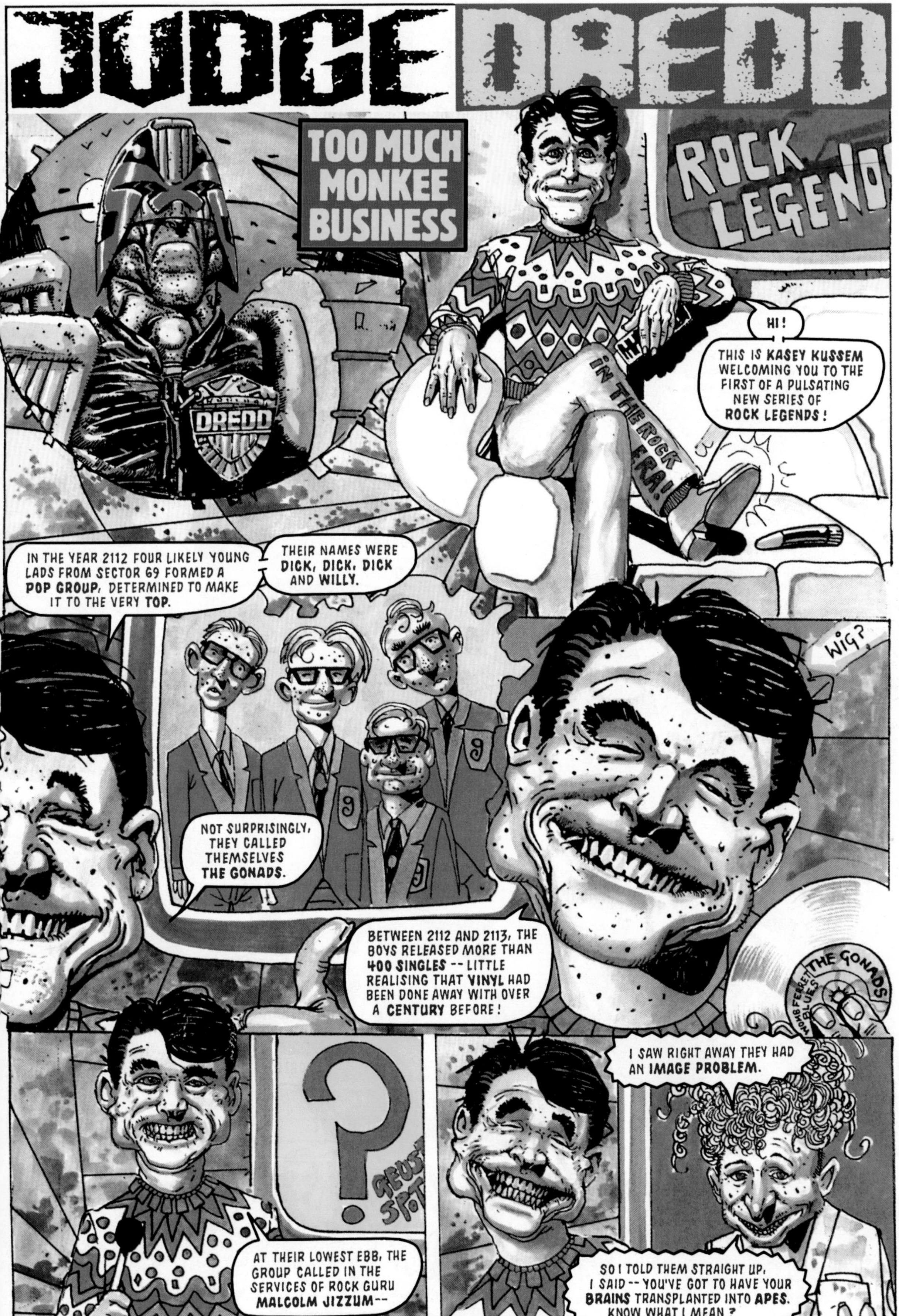
JUDGE DREDD
TOO MUCH MONKEE BUSINESS
ROCK LEGENDS
DREDD
IN THE ROCK ERA!
HI!
THIS IS KASEY KUSSEM WELCOMING YOU TO THE FIRST OF A PULSATING NEW SERIES OF ROCK LEGENDS!
IN THE YEAR 2112 FOUR LIKELY YOUNG LADS FROM SECTOR 69 FORMED A POP GROUP, DETERMINED TO MAKE IT TO THE VERY TOP.
THEIR NAMES WERE DICK, DICK, DICK AND WILLY.
WIG?
NOT SURPRISINGLY, THEY CALLED THEMSELVES THE GONADS.
BETWEEN 2112 AND 2113, THE BOYS RELEASED MORE THAN 400 SINGLES -- LITTLE REALISING THAT VINYL HAD BEEN DONE AWAY WITH OVER A CENTURY BEFORE!
THE GONADS
AT THEIR LOWEST EBB, THE GROUP CALLED IN THE SERVICES OF ROCK GURU MALCOLM JIZZUM--
I SAW RIGHT AWAY THEY HAD AN IMAGE PROBLEM.
SO I TOLD THEM STRAIGHT UP, I SAID -- YOU'VE GOT TO HAVE YOUR BRAINS TRANSPLANTED INTO APES. KNOW WHAT I MEAN?

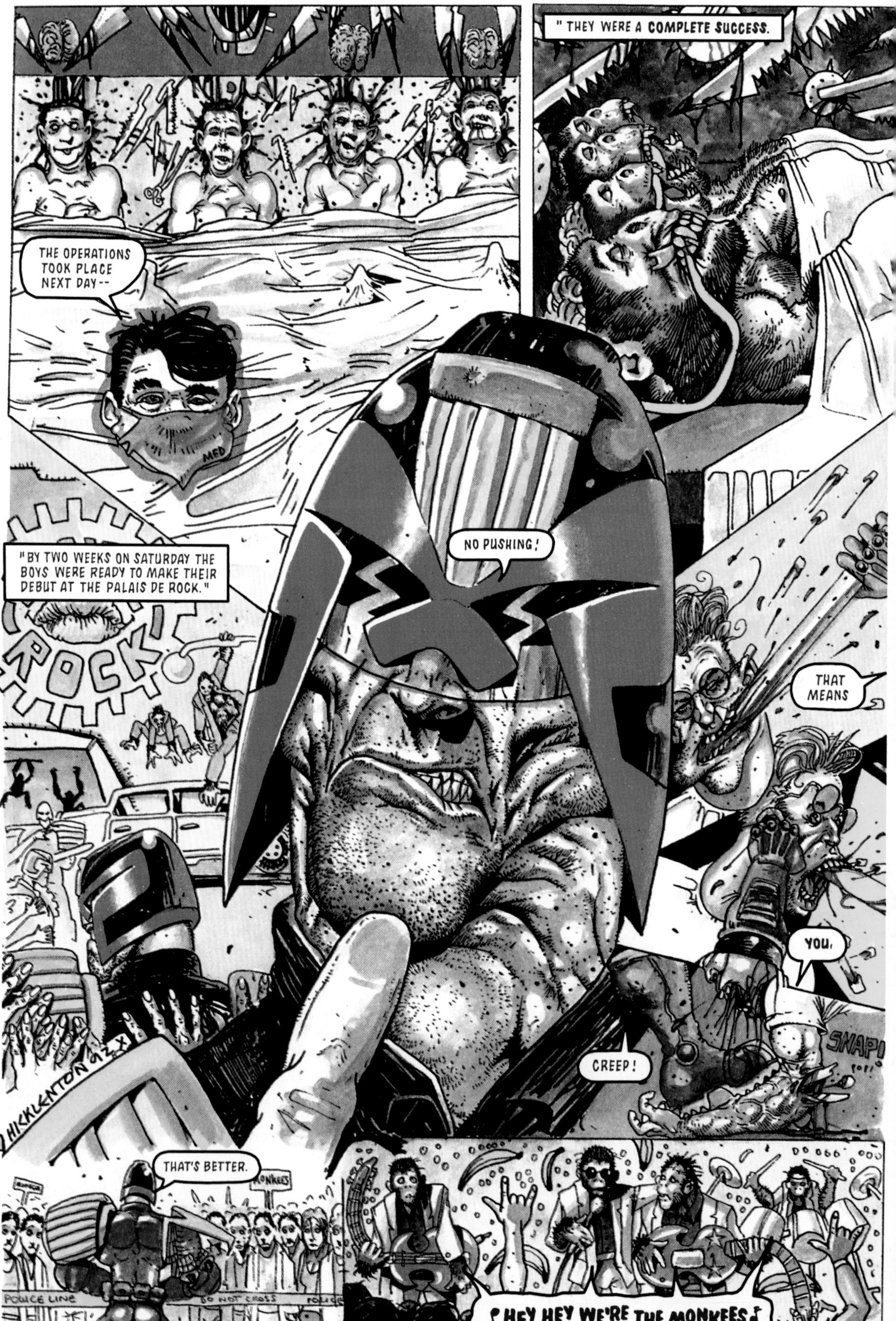
THE OPERATIONS TOOK PLACE NEXT DAY--
MED
"THEY WERE A COMPLETE SUCCESS.
"BY TWO WEEKS ON SATURDAY THE BOYS WERE READY TO MAKE THEIR DEBUT AT THE PALAIS DE ROCK."
ROCK
NO PUSHING!
THAT MEANS
YOU,
SNAP!
CREEP!
HICKLENTON 92 X
THAT'S BETTER.
MONKEES
POLICE LINE
DO NOT CROSS
HEY HEY WE'RE THE MONKEES

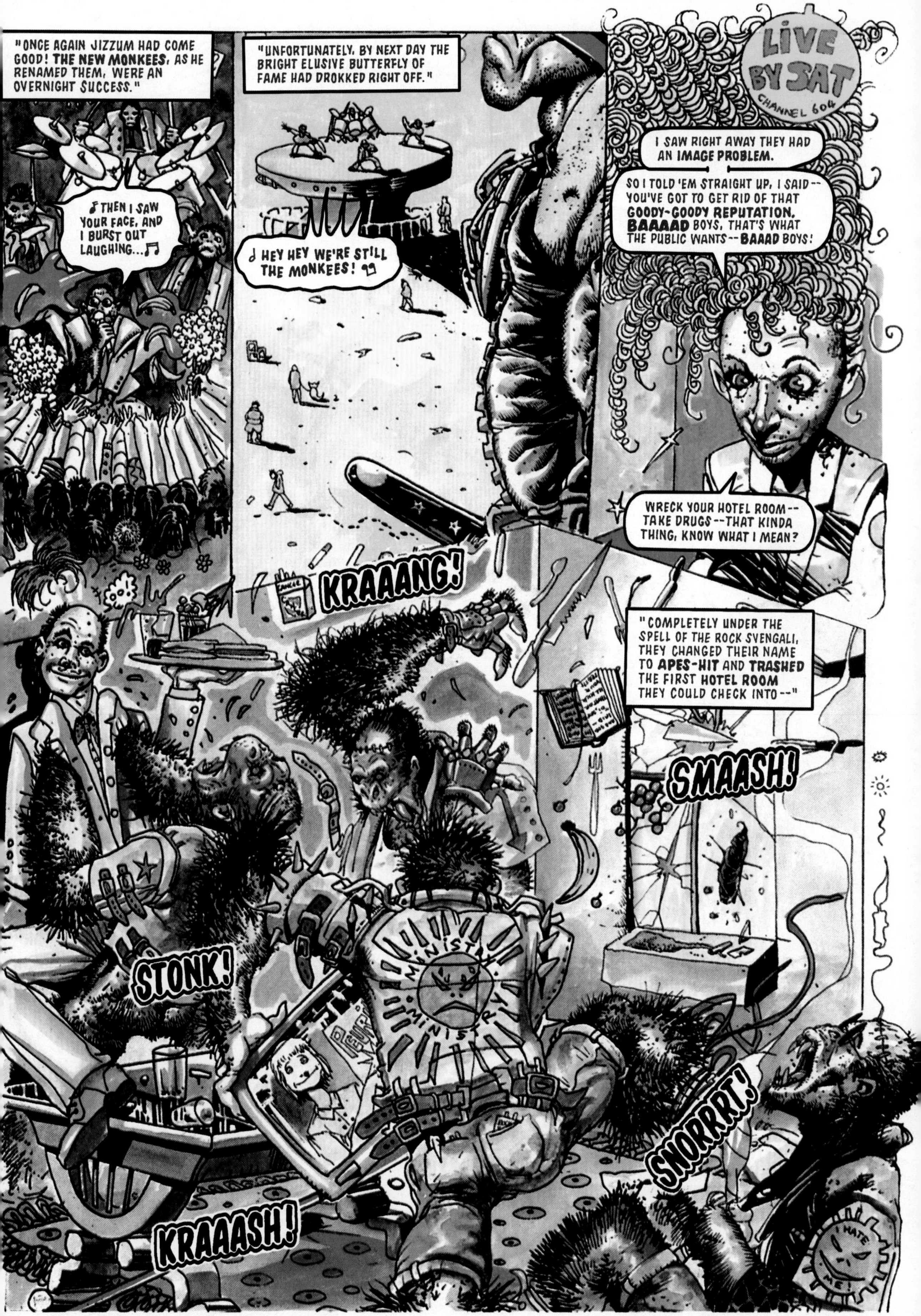
"ONCE AGAIN JIZZUM HAD COME GOOD! THE NEW MONKEES, AS HE RENAMED THEM, WERE AN OVERNIGHT SUCCESS."
THEN I SAW YOUR FACE, AND I BURST OUT LAUGHING...
"UNFORTUNATELY, BY NEXT DAY THE BRIGHT ELUSIVE BUTTERFLY OF FAME HAD DROKKED RIGHT OFF."
HEY HEY WE'RE STILL THE MONKEES!
LIVE BY SAT
CHANNEL 604
I SAW RIGHT AWAY THEY HAD AN IMAGE PROBLEM.
SO I TOLD 'EM STRAIGHT UP, I SAID-- YOU'VE GOT TO GET RID OF THAT GOODY-GOODY REPUTATION. BAAAAD BOYS, THAT'S WHAT THE PUBLIC WANTS--BAAAD BOYS!
WRECK YOUR HOTEL ROOM-- TAKE DRUGS--THAT KINDA THING, KNOW WHAT I MEAN?
KRAAANG!
"COMPLETELY UNDER THE SPELL OF THE ROCK SVENGALI, THEY CHANGED THEIR NAME TO APES-HIT AND TRASHED THE FIRST HOTEL ROOM THEY COULD CHECK INTO--"
SMAASH!
STONK!
MINISTRY
SNORRRT!
KRAAASH!
I HATE ME!

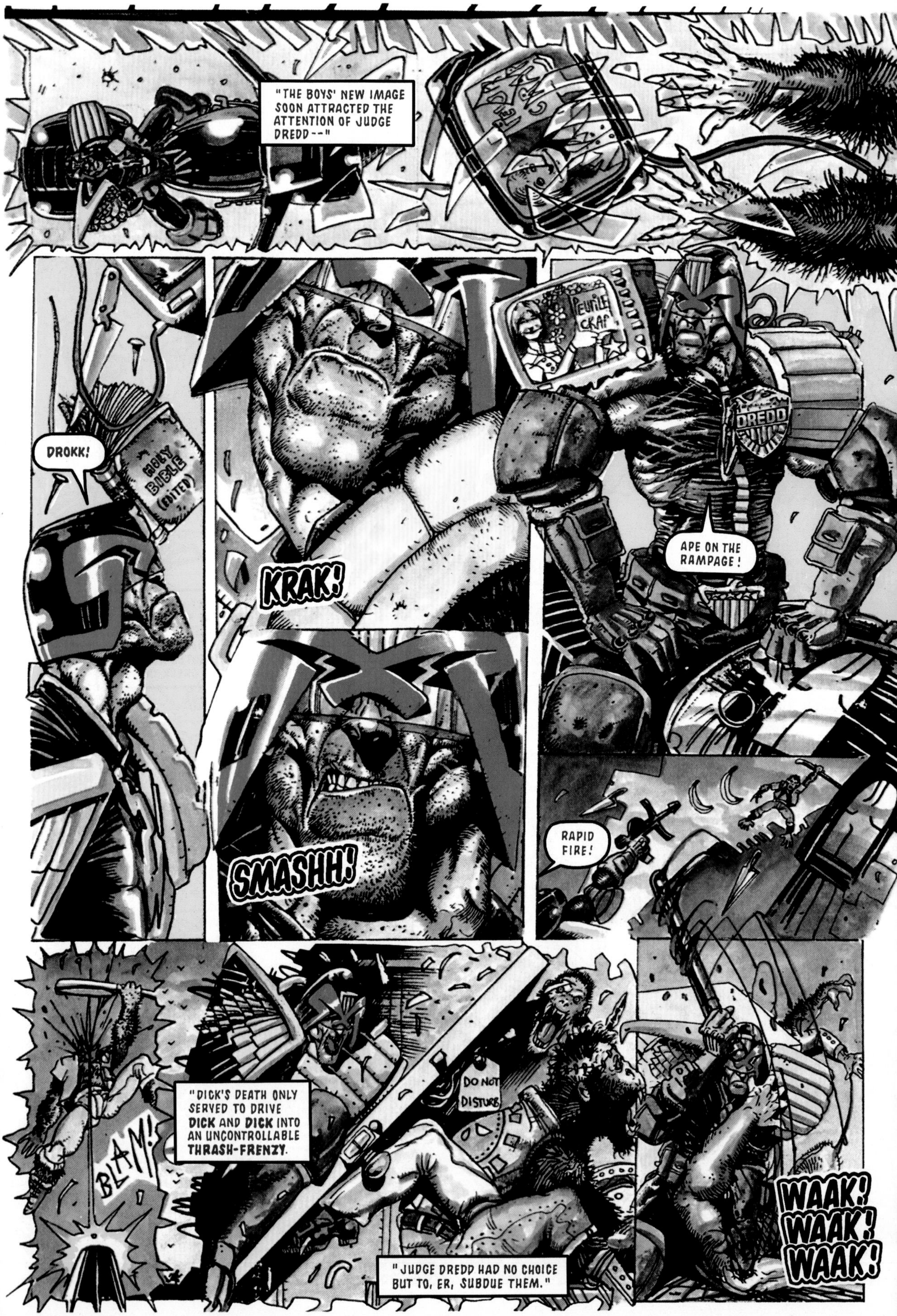

"THE BOYS' NEW IMAGE SOON ATTRACTED THE ATTENTION OF JUDGE DREDD--"
DROKK!
HOLY BIBLE (EDITED)
KRAK!
APE ON THE RAMPAGE!
DREDD
SMASHH!
RAPID FIRE!
"DICK'S DEATH ONLY SERVED TO DRIVE DICK AND DICK INTO AN UNCONTROLLABLE THRASH-FRENZY.
BLAM!
DO NOT DISTURB
"JUDGE DREDD HAD NO CHOICE BUT TO, ER, SUBDUE THEM."
WAAK! WAAK! WAAK!

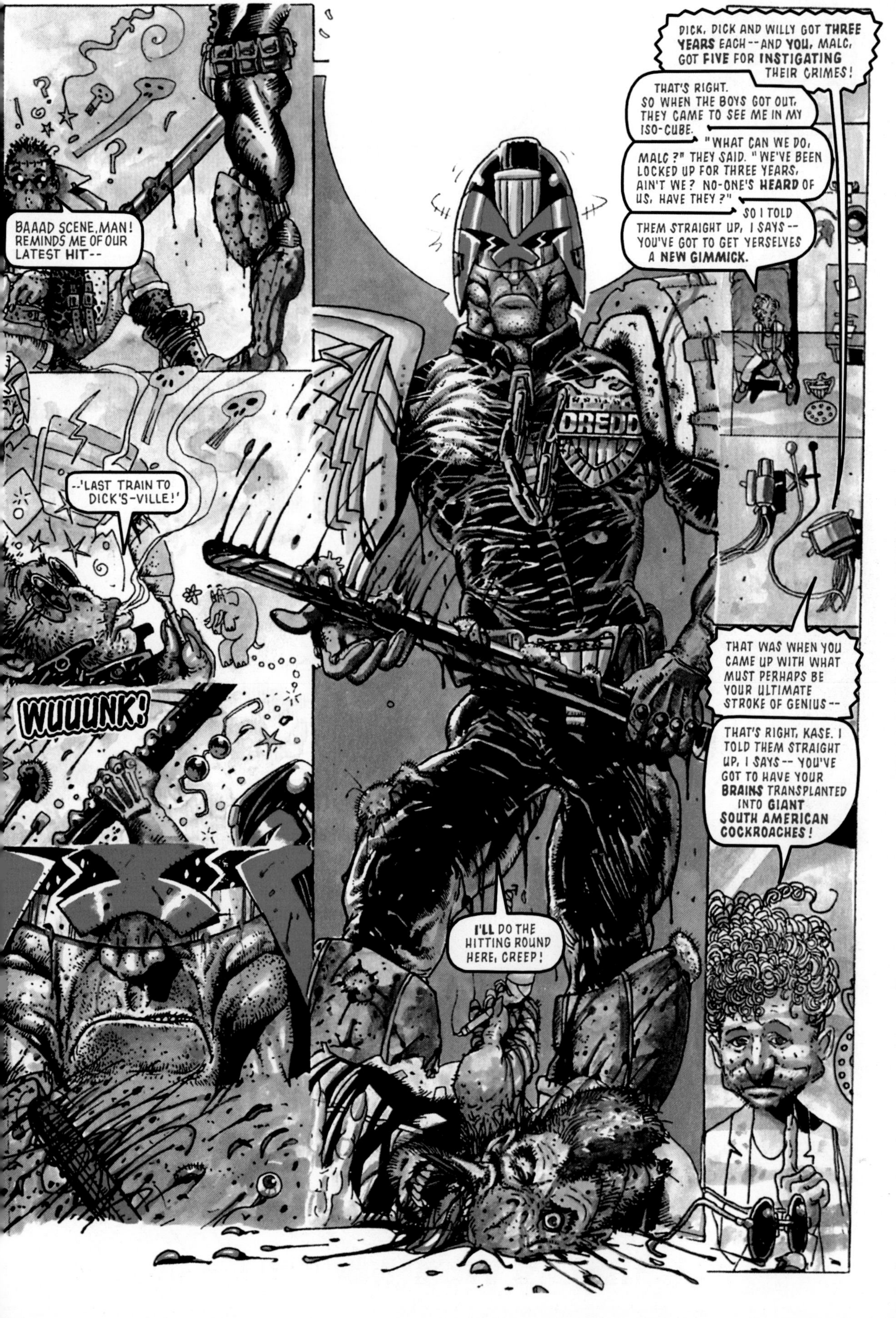
BAAAD SCENE, MAN! REMINDS ME OF OUR LATEST HIT--
--'LAST TRAIN TO DICK'S-VILLE!'
WUUUNK!
DICK, DICK AND WILLY GOT THREE YEARS EACH--AND YOU, MALC, GOT FIVE FOR INSTIGATING THEIR CRIMES!
THAT'S RIGHT. SO WHEN THE BOYS GOT OUT, THEY CAME TO SEE ME IN MY ISO-CUBE.
"WHAT CAN WE DO, MALC?" THEY SAID. "WE'VE BEEN LOCKED UP FOR THREE YEARS, AIN'T WE? NO-ONE'S HEARD OF US, HAVE THEY?"
SO I TOLD THEM STRAIGHT UP, I SAYS-- YOU'VE GOT TO GET YERSELVES A NEW GIMMICK.
THAT WAS WHEN YOU CAME UP WITH WHAT MUST PERHAPS BE YOUR ULTIMATE STROKE OF GENIUS--
THAT'S RIGHT, KASE. I TOLD THEM STRAIGHT UP, I SAYS-- YOU'VE GOT TO HAVE YOUR BRAINS TRANSPLANTED INTO GIANT SOUTH AMERICAN COCKROACHES!
I'LL DO THE HITTING ROUND HERE, CREEP!
DREDD

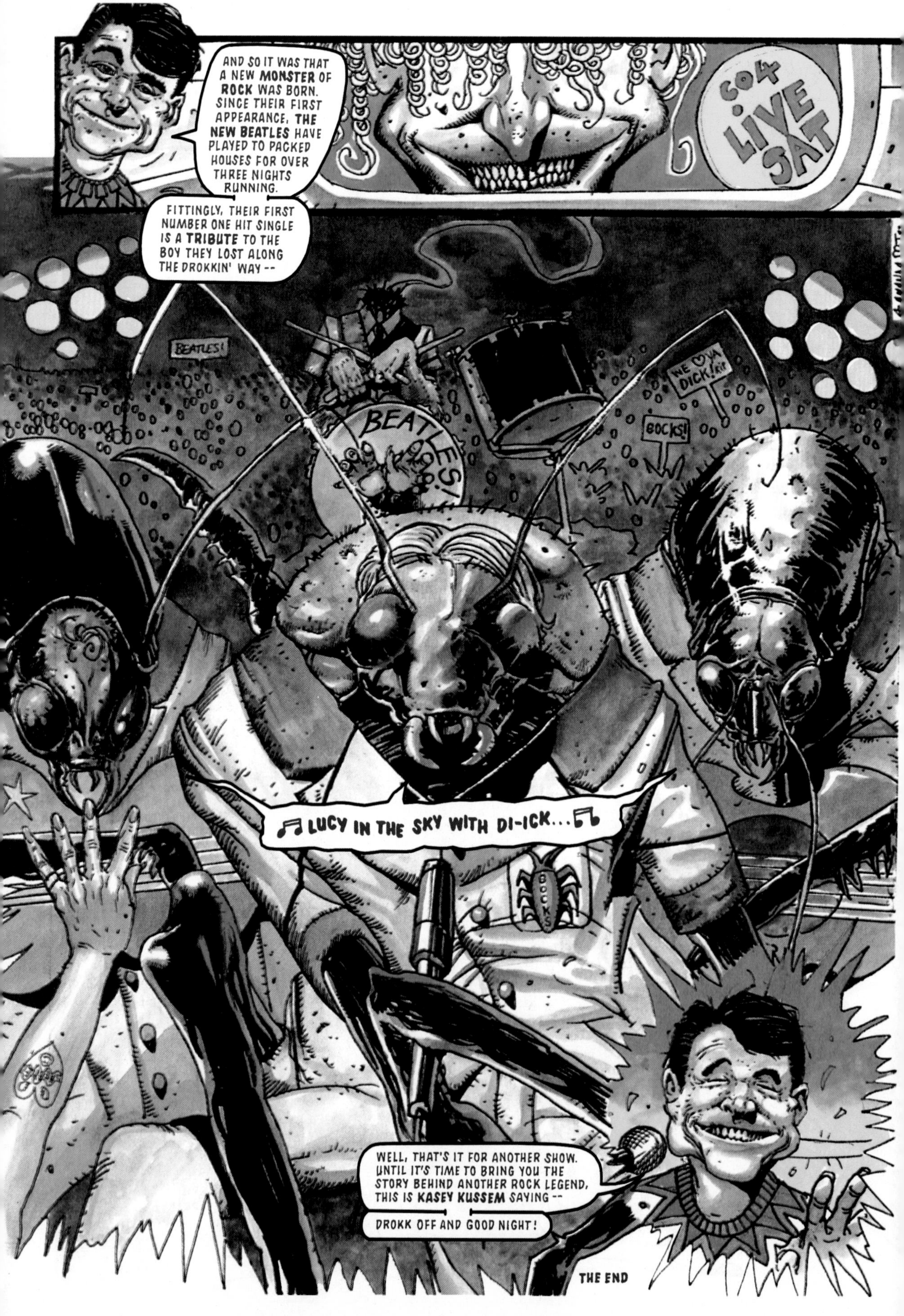

AND SO IT WAS THAT A NEW MONSTER OF ROCK WAS BORN. SINCE THEIR FIRST APPEARANCE, THE NEW BEATLES HAVE PLAYED TO PACKED HOUSES FOR OVER THREE NIGHTS RUNNING.
FITTINGLY, THEIR FIRST NUMBER ONE HIT SINGLE IS A TRIBUTE TO THE BOY THEY LOST ALONG THE DROKKIN' WAY --
C04 LIVE SAT
BEATLES!
BEATLES!
WE ♥ YA DICK!
BOCKS!
♫ LUCY IN THE SKY WITH DI-ICK... ♫
BOCKS
WELL, THAT'S IT FOR ANOTHER SHOW. UNTIL IT'S TIME TO BRING YOU THE STORY BEHIND ANOTHER ROCK LEGEND, THIS IS KASEY KUSSEM SAYING --
DROKK OFF AND GOOD NIGHT!
THE END

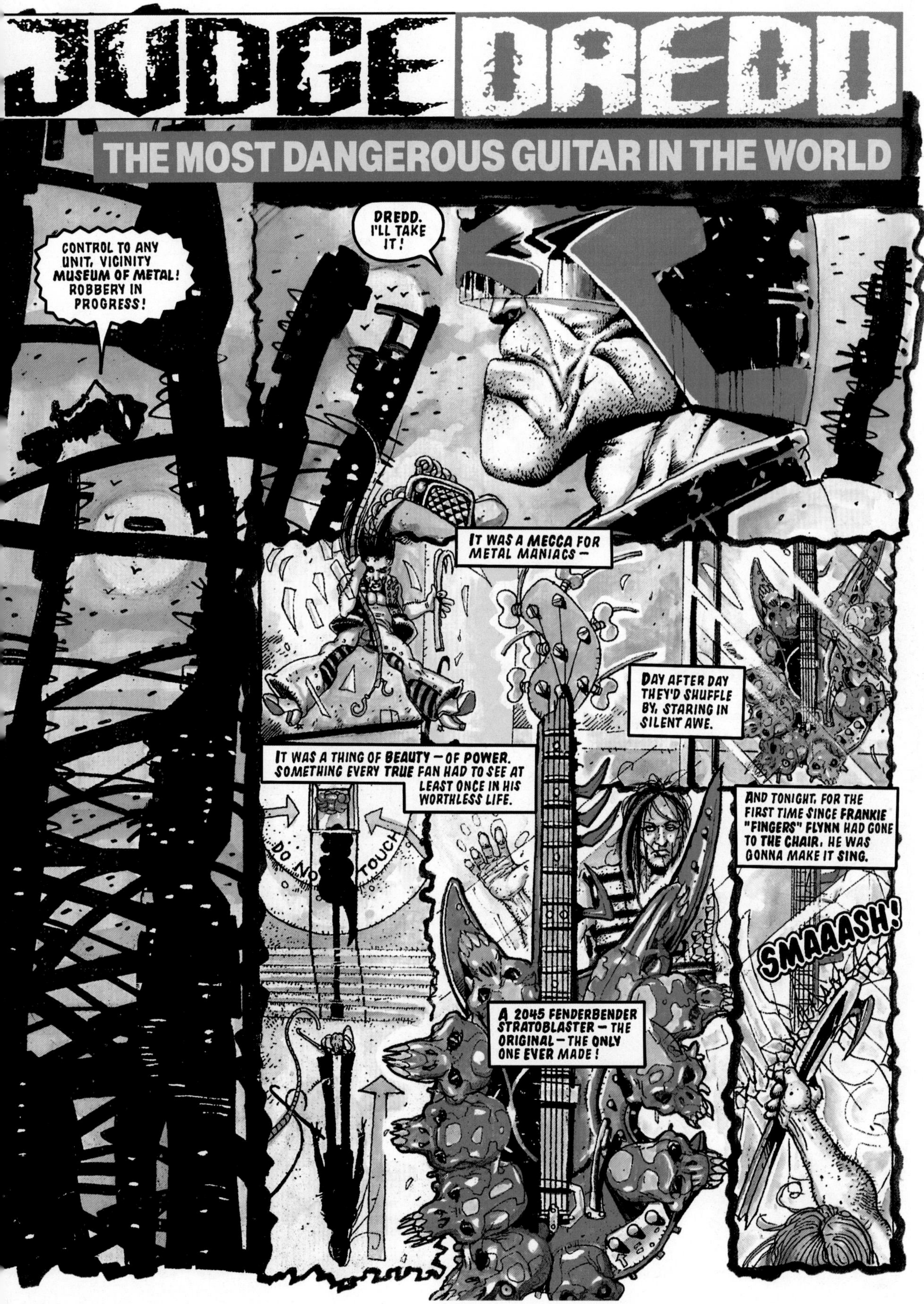
JUDGE DREDD
THE MOST DANGEROUS GUITAR IN THE WORLD
CONTROL TO ANY UNIT, VICINITY MUSEUM OF METAL! ROBBERY IN PROGRESS!
DREDD. I'LL TAKE IT!
IT WAS A MECCA FOR METAL MANIACS —
DAY AFTER DAY THEY'D SHUFFLE BY, STARING IN SILENT AWE.
IT WAS A THING OF BEAUTY — OF POWER. SOMETHING EVERY TRUE FAN HAD TO SEE AT LEAST ONCE IN HIS WORTHLESS LIFE.
DO NO
TOUCH
A 2045 FENDERBENDER STRATOBLASTER — THE ORIGINAL — THE ONLY ONE EVER MADE!
AND TONIGHT, FOR THE FIRST TIME SINCE FRANKIE "FINGERS" FLYNN HAD GONE TO THE CHAIR, HE WAS GONNA MAKE IT SING.
SMAAASH!

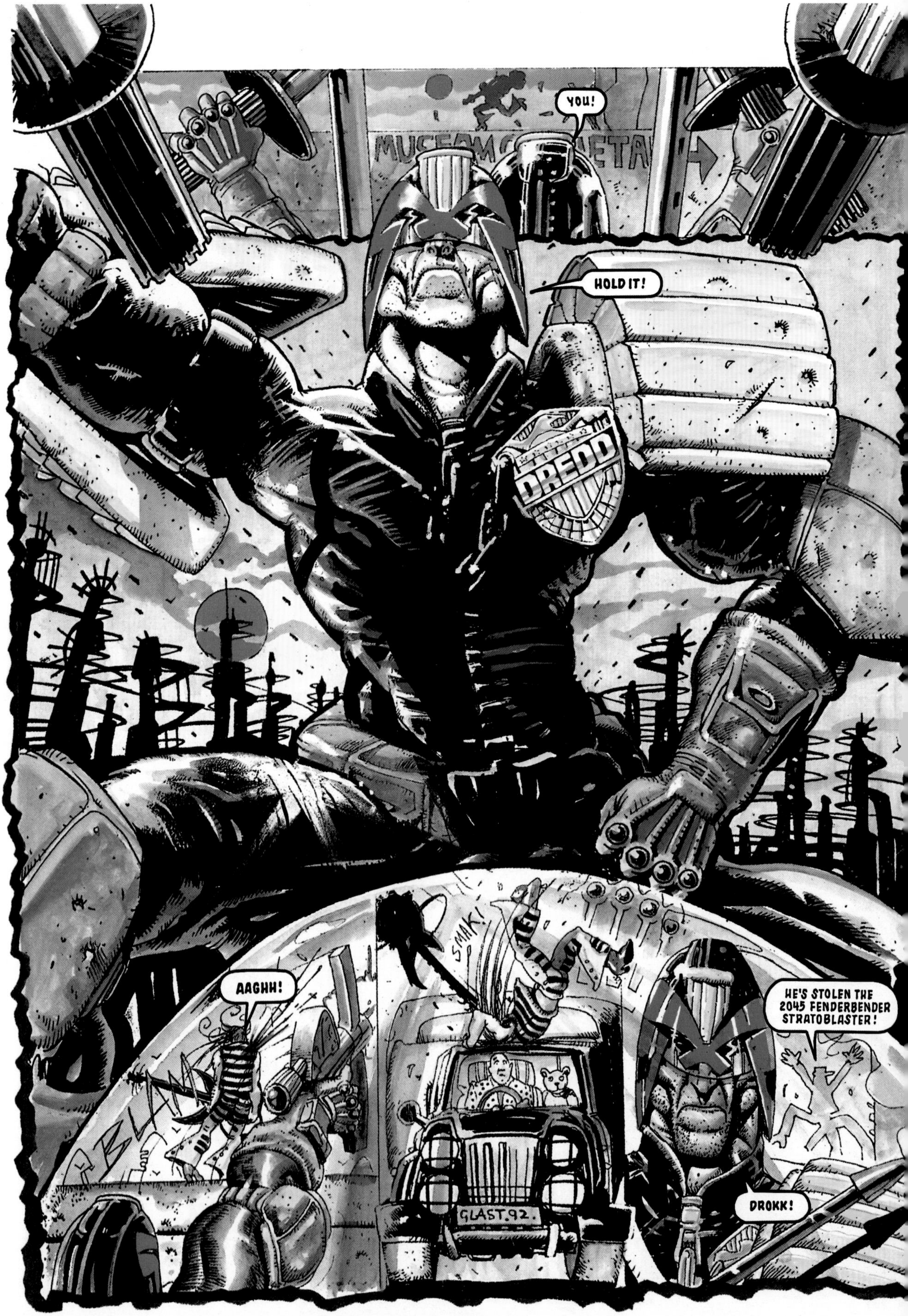
YOU!
HOLD IT!
AAGHH!
SMAK!
HE'S STOLEN THE 2045 FENDERBENDER STRATOBLASTER!
GLAST.92.
DROKK!

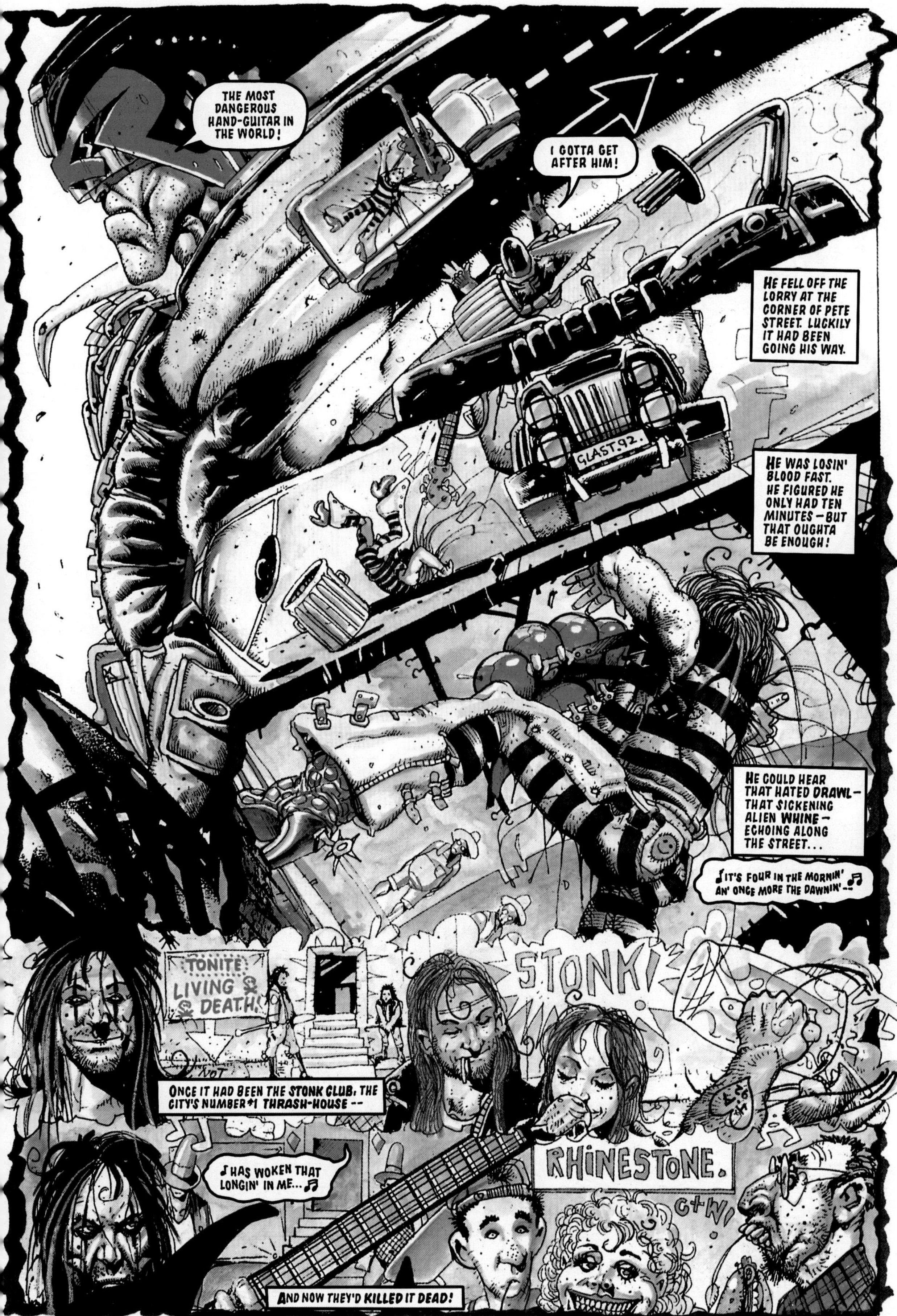
THE MOST DANGEROUS HAND-GUITAR IN THE WORLD!
I GOTTA GET AFTER HIM!
HE FELL OFF THE LORRY AT THE CORNER OF PETE STREET. LUCKILY IT HAD BEEN GOING HIS WAY.
GLAST.92.
HE WAS LOSIN' BLOOD FAST. HE FIGURED HE ONLY HAD TEN MINUTES – BUT THAT OUGHTA BE ENOUGH!
HE COULD HEAR THAT HATED DRAWL – THAT SICKENING ALIEN WHINE – ECHOING ALONG THE STREET...
♪IT'S FOUR IN THE MORNIN' AN' ONCE MORE THE DAWNIN' --♫
TONITE LIVING DEATH!
STONK!
ONCE IT HAD BEEN THE STONK CLUB: THE CITY'S NUMBER #1 THRASH-HOUSE --
♪HAS WOKEN THAT LONGIN' IN ME...♫
RHINESTONE.
AND NOW THEY'D KILLED IT DEAD!

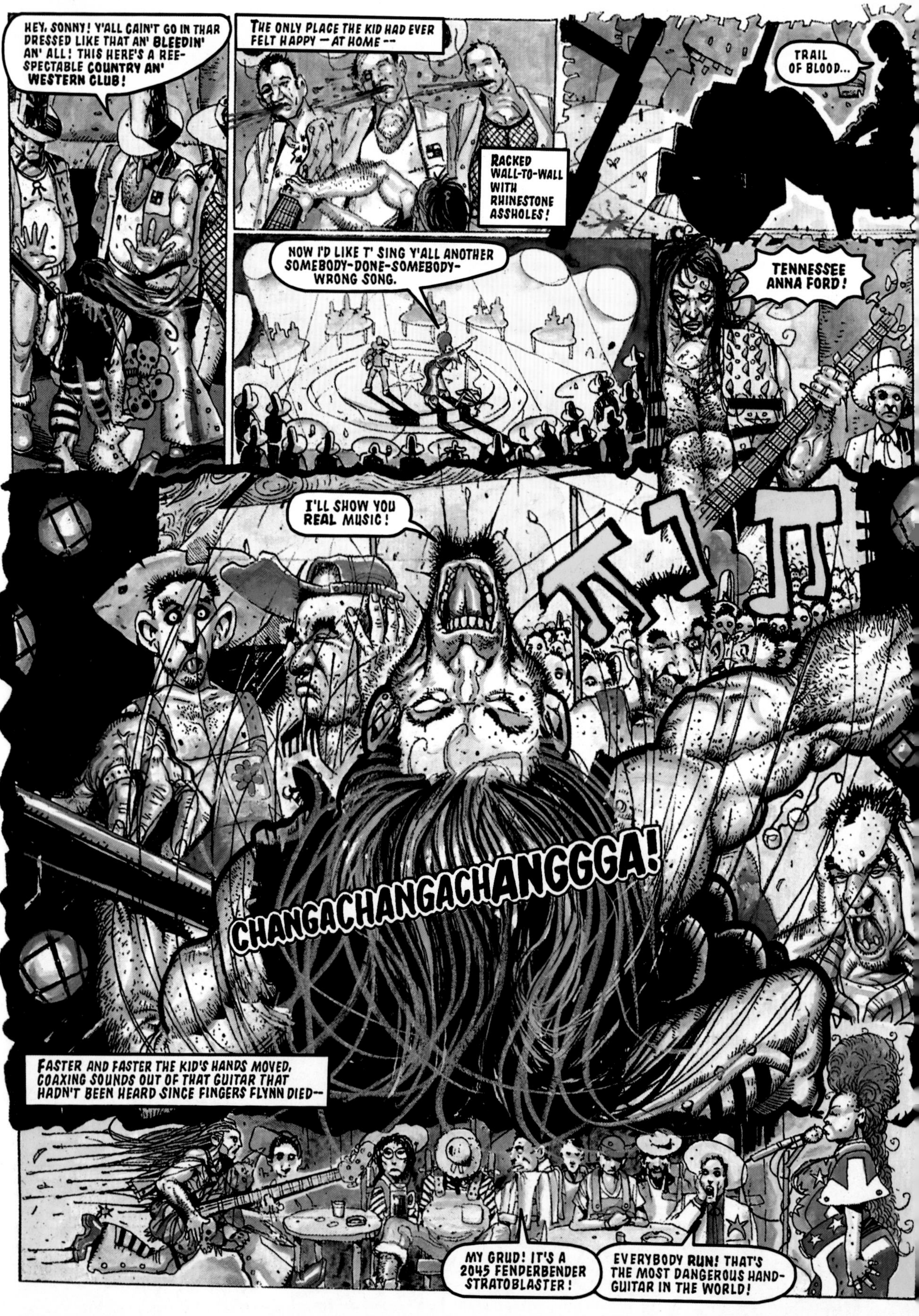
HEY, SONNY! Y'ALL CAIN'T GO IN THAR DRESSED LIKE THAT AN' BLEEDIN' AN' ALL! THIS HERE'S A REE-SPECTABLE COUNTRY AN' WESTERN CLUB!
THE ONLY PLACE THE KID HAD EVER FELT HAPPY — AT HOME --
RACKED WALL-TO-WALL WITH RHINESTONE ASSHOLES!
TRAIL OF BLOOD...
NOW I'D LIKE T' SING Y'ALL ANOTHER SOMEBODY-DONE-SOMEBODY-WRONG SONG.
TENNESSEE ANNA FORD!
I'LL SHOW YOU REAL MUSIC!
CHANGACHANGACHANGGGA!
FASTER AND FASTER THE KID'S HANDS MOVED, COAXING SOUNDS OUT OF THAT GUITAR THAT HADN'T BEEN HEARD SINCE FINGERS FLYNN DIED--
MY GRUD! IT'S A 2045 FENDERBENDER STRATOBLASTER!
EVERYBODY RUN! THAT'S THE MOST DANGEROUS HAND-GUITAR IN THE WORLD!

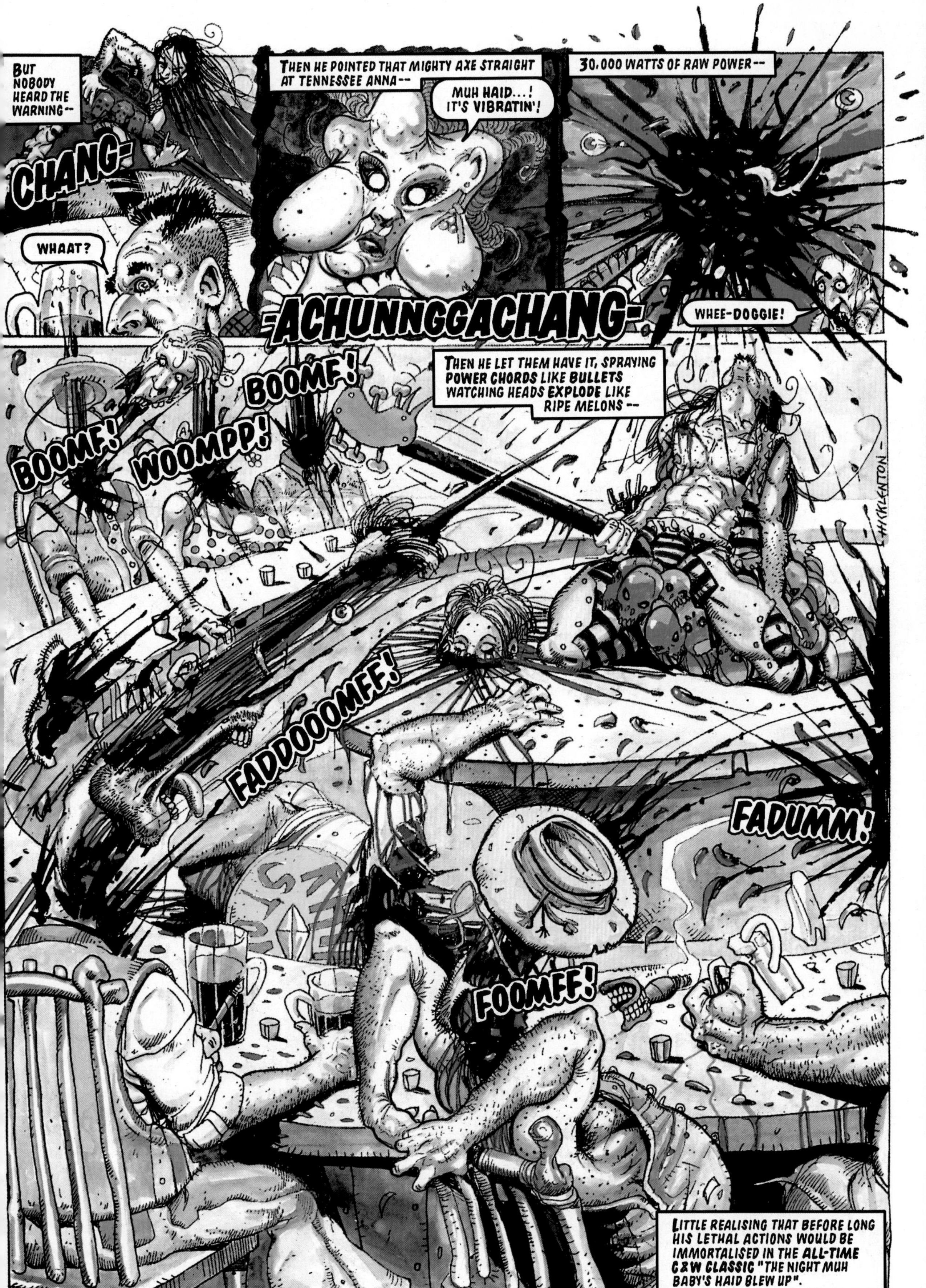

BUT NOBODY HEARD THE WARNING--
CHANG-
WHAAT?
THEN HE POINTED THAT MIGHTY AXE STRAIGHT AT TENNESSEE ANNA--
MUH HAID...! IT'S VIBRATIN'!
30,000 WATTS OF RAW POWER--
-ACHUNNGGACHANG-
WHEE-DOGGIE!
THEN HE LET THEM HAVE IT, SPRAYING POWER CHORDS LIKE BULLETS WATCHING HEADS EXPLODE LIKE RIPE MELONS--
BOOMF!
BOOMF!
WOOMPP!
FADDOOOMFF!
FADUMM!
FOOMFF!
HICKLENTON
LITTLE REALISING THAT BEFORE LONG HIS LETHAL ACTIONS WOULD BE IMMORTALISED IN THE ALL-TIME C&W CLASSIC "THE NIGHT MUH BABY'S HAID BLEW UP".

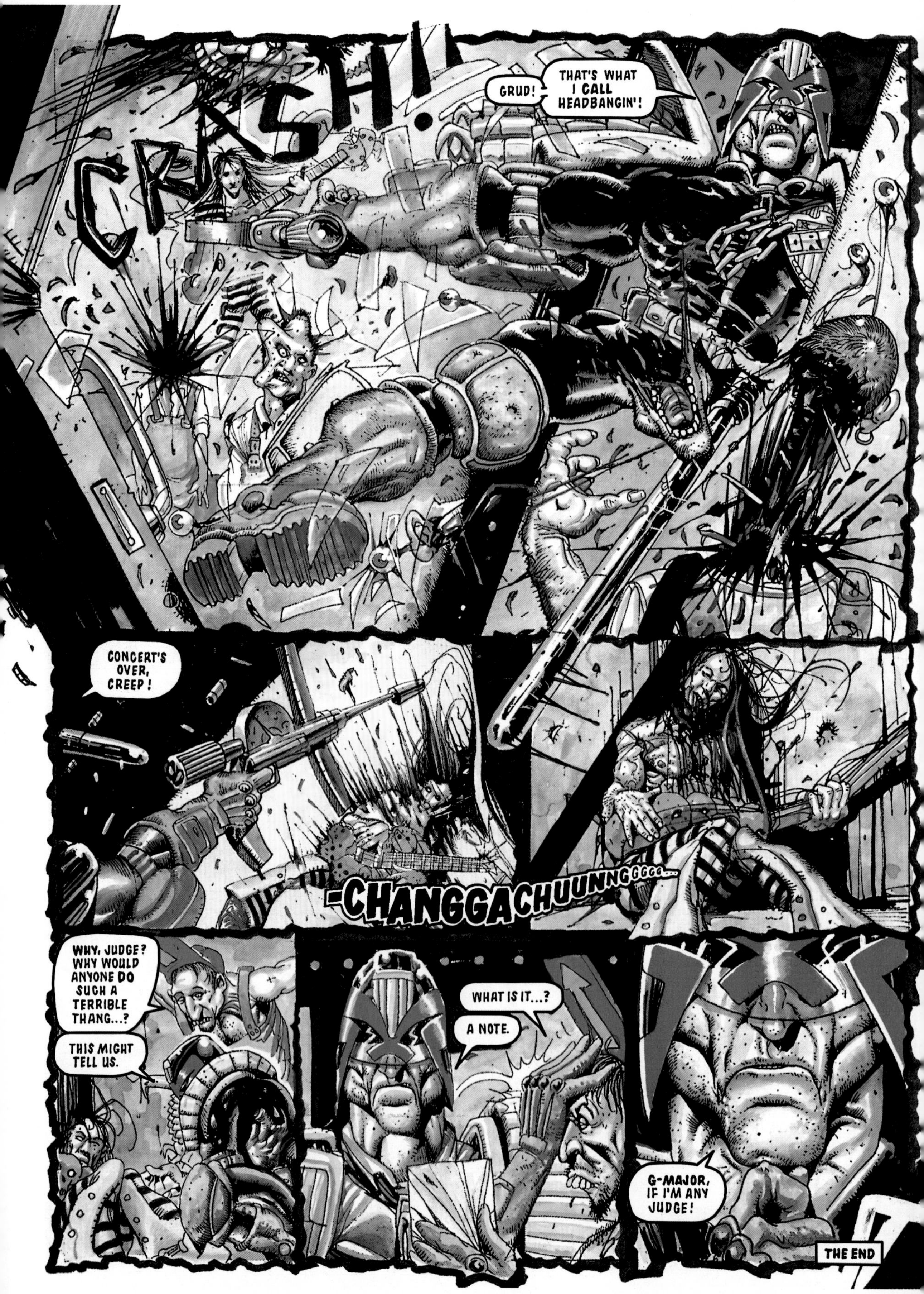
CRASH!
GRUD!
THAT'S WHAT I CALL HEADBANGIN'!
CONCERT'S OVER, CREEP!
-CHANGGACHUUNNGGGG...
WHY, JUDGE? WHY WOULD ANYONE DO SUCH A TERRIBLE THANG...?
THIS MIGHT TELL US.
WHAT IS IT...?
A NOTE.
G-MAJOR, IF I'M ANY JUDGE!
THE END

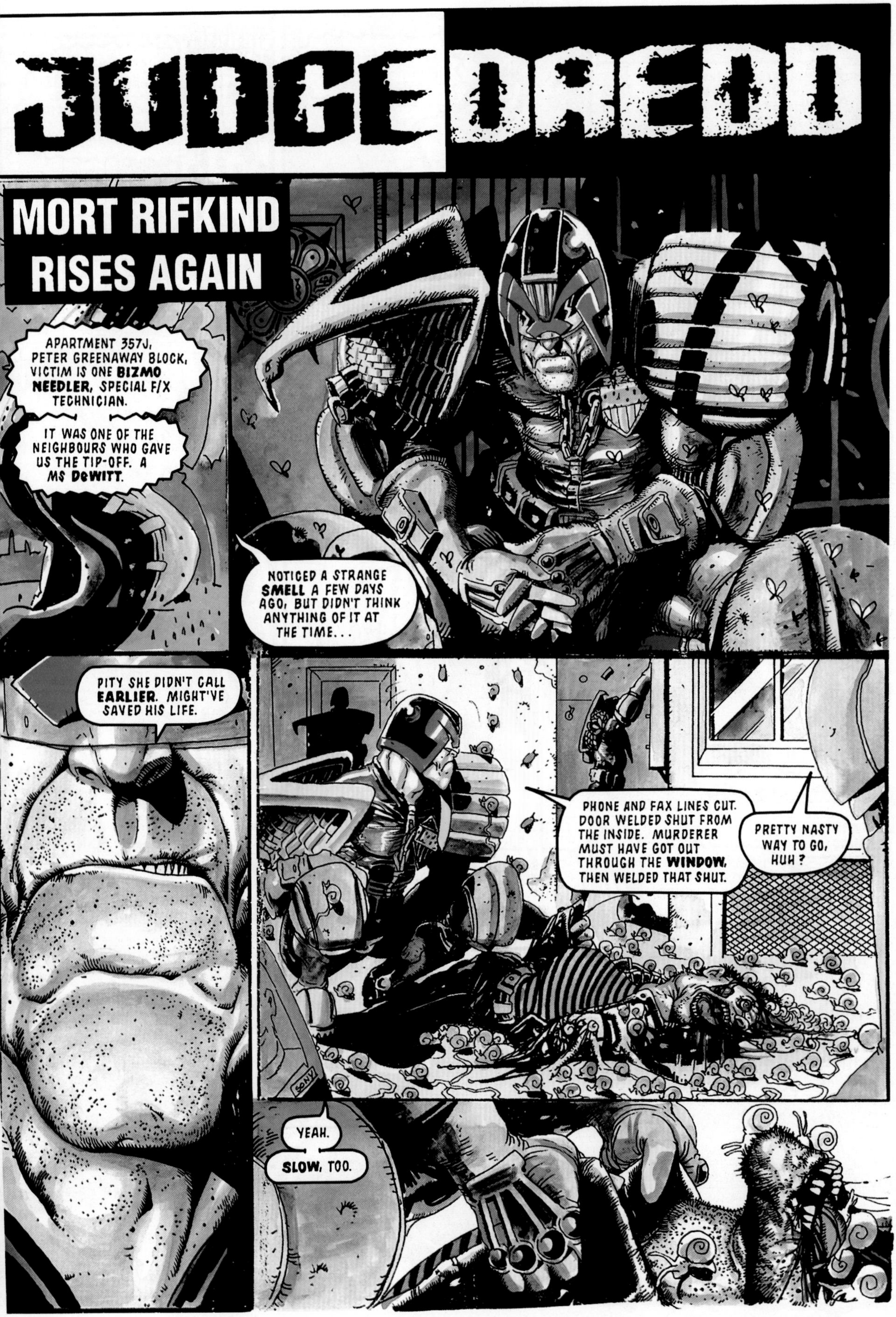
JUDGE DREDD
MORT RIFKIND RISES AGAIN
APARTMENT 357J, PETER GREENAWAY BLOCK, VICTIM IS ONE BIZMO NEEDLER, SPECIAL F/X TECHNICIAN.
IT WAS ONE OF THE NEIGHBOURS WHO GAVE US THE TIP-OFF. A MS DeWITT.
NOTICED A STRANGE SMELL A FEW DAYS AGO, BUT DIDN'T THINK ANYTHING OF IT AT THE TIME...
PITY SHE DIDN'T CALL EARLIER. MIGHT'VE SAVED HIS LIFE.
PHONE AND FAX LINES CUT. DOOR WELDED SHUT FROM THE INSIDE. MURDERER MUST HAVE GOT OUT THROUGH THE WINDOW, THEN WELDED THAT SHUT.
PRETTY NASTY WAY TO GO, HUH ?
YEAH.
SLOW, TOO.

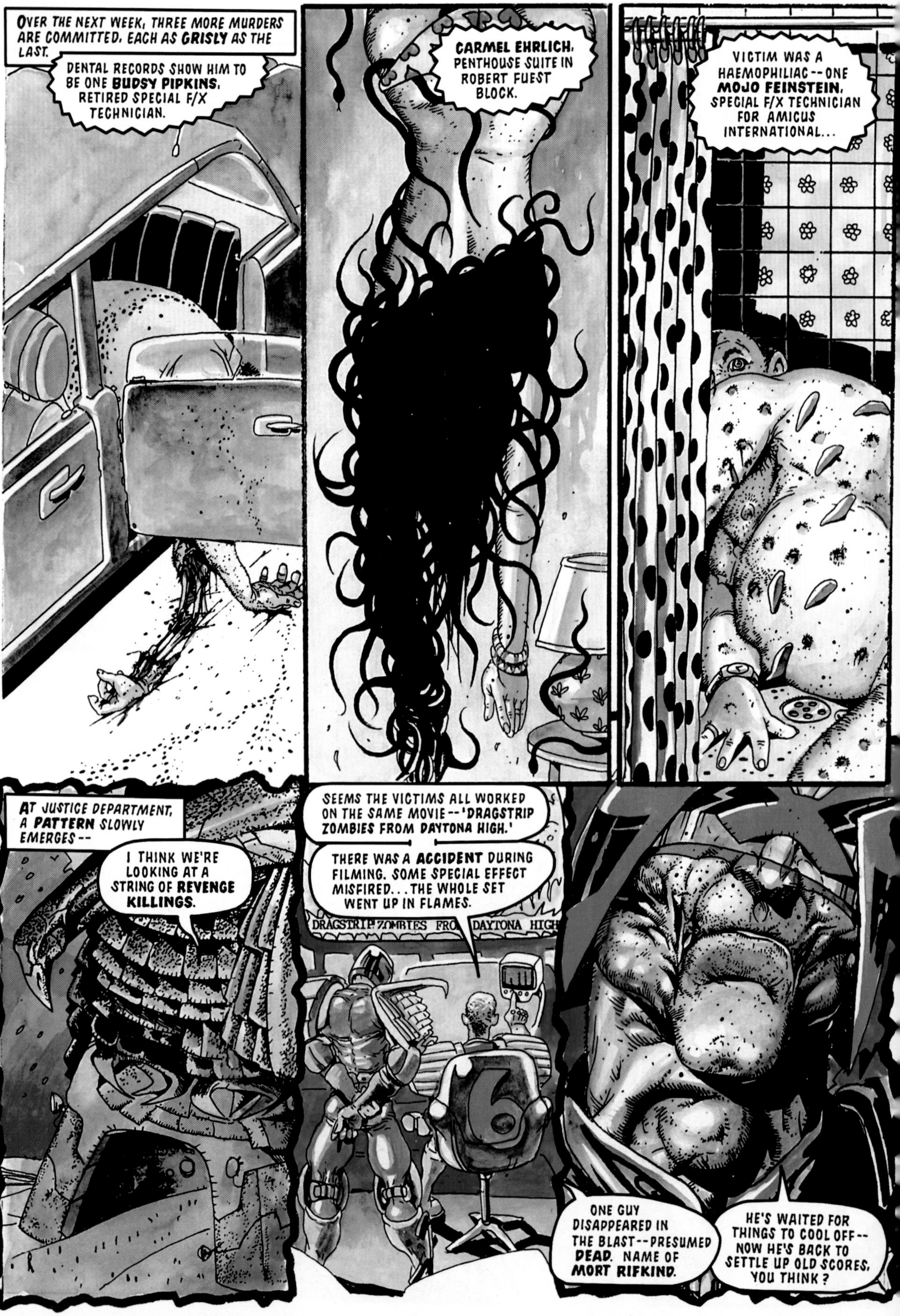
OVER THE NEXT WEEK, THREE MORE MURDERS ARE COMMITTED, EACH AS GRISLY AS THE LAST.
DENTAL RECORDS SHOW HIM TO BE ONE BUDSY PIPKINS, RETIRED SPECIAL F/X TECHNICIAN.
CARMEL EHRLICH, PENTHOUSE SUITE IN ROBERT FUEST BLOCK.
VICTIM WAS A HAEMOPHILIAC--ONE MOJO FEINSTEIN, SPECIAL F/X TECHNICIAN FOR AMICUS INTERNATIONAL...
AT JUSTICE DEPARTMENT, A PATTERN SLOWLY EMERGES--
I THINK WE'RE LOOKING AT A STRING OF REVENGE KILLINGS.
SEEMS THE VICTIMS ALL WORKED ON THE SAME MOVIE--'DRAGSTRIP ZOMBIES FROM DAYTONA HIGH.'
THERE WAS A ACCIDENT DURING FILMING. SOME SPECIAL EFFECT MISFIRED...THE WHOLE SET WENT UP IN FLAMES.
DRAGSTRIP ZOMBIES FROM DAYTONA HIGH
ONE GUY DISAPPEARED IN THE BLAST--PRESUMED DEAD. NAME OF MORT RIFKIND.
HE'S WAITED FOR THINGS TO COOL OFF--NOW HE'S BACK TO SETTLE UP OLD SCORES, YOU THINK?

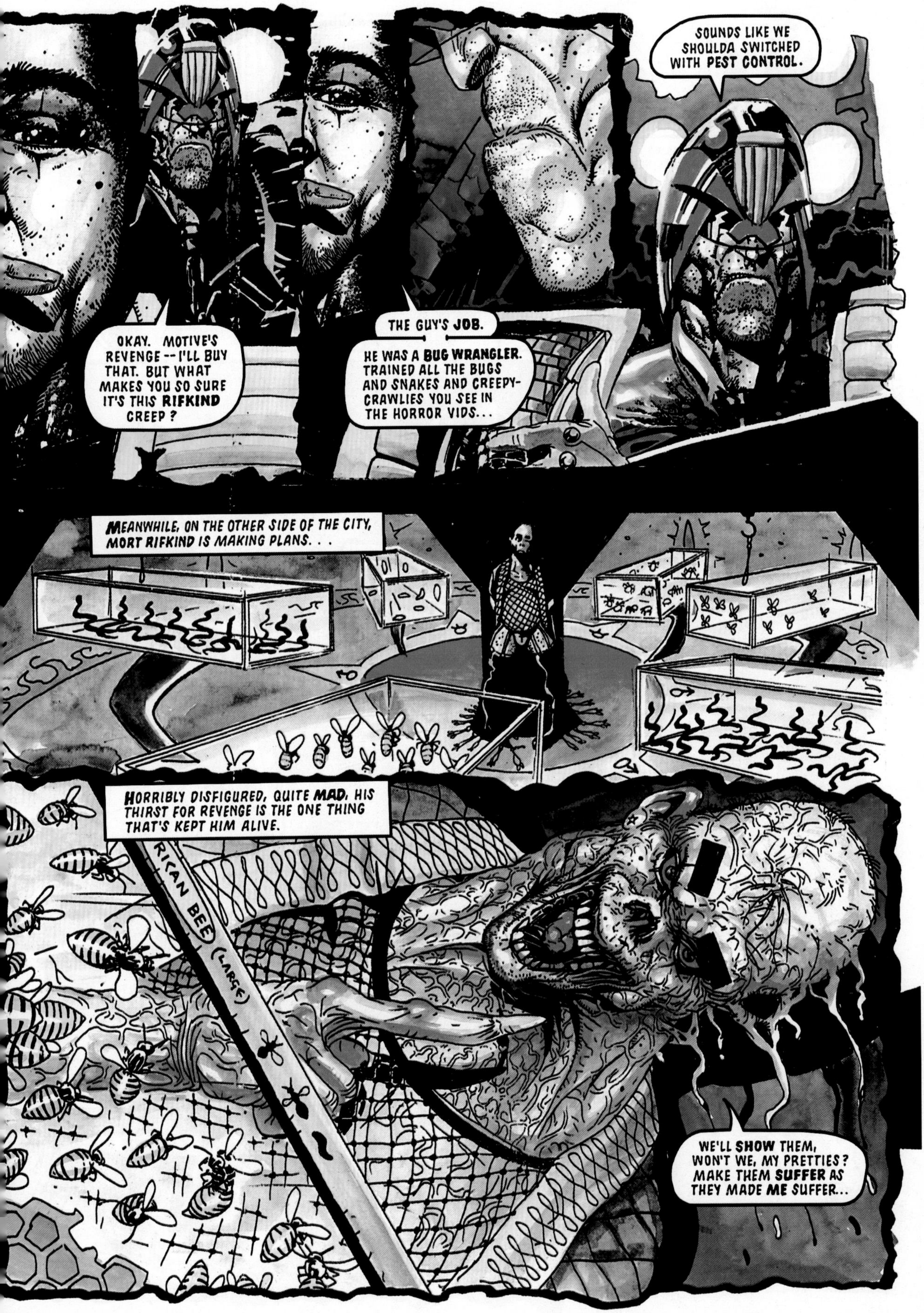
OKAY. MOTIVE'S REVENGE -- I'LL BUY THAT. BUT WHAT MAKES YOU SO SURE IT'S THIS **RIFKIND** CREEP ?
THE GUY'S **JOB**.
HE WAS A **BUG WRANGLER**. TRAINED ALL THE BUGS AND SNAKES AND CREEPY-CRAWLIES YOU SEE IN THE HORROR VIDS...
SOUNDS LIKE WE SHOULDA SWITCHED WITH **PEST CONTROL**.
MEANWHILE, ON THE OTHER SIDE OF THE CITY, MORT RIFKIND IS MAKING PLANS. . .
HORRIBLY DISFIGURED, QUITE **MAD**, HIS THIRST FOR REVENGE IS THE ONE THING THAT'S KEPT HIM ALIVE.
RICAN BEE
(LARGE)
WE'LL **SHOW** THEM, WON'T WE, MY PRETTIES? MAKE THEM **SUFFER** AS THEY MADE **ME** SUFFER...

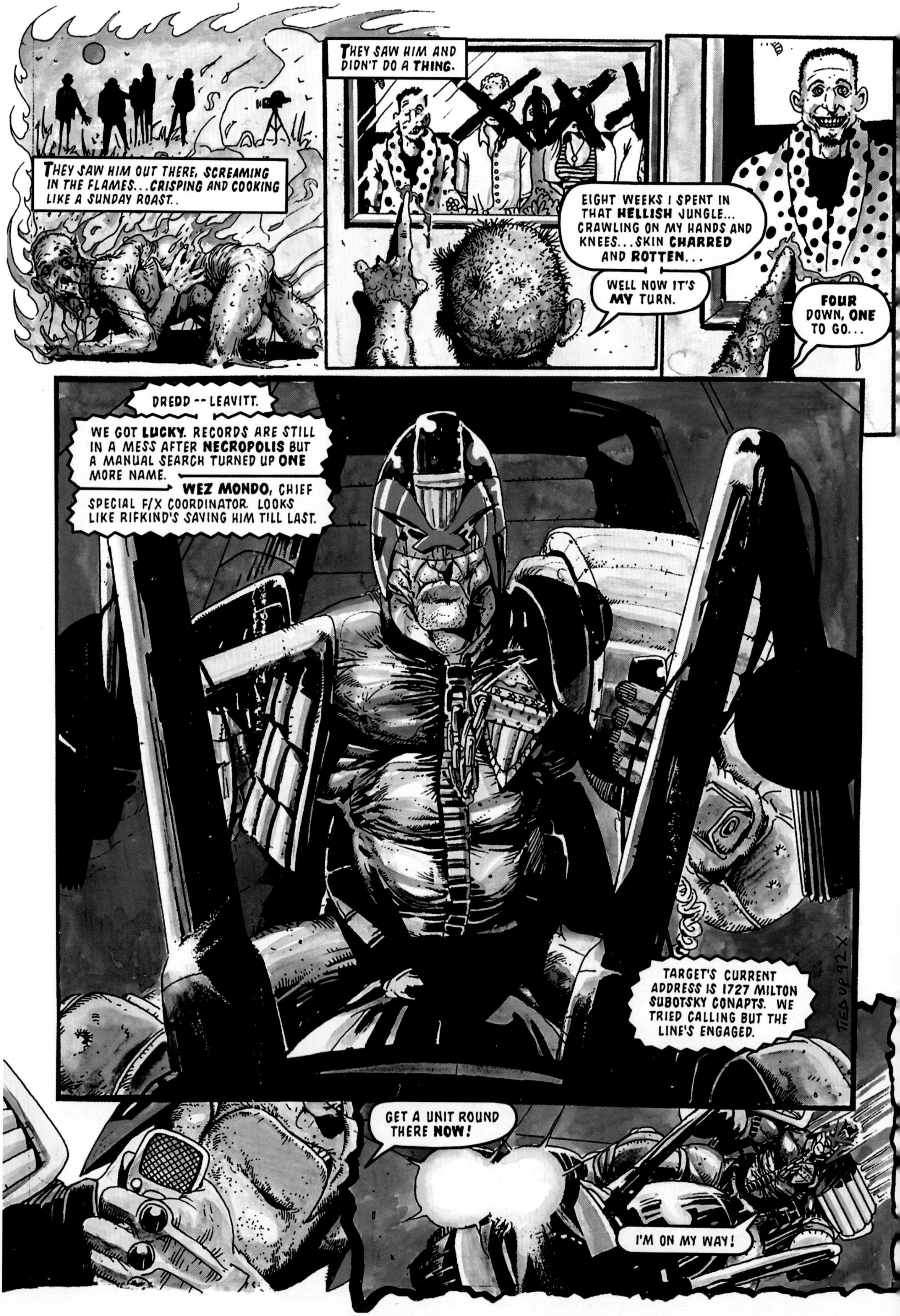
THEY SAW HIM OUT THERE, SCREAMING IN THE FLAMES...CRISPING AND COOKING LIKE A SUNDAY ROAST..
THEY SAW HIM AND DIDN'T DO A THING.
EIGHT WEEKS I SPENT IN THAT HELLISH JUNGLE... CRAWLING ON MY HANDS AND KNEES...SKIN CHARRED AND ROTTEN...
WELL NOW IT'S MY TURN.
FOUR DOWN, ONE TO GO...
DREDD -- LEAVITT.
WE GOT LUCKY. RECORDS ARE STILL IN A MESS AFTER NECROPOLIS BUT A MANUAL SEARCH TURNED UP ONE MORE NAME.
WEZ MONDO, CHIEF SPECIAL F/X COORDINATOR. LOOKS LIKE RIFKIND'S SAVING HIM TILL LAST.
TARGET'S CURRENT ADDRESS IS 1727 MILTON SUBOTSKY CONAPTS. WE TRIED CALLING BUT THE LINE'S ENGAGED.
GET A UNIT ROUND THERE NOW!
I'M ON MY WAY!

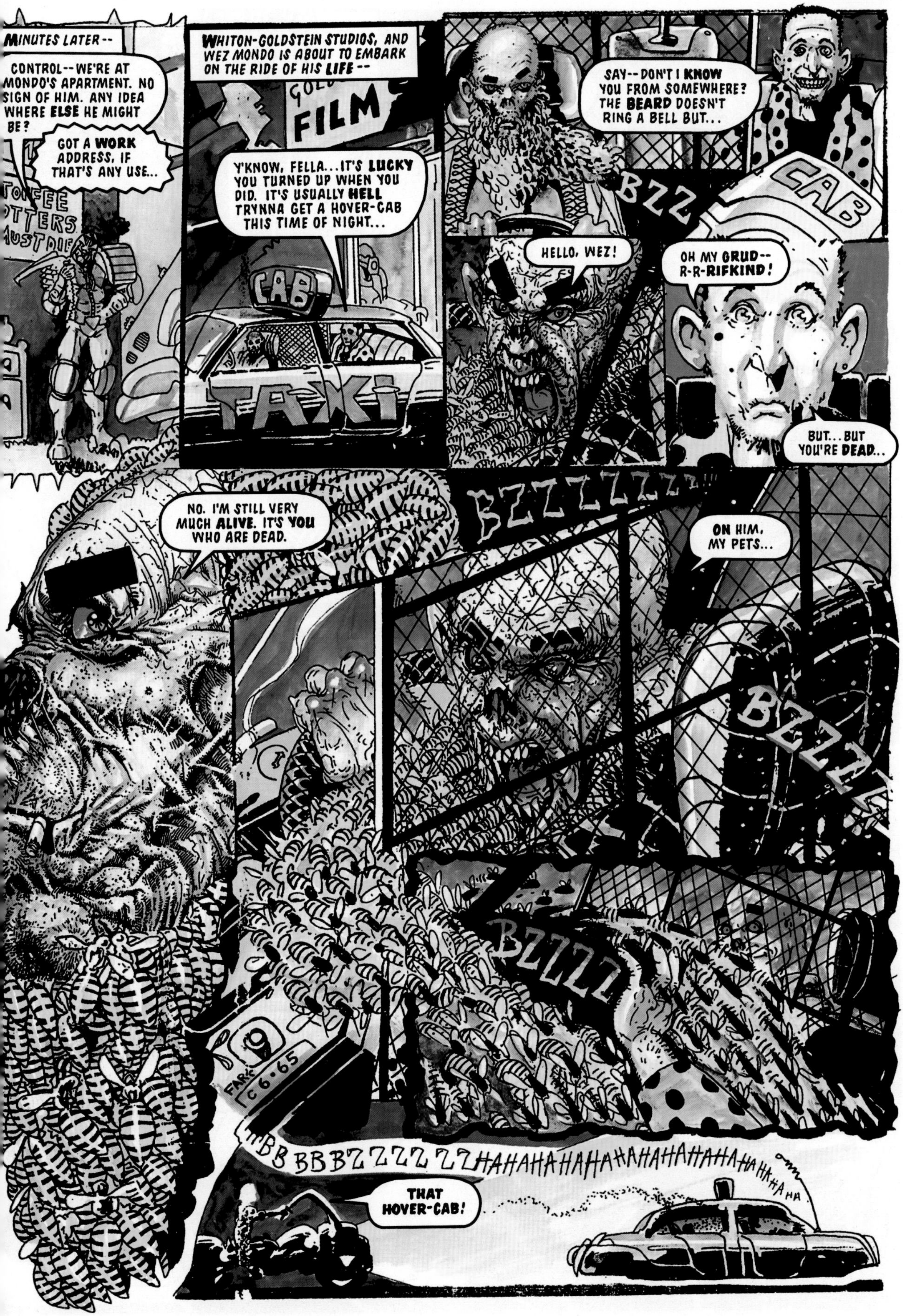
MINUTES LATER--
CONTROL--WE'RE AT MONDO'S APARTMENT. NO SIGN OF HIM. ANY IDEA WHERE ELSE HE MIGHT BE?
GOT A WORK ADDRESS, IF THAT'S ANY USE...
WHITON-GOLDSTEIN STUDIOS, AND WEZ MONDO IS ABOUT TO EMBARK ON THE RIDE OF HIS LIFE--
FILM
Y'KNOW, FELLA...IT'S LUCKY YOU TURNED UP WHEN YOU DID. IT'S USUALLY HELL TRYNNA GET A HOVER-CAB THIS TIME OF NIGHT...
CAB
TAXI
SAY--DON'T I KNOW YOU FROM SOMEWHERE? THE BEARD DOESN'T RING A BELL BUT...
BZZ
CAB
HELLO, WEZ!
OH MY GRUD-- R-R-RIFKIND!
BUT...BUT YOU'RE DEAD...
NO. I'M STILL VERY MUCH ALIVE. IT'S YOU WHO ARE DEAD.
BZZZZZZZ
ON HIM, MY PETS...
BZZZ
BZZZZ
FARE C 6·65
BBBBBZZZZZZZHAHAHAHAHAHAHAHAHAHAHAHAHA
THAT HOVER-CAB!

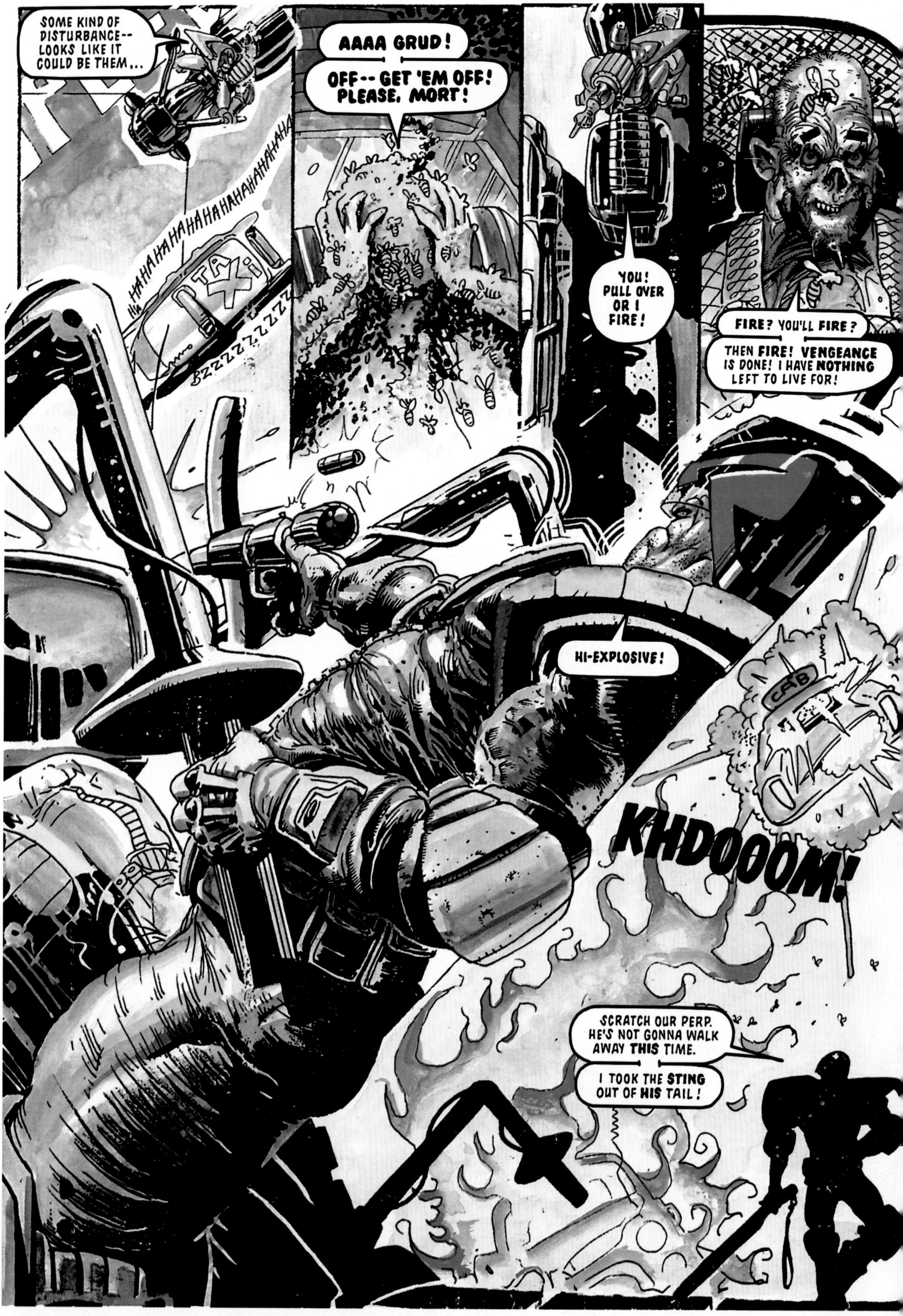
SOME KIND OF DISTURBANCE-- LOOKS LIKE IT COULD BE THEM...
HAHAHAHAHAHAHAHAHAHAHAHAHAHAHA
BZZZZZZZZZZ
AAAA GRUD!
OFF-- GET 'EM OFF! PLEASE, MORT!
YOU! PULL OVER OR I FIRE!
FIRE? YOU'LL FIRE?
THEN FIRE! VENGEANCE IS DONE! I HAVE NOTHING LEFT TO LIVE FOR!
HI-EXPLOSIVE!
KHDOOOM!
SCRATCH OUR PERP. HE'S NOT GONNA WALK AWAY THIS TIME.
I TOOK THE STING OUT OF HIS TAIL!

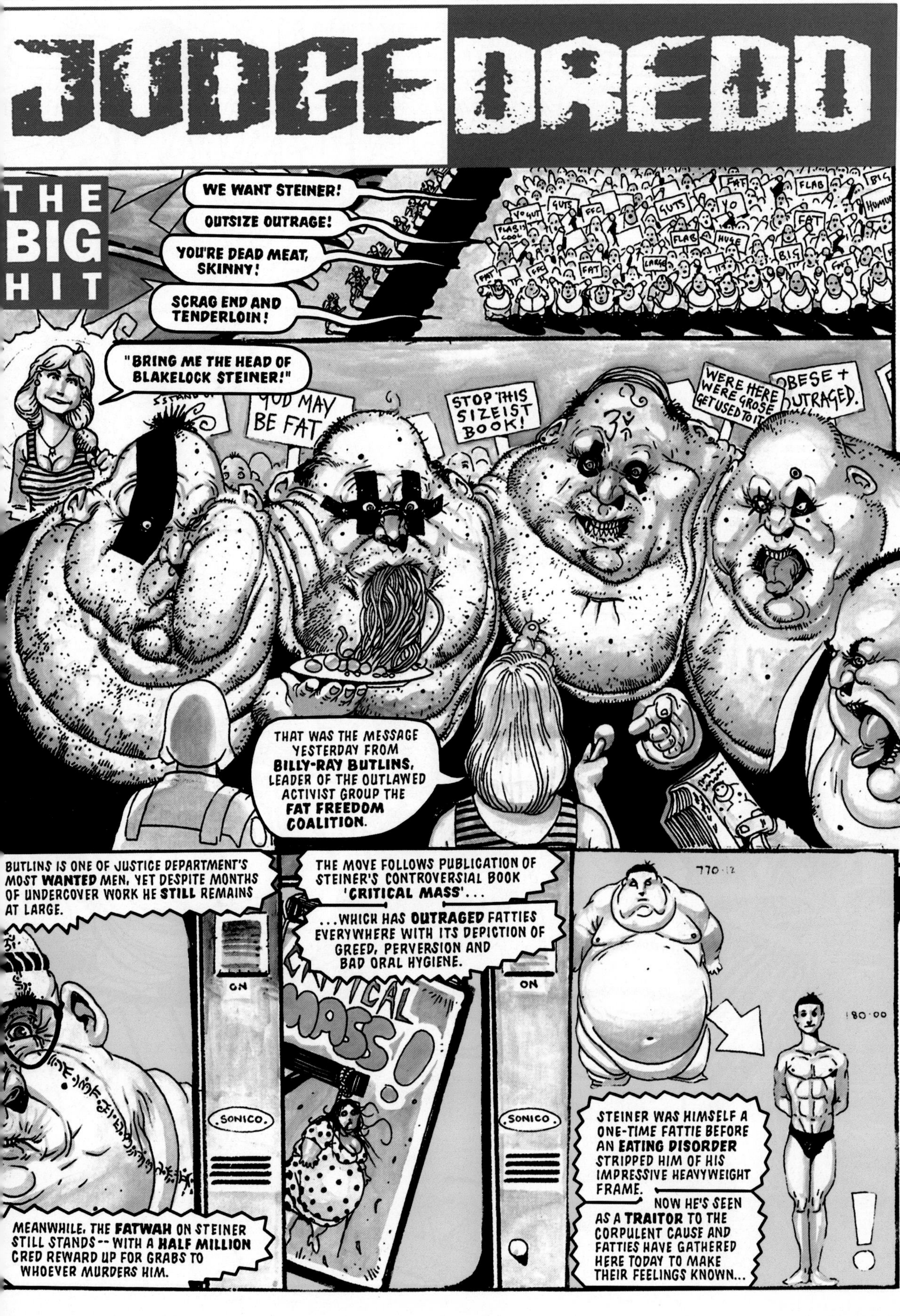

JUDGE DREDD
THE BIG HIT
WE WANT STEINER!
OUTSIZE OUTRAGE!
YOU'RE DEAD MEAT, SKINNY!
SCRAG END AND TENDERLOIN!
"BRING ME THE HEAD OF BLAKELOCK STEINER!"
GOD MAY BE FAT
STOP THIS SIZEIST BOOK!
WERE HERE WERE GROSE GET USED TO IT
OBESE + OUTRAGED.
THAT WAS THE MESSAGE YESTERDAY FROM BILLY-RAY BUTLINS, LEADER OF THE OUTLAWED ACTIVIST GROUP THE FAT FREEDOM COALITION.
BUTLINS IS ONE OF JUSTICE DEPARTMENT'S MOST WANTED MEN, YET DESPITE MONTHS OF UNDERCOVER WORK HE STILL REMAINS AT LARGE.
ON
SONICO
MEANWHILE, THE FATWAH ON STEINER STILL STANDS -- WITH A HALF MILLION CRED REWARD UP FOR GRABS TO WHOEVER MURDERS HIM.
THE MOVE FOLLOWS PUBLICATION OF STEINER'S CONTROVERSIAL BOOK 'CRITICAL MASS'...
...WHICH HAS OUTRAGED FATTIES EVERYWHERE WITH ITS DEPICTION OF GREED, PERVERSION AND BAD ORAL HYGIENE.
CRITICAL MASS!
ON
SONICO
770.12
180.00
STEINER WAS HIMSELF A ONE-TIME FATTIE BEFORE AN EATING DISORDER STRIPPED HIM OF HIS IMPRESSIVE HEAVYWEIGHT FRAME.
NOW HE'S SEEN AS A TRAITOR TO THE CORPULENT CAUSE AND FATTIES HAVE GATHERED HERE TODAY TO MAKE THEIR FEELINGS KNOWN...
!

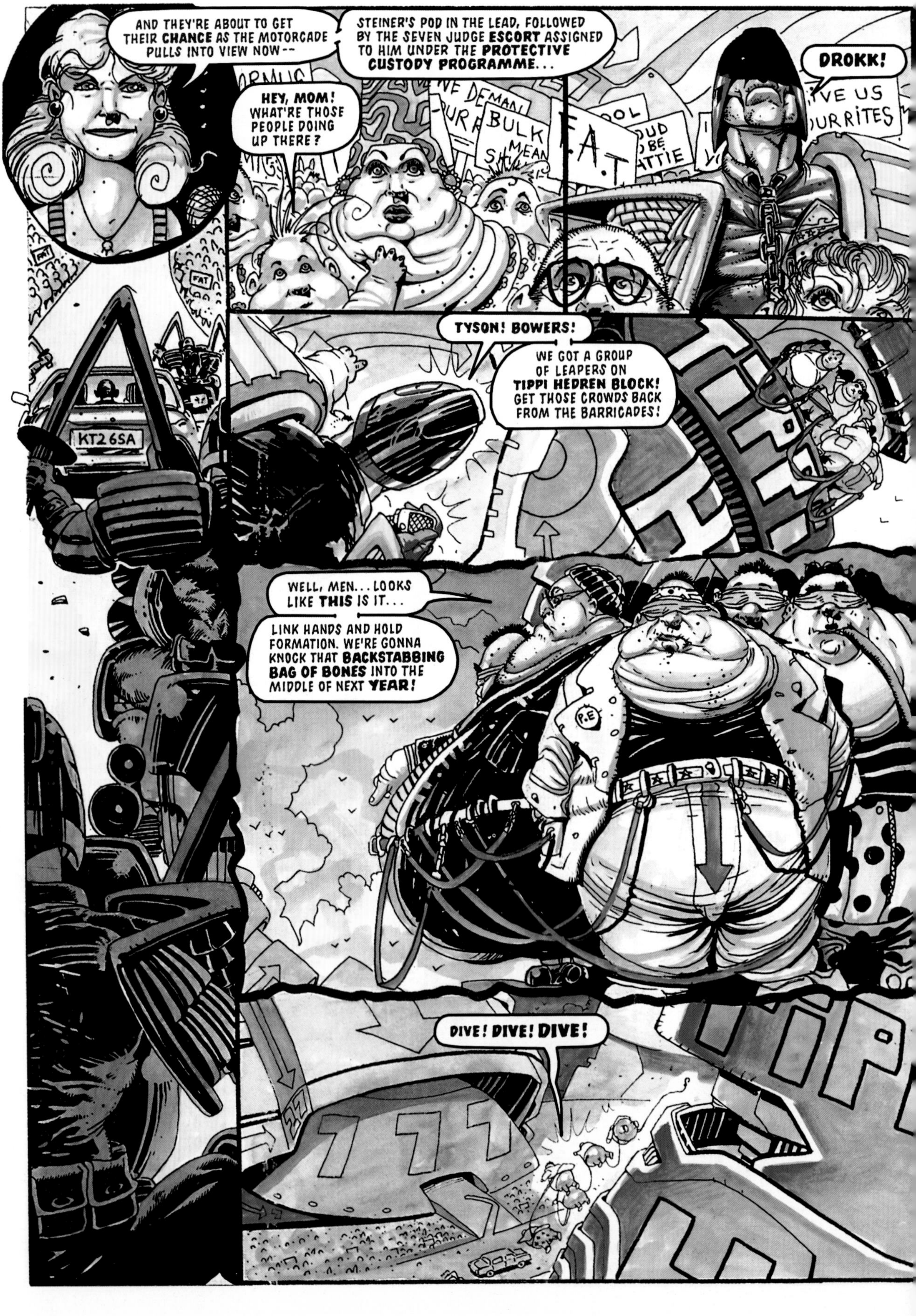

AND THEY'RE ABOUT TO GET THEIR CHANCE AS THE MOTORCADE PULLS INTO VIEW NOW--
STEINER'S POD IN THE LEAD, FOLLOWED BY THE SEVEN JUDGE ESCORT ASSIGNED TO HIM UNDER THE PROTECTIVE CUSTODY PROGRAMME...
HEY, MOM! WHAT'RE THOSE PEOPLE DOING UP THERE?
BULK
DROKK!
KT2 6SA
TYSON! BOWERS!
WE GOT A GROUP OF LEAPERS ON TIPPI HEDREN BLOCK! GET THOSE CROWDS BACK FROM THE BARRICADES!
WELL, MEN... LOOKS LIKE THIS IS IT...
LINK HANDS AND HOLD FORMATION. WE'RE GONNA KNOCK THAT BACKSTABBING BAG OF BONES INTO THE MIDDLE OF NEXT YEAR!
P.E
DIVE! DIVE! DIVE!

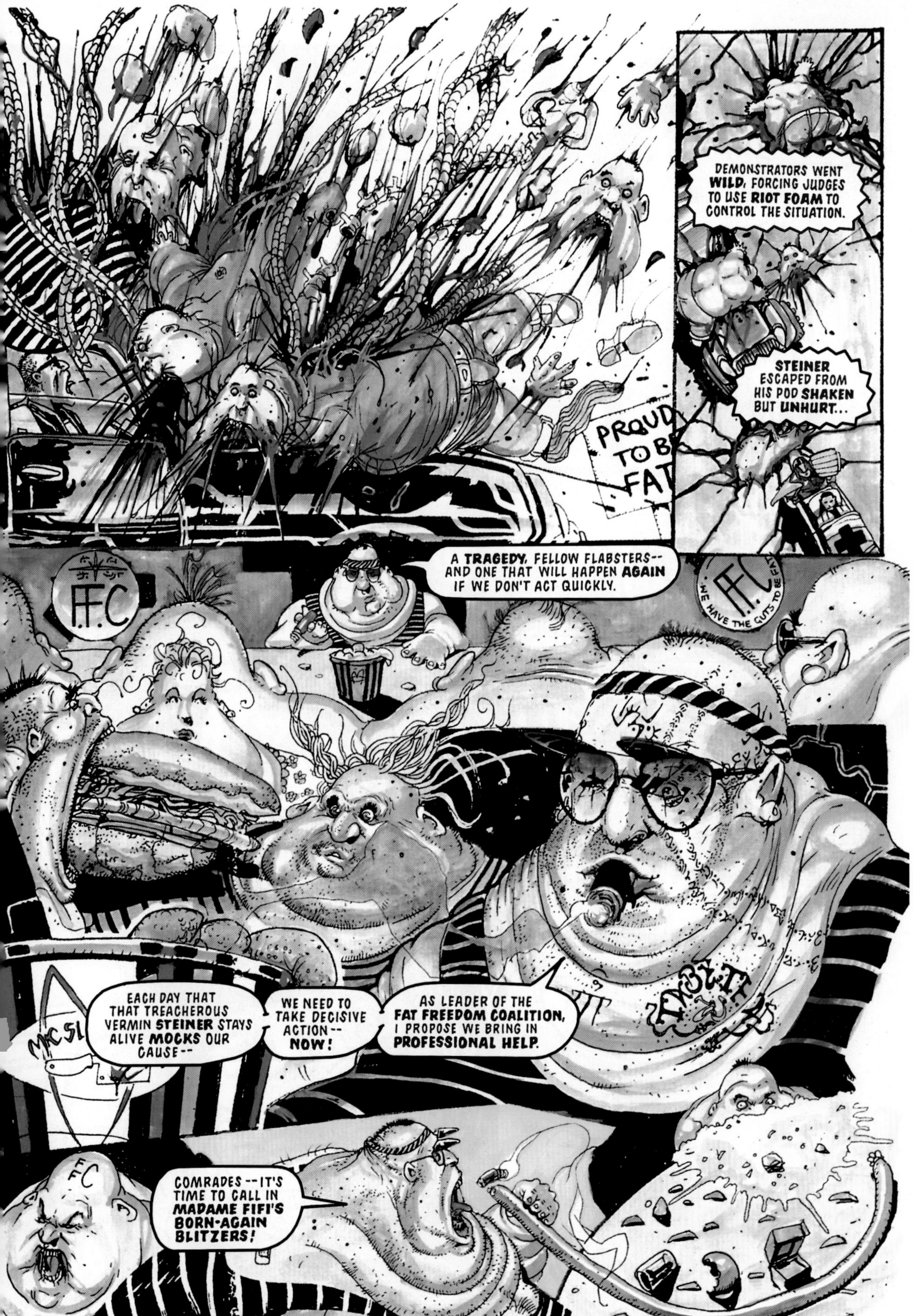
DEMONSTRATORS WENT WILD, FORCING JUDGES TO USE RIOT FOAM TO CONTROL THE SITUATION.
PROUD TO BE FAT
STEINER ESCAPED FROM HIS POD SHAKEN BUT UNHURT...
FFC
A TRAGEDY, FELLOW FLABSTERS--AND ONE THAT WILL HAPPEN AGAIN IF WE DON'T ACT QUICKLY.
FFC
WE HAVE THE GUTS TO BE FAT
EACH DAY THAT THAT TREACHEROUS VERMIN STEINER STAYS ALIVE MOCKS OUR CAUSE--
WE NEED TO TAKE DECISIVE ACTION--NOW!
AS LEADER OF THE FAT FREEDOM COALITION, I PROPOSE WE BRING IN PROFESSIONAL HELP.
FFC
COMRADES--IT'S TIME TO CALL IN MADAME FIFI'S BORN-AGAIN BLITZERS!

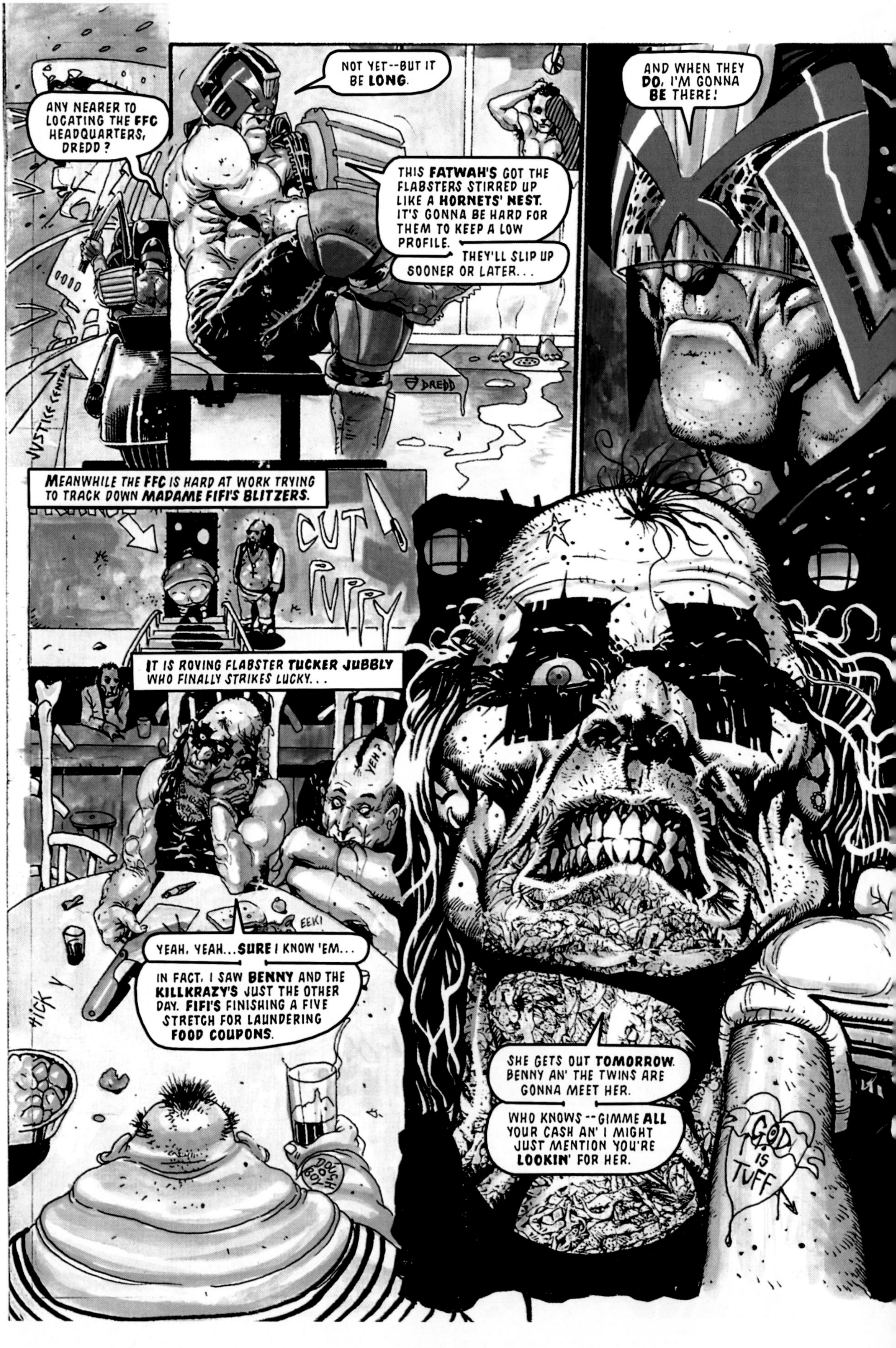

ANY NEARER TO LOCATING THE **FFC** HEADQUARTERS, DREDD?
NOT YET--BUT IT BE **LONG**.
THIS **FATWAH'S** GOT THE FLABSTERS STIRRED UP LIKE A **HORNETS' NEST**. IT'S GONNA BE HARD FOR THEM TO KEEP A LOW PROFILE.
THEY'LL SLIP UP SOONER OR LATER...
JUSTICE CENTRAL
DREDD
AND WHEN THEY **DO**, I'M GONNA **BE** THERE!
MEANWHILE THE **FFC** IS HARD AT WORK TRYING TO TRACK DOWN **MADAME FIFI'S BLITZERS**.
CUT PUPPY
IT IS ROVING FLABSTER **TUCKER JUBBLY** WHO FINALLY STRIKES LUCKY...
YEH?
EEK!
YEAH, YEAH...**SURE** I KNOW 'EM...
IN FACT, I SAW **BENNY** AND THE **KILLKRAZY'S** JUST THE OTHER DAY. **FIFI'S** FINISHING A FIVE STRETCH FOR LAUNDERING **FOOD COUPONS**.
HICK
DOUGH BOY
SHE GETS OUT **TOMORROW**. BENNY AN' THE TWINS ARE GONNA MEET HER.
WHO KNOWS--GIMME **ALL** YOUR CASH AN' I MIGHT JUST MENTION YOU'RE **LOOKIN'** FOR HER.
GOD IS TUFF

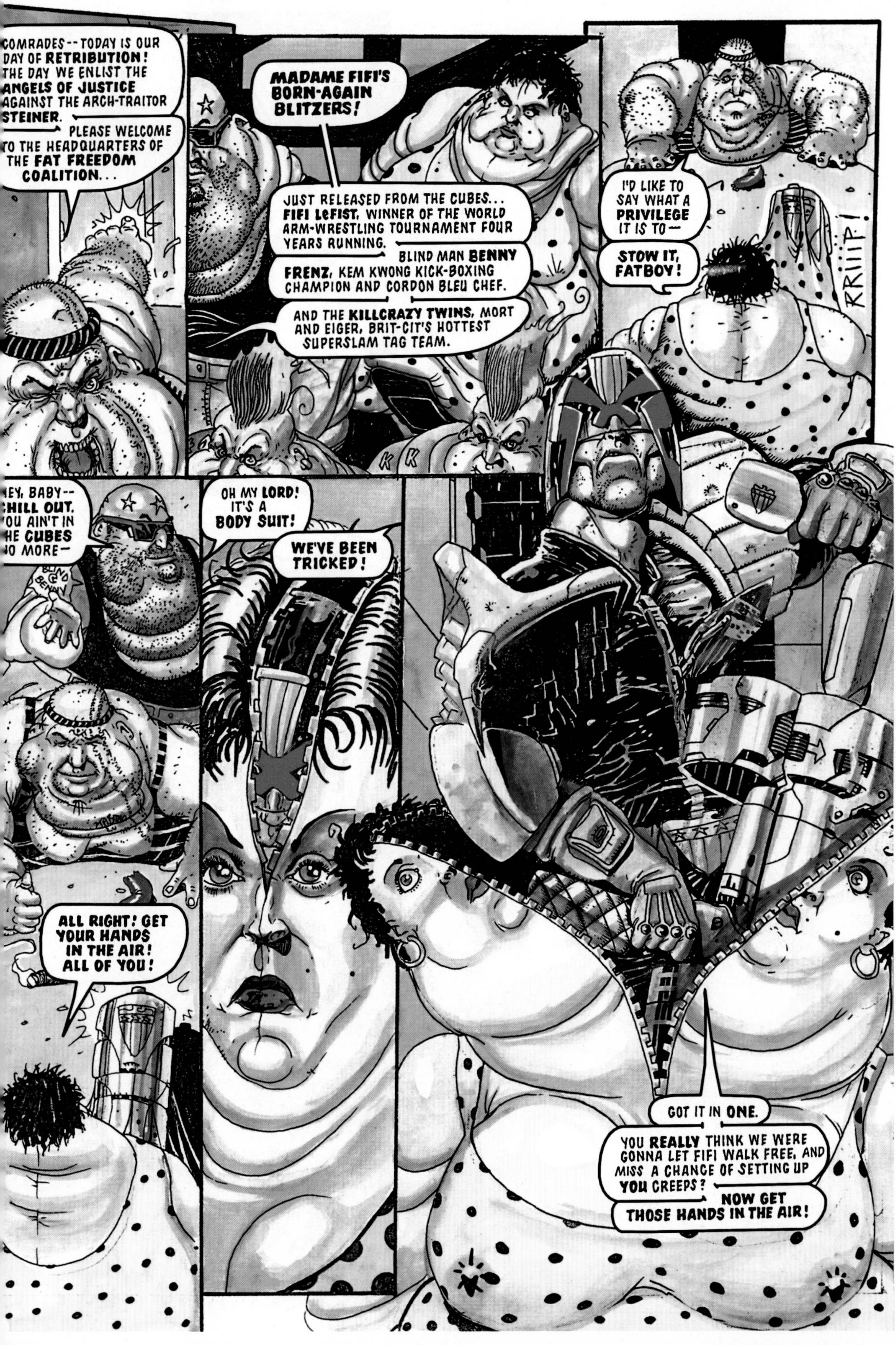
COMRADES--TODAY IS OUR DAY OF RETRIBUTION! THE DAY WE ENLIST THE ANGELS OF JUSTICE AGAINST THE ARCH-TRAITOR STEINER.
PLEASE WELCOME TO THE HEADQUARTERS OF THE FAT FREEDOM COALITION...
MADAME FIFI'S BORN-AGAIN BLITZERS!
JUST RELEASED FROM THE CUBES... FIFI LeFIST, WINNER OF THE WORLD ARM-WRESTLING TOURNAMENT FOUR YEARS RUNNING.
BLIND MAN BENNY FRENZ, KEM KWONG KICK-BOXING CHAMPION AND CORDON BLEU CHEF.
AND THE KILLCRAZY TWINS, MORT AND EIGER, BRIT-CIT'S HOTTEST SUPERSLAM TAG TEAM.
I'D LIKE TO SAY WHAT A PRIVILEGE IT IS TO—
STOW IT, FATBOY!
KRIIIP!
HEY, BABY--CHILL OUT. YOU AIN'T IN THE CUBES NO MORE—
OH MY LORD! IT'S A BODY SUIT!
WE'VE BEEN TRICKED!
ALL RIGHT! GET YOUR HANDS IN THE AIR! ALL OF YOU!
GOT IT IN ONE.
YOU REALLY THINK WE WERE GONNA LET FIFI WALK FREE, AND MISS A CHANCE OF SETTING UP YOU CREEPS?
NOW GET THOSE HANDS IN THE AIR!

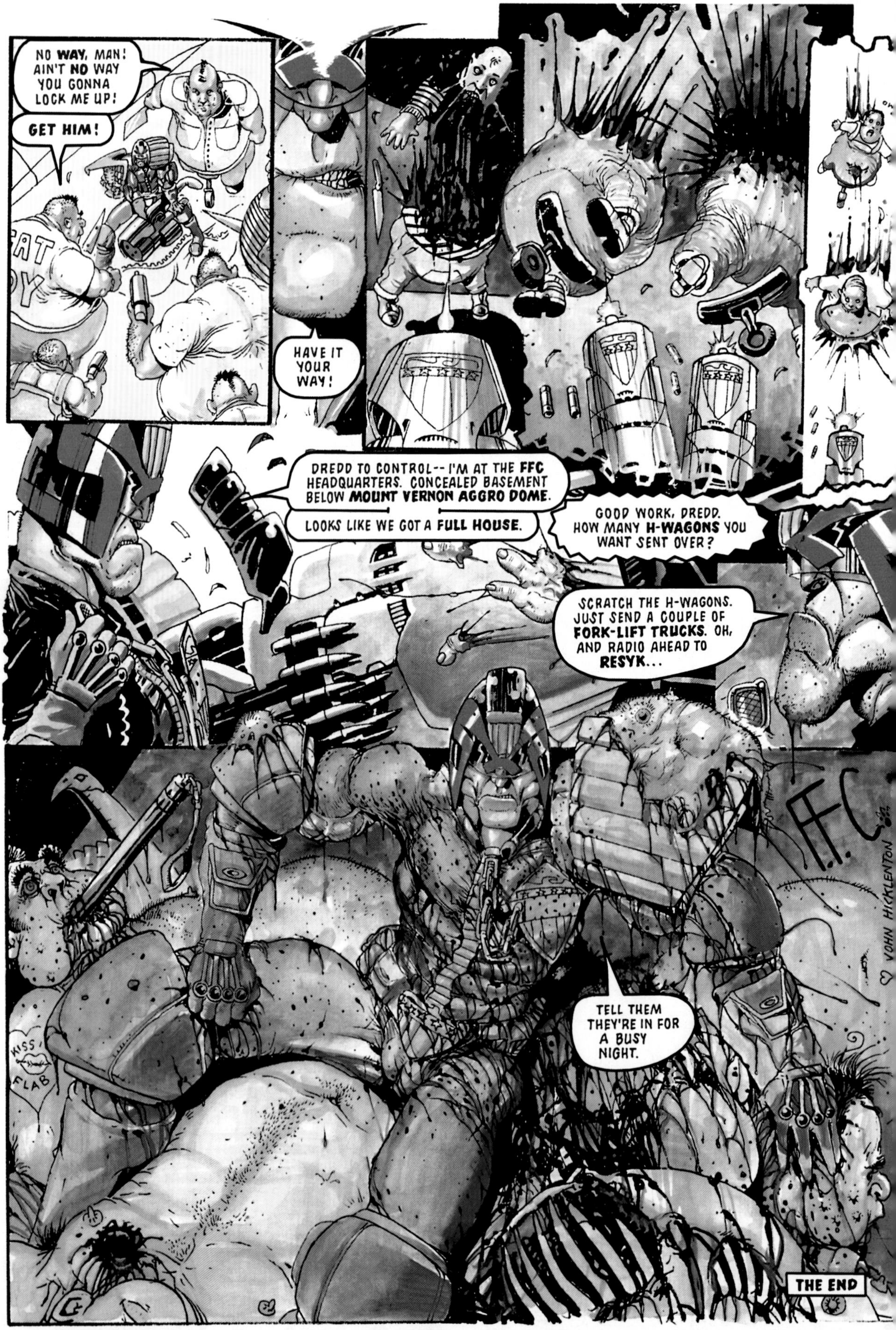

NO WAY, MAN! AIN'T NO WAY YOU GONNA LOCK ME UP!
GET HIM!
HAVE IT YOUR WAY!
DREDD TO CONTROL-- I'M AT THE FFC HEADQUARTERS. CONCEALED BASEMENT BELOW MOUNT VERNON AGGRO DOME.
LOOKS LIKE WE GOT A FULL HOUSE.
GOOD WORK, DREDD. HOW MANY H-WAGONS YOU WANT SENT OVER?
SCRATCH THE H-WAGONS. JUST SEND A COUPLE OF FORK-LIFT TRUCKS. OH, AND RADIO AHEAD TO RESYK...
TELL THEM THEY'RE IN FOR A BUSY NIGHT.
F.F.C.
JOHN HICKLENTON
KISS FLAB
THE END

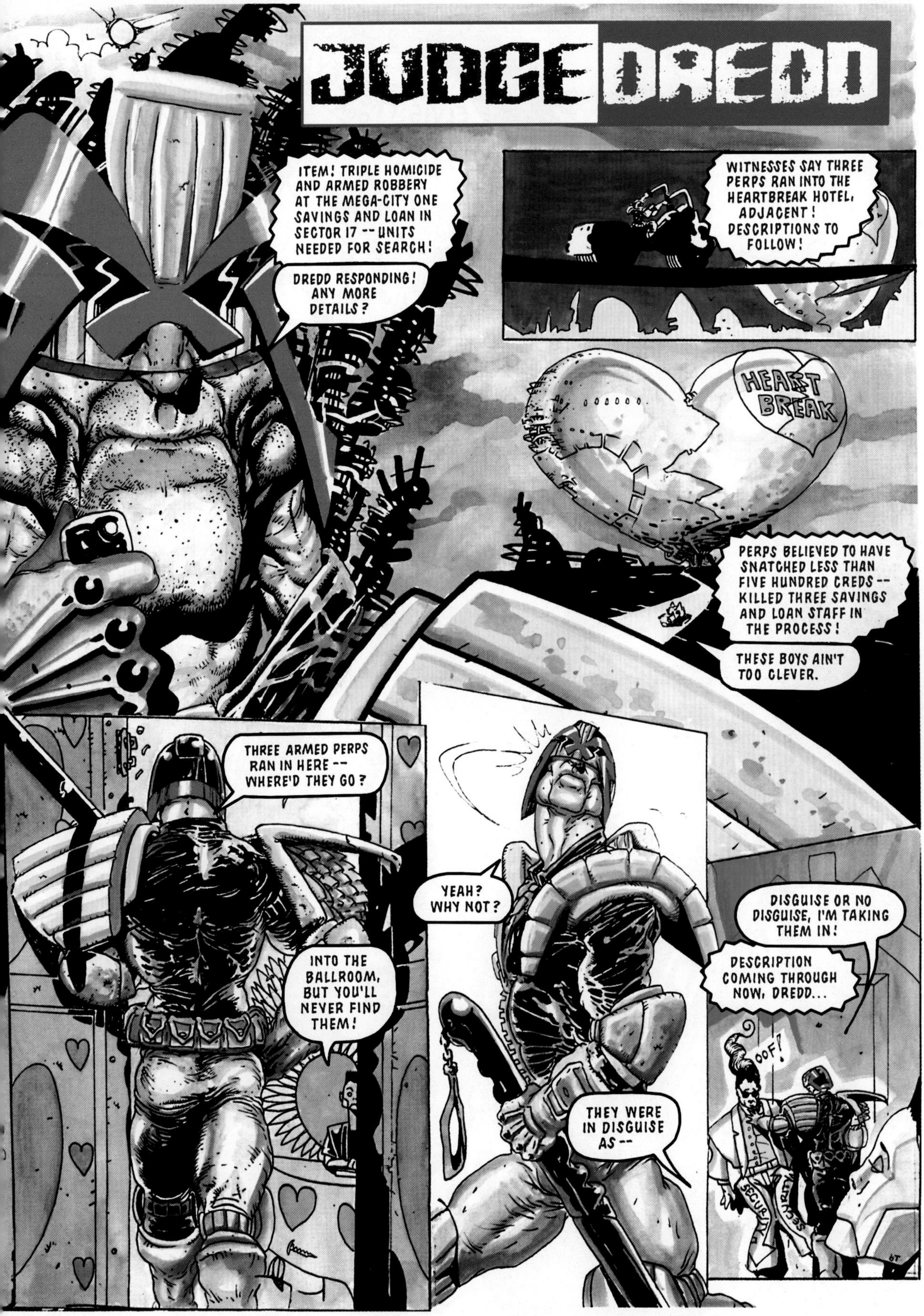
JUDGE DREDD
ITEM! TRIPLE HOMICIDE AND ARMED ROBBERY AT THE MEGA-CITY ONE SAVINGS AND LOAN IN SECTOR 17 -- UNITS NEEDED FOR SEARCH!
DREDD RESPONDING! ANY MORE DETAILS?
WITNESSES SAY THREE PERPS RAN INTO THE HEARTBREAK HOTEL, ADJACENT! DESCRIPTIONS TO FOLLOW!
HEART BREAK
PERPS BELIEVED TO HAVE SNATCHED LESS THAN FIVE HUNDRED CREDS -- KILLED THREE SAVINGS AND LOAN STAFF IN THE PROCESS!
THESE BOYS AIN'T TOO CLEVER.
THREE ARMED PERPS RAN IN HERE -- WHERE'D THEY GO?
INTO THE BALLROOM, BUT YOU'LL NEVER FIND THEM!
YEAH? WHY NOT?
THEY WERE IN DISGUISE AS --
DISGUISE OR NO DISGUISE, I'M TAKING THEM IN!
DESCRIPTION COMING THROUGH NOW, DREDD...
OOF!
SECURITY
SECURITY

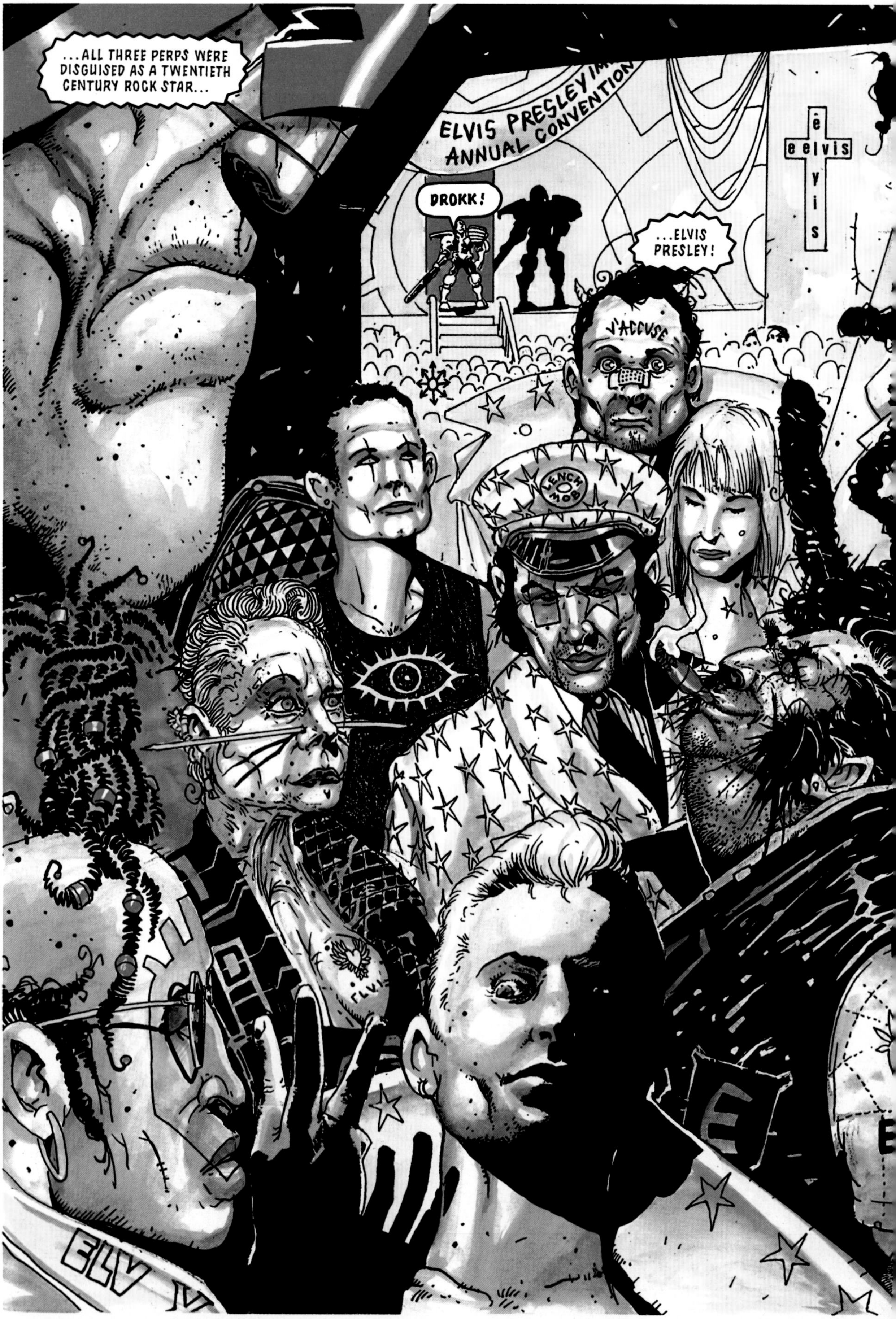
...ALL THREE PERPS WERE DISGUISED AS A TWENTIETH CENTURY ROCK STAR...
ELVIS PRESLEY IM
ANNUAL CONVENTION
eelvis
DROKK!
...ELVIS PRESLEY!
J'ACCUSE
LENCH MOB
ELV

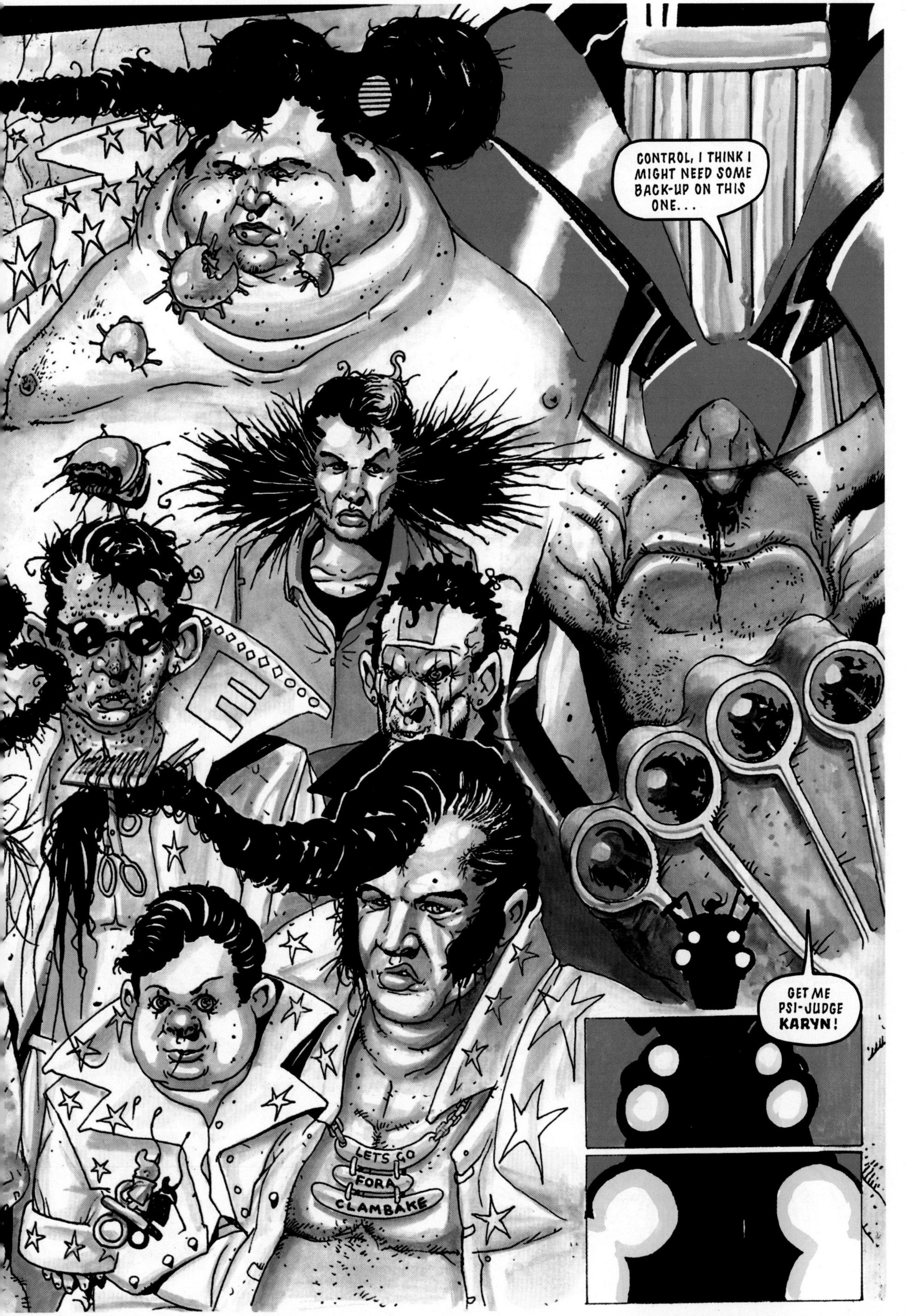
CONTROL, I THINK I MIGHT NEED SOME BACK-UP ON THIS ONE...
LETS GO FORA CLAMBAKE
GET ME PSI-JUDGE KARYN!

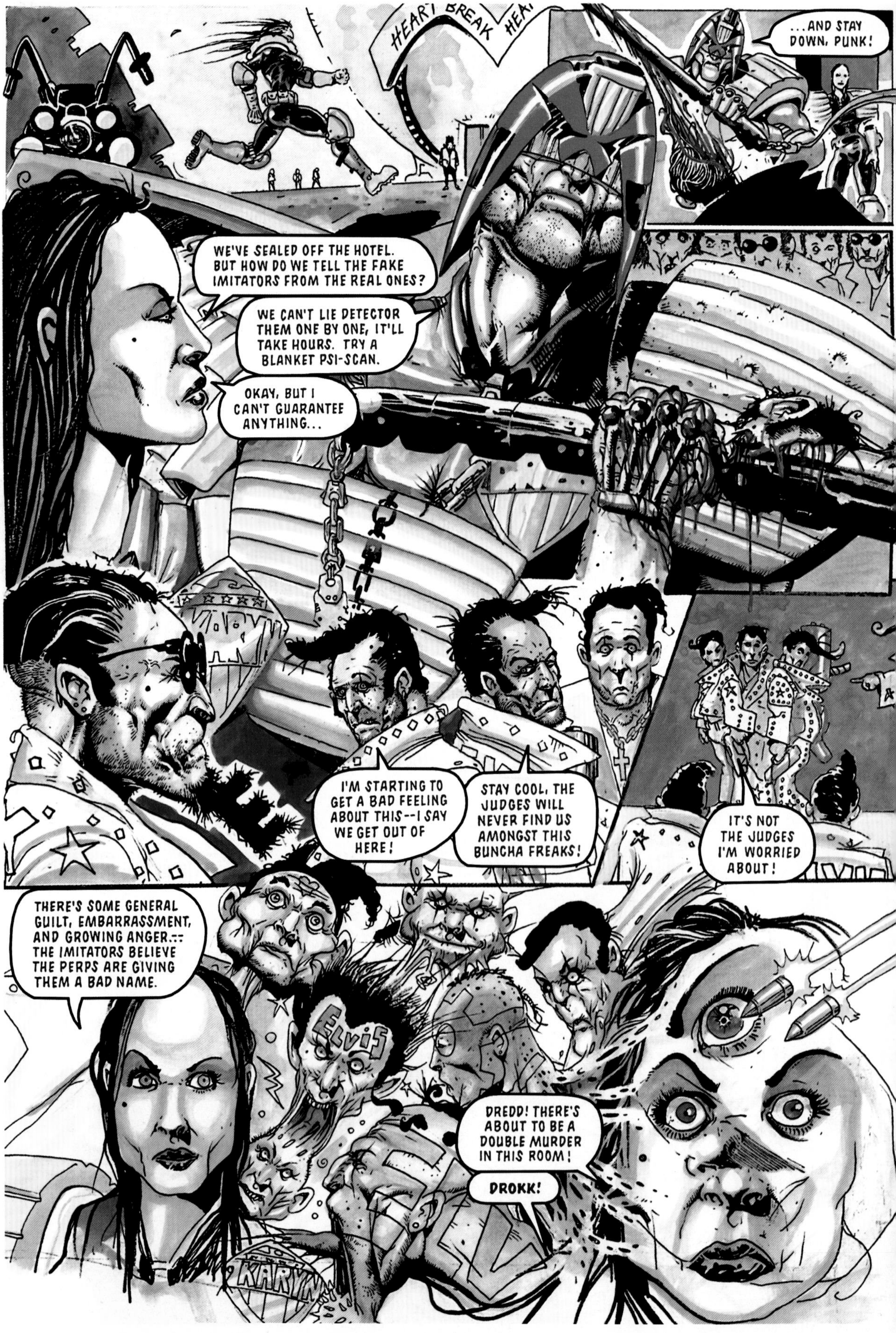
HEART BREAK HEAR
...AND STAY DOWN, PUNK!
WE'VE SEALED OFF THE HOTEL. BUT HOW DO WE TELL THE FAKE IMITATORS FROM THE REAL ONES?
WE CAN'T LIE DETECTOR THEM ONE BY ONE, IT'LL TAKE HOURS. TRY A BLANKET PSI-SCAN.
OKAY, BUT I CAN'T GUARANTEE ANYTHING...
I'M STARTING TO GET A BAD FEELING ABOUT THIS--I SAY WE GET OUT OF HERE!
STAY COOL, THE JUDGES WILL NEVER FIND US AMONGST THIS BUNCHA FREAKS!
IT'S NOT THE JUDGES I'M WORRIED ABOUT!
THERE'S SOME GENERAL GUILT, EMBARRASSMENT, AND GROWING ANGER... THE IMITATORS BELIEVE THE PERPS ARE GIVING THEM A BAD NAME.
ELVIS
DREDD! THERE'S ABOUT TO BE A DOUBLE MURDER IN THIS ROOM!
DROKK!
KARYN

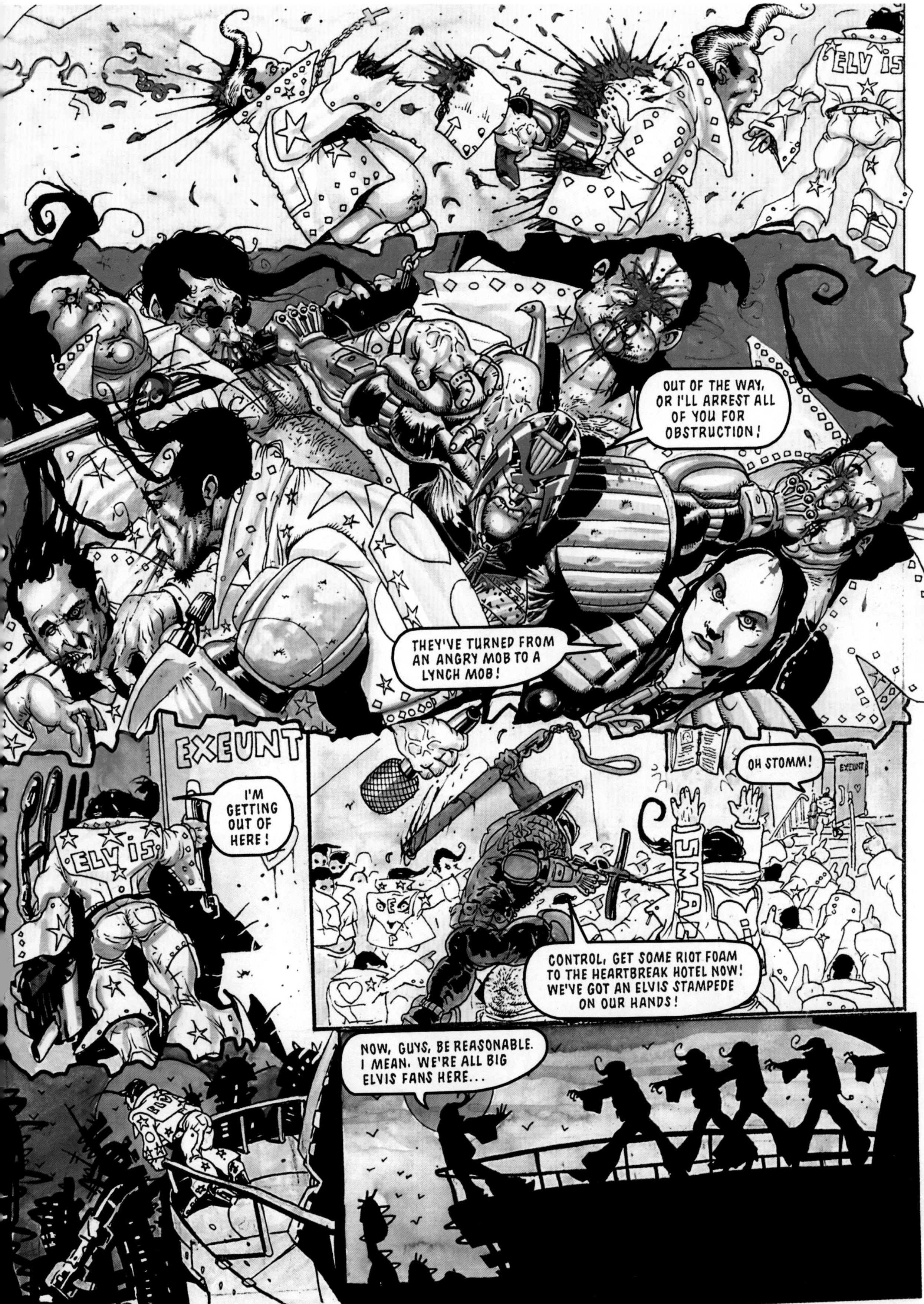
ELV IS
OUT OF THE WAY, OR I'LL ARREST ALL OF YOU FOR OBSTRUCTION!
THEY'VE TURNED FROM AN ANGRY MOB TO A LYNCH MOB!
EXEUNT
I'M GETTING OUT OF HERE!
ELV IS
OH STOMM!
CONTROL, GET SOME RIOT FOAM TO THE HEARTBREAK HOTEL NOW! WE'VE GOT AN ELVIS STAMPEDE ON OUR HANDS!
NOW, GUYS, BE REASONABLE. I MEAN, WE'RE ALL BIG ELVIS FANS HERE...

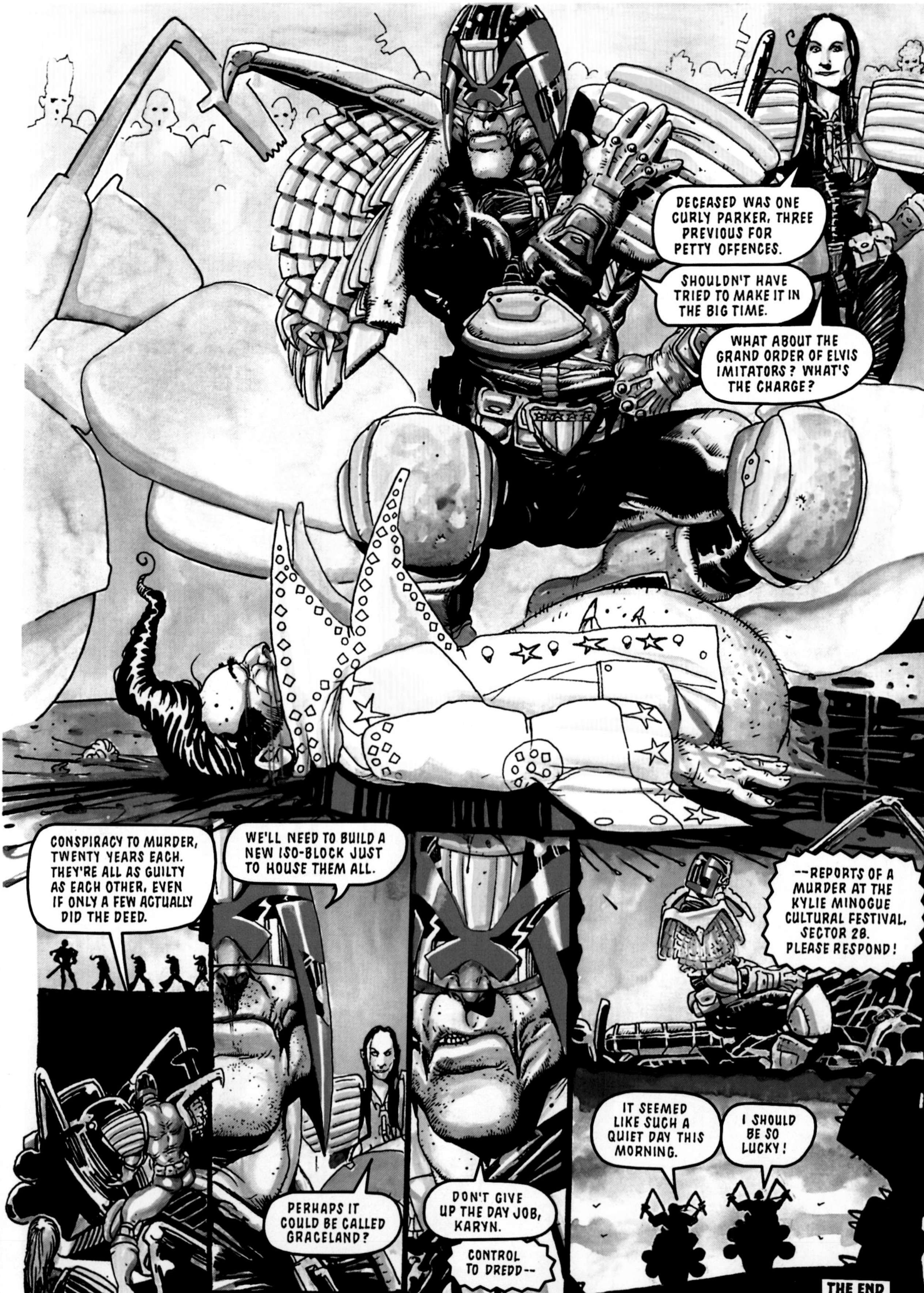
DECEASED WAS ONE CURLY PARKER, THREE PREVIOUS FOR PETTY OFFENCES.
SHOULDN'T HAVE TRIED TO MAKE IT IN THE BIG TIME.
WHAT ABOUT THE GRAND ORDER OF ELVIS IMITATORS? WHAT'S THE CHARGE?
CONSPIRACY TO MURDER, TWENTY YEARS EACH. THEY'RE ALL AS GUILTY AS EACH OTHER, EVEN IF ONLY A FEW ACTUALLY DID THE DEED.
WE'LL NEED TO BUILD A NEW ISO-BLOCK JUST TO HOUSE THEM ALL.
PERHAPS IT COULD BE CALLED GRACELAND?
DON'T GIVE UP THE DAY JOB, KARYN.
CONTROL TO DREDD--
--REPORTS OF A MURDER AT THE KYLIE MINOGUE CULTURAL FESTIVAL, SECTOR 28. PLEASE RESPOND!
IT SEEMED LIKE SUCH A QUIET DAY THIS MORNING.
I SHOULD BE SO LUCKY!
THE END

JUDGE DREDD

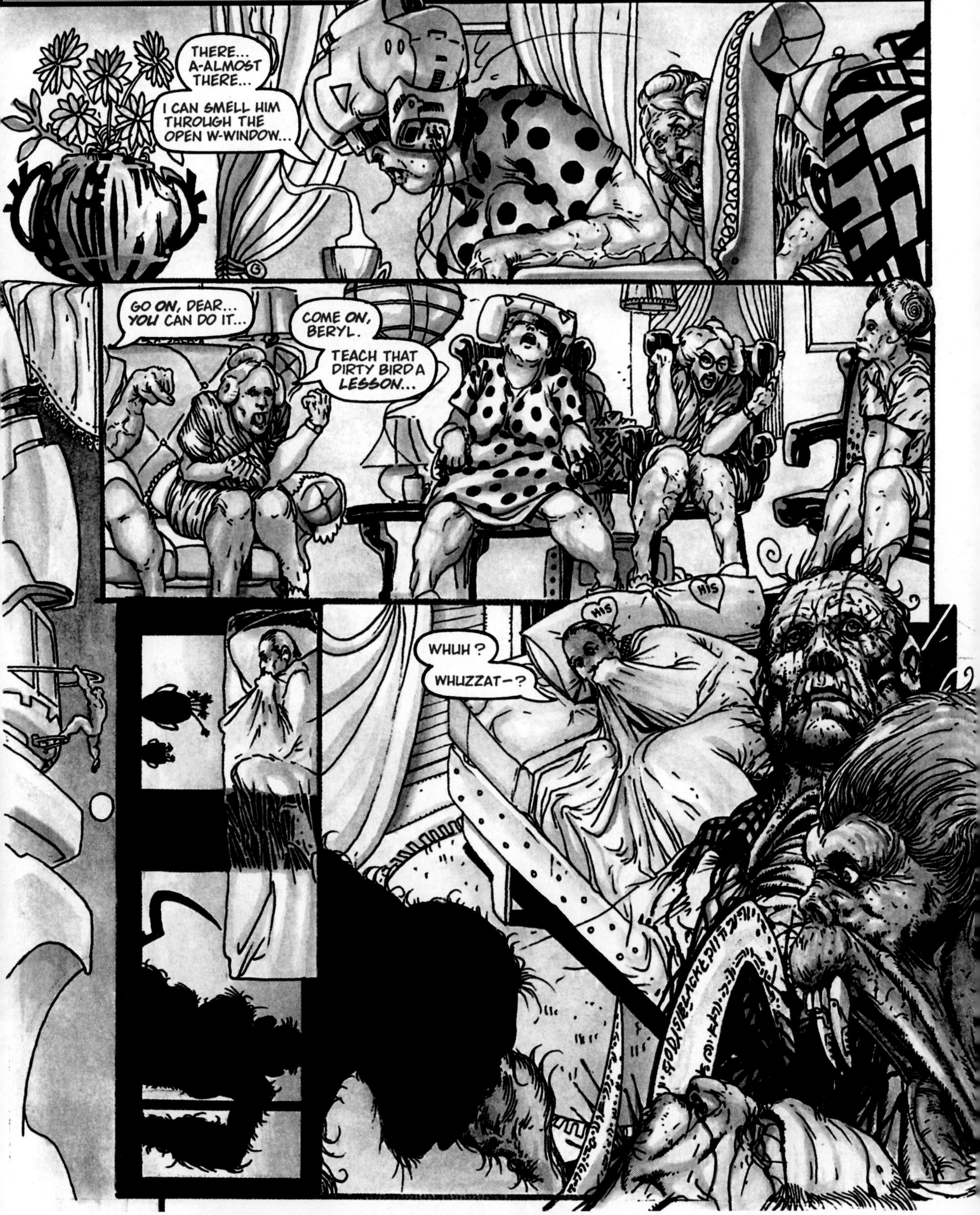

THERE... A-ALMOST THERE...
I CAN SMELL HIM THROUGH THE OPEN W-WINDOW...
GO ON, DEAR... YOU CAN DO IT...
COME ON, BERYL.
TEACH THAT DIRTY BIRD A LESSON...
HIS
HIS
WHUH ?
WHUZZAT-?

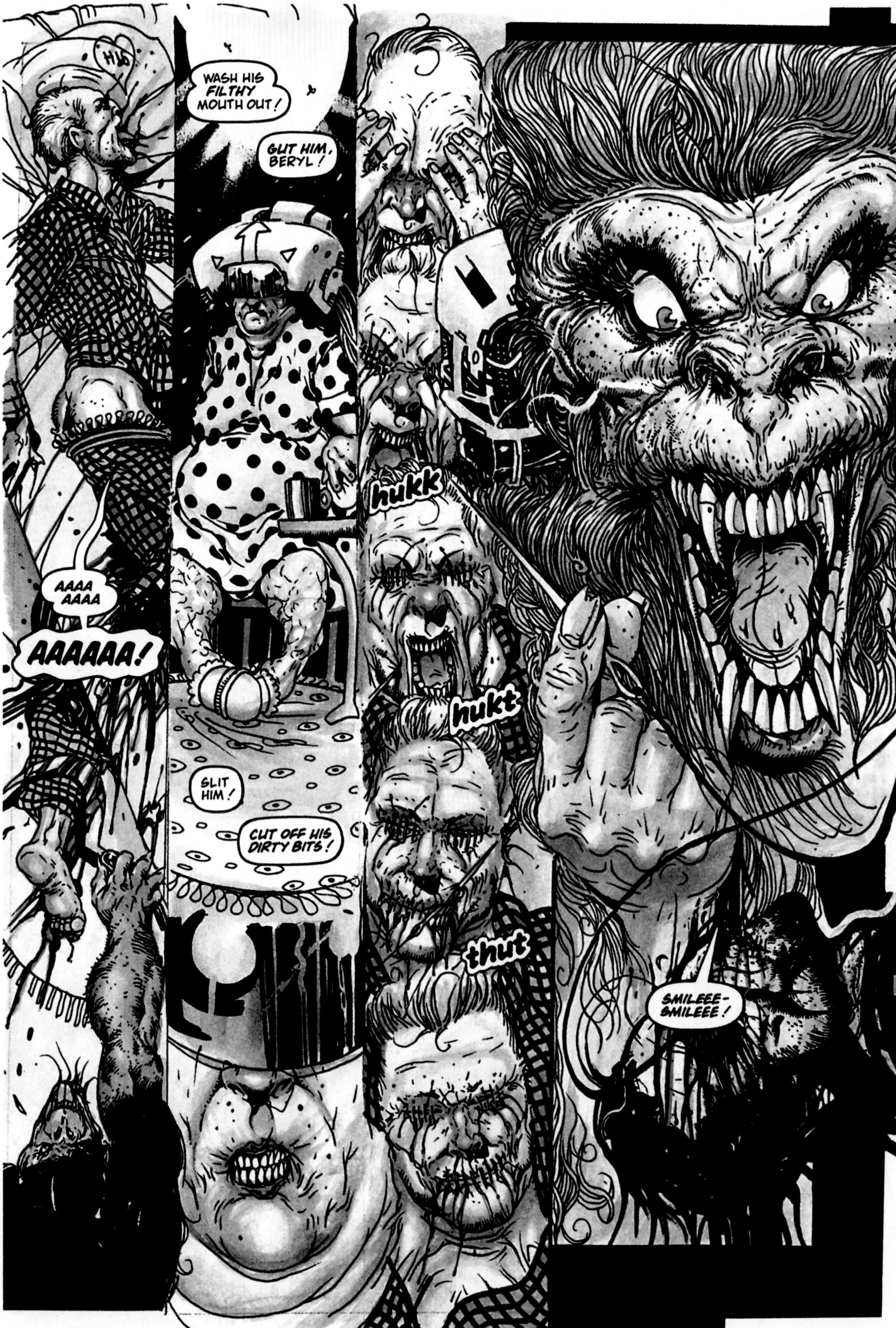
HIS
WASH HIS FILTHY MOUTH OUT!
GUT HIM, BERYL!
AAAA AAAA
AAAAAA!
hukk
hukt
SLIT HIM!
CUT OFF HIS DIRTY BITS!
thut
SMILEEE-SMILEEE!

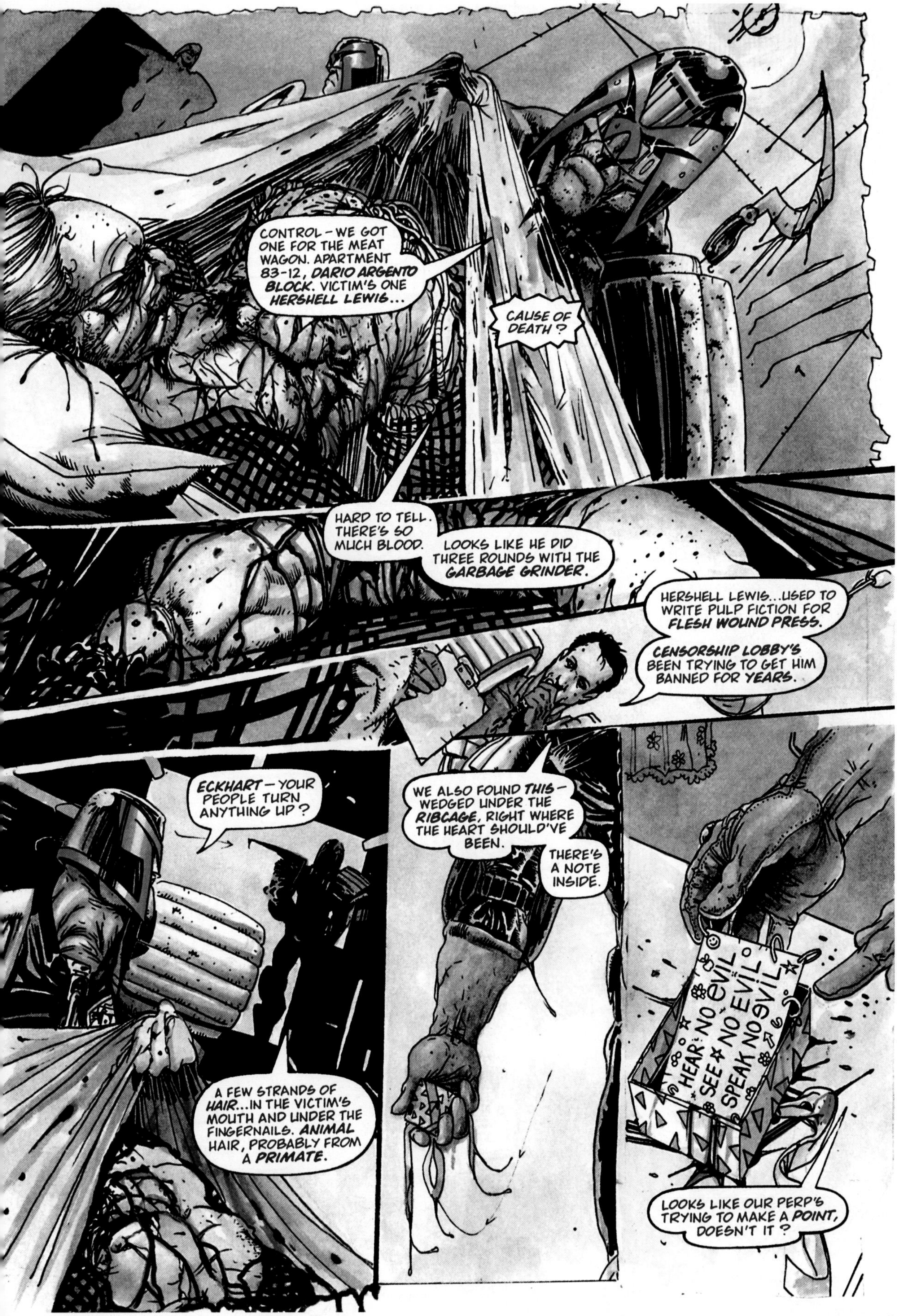
CONTROL – WE GOT ONE FOR THE MEAT WAGON. APARTMENT 83-12, DARIO ARGENTO BLOCK. VICTIM'S ONE HERSHELL LEWIS...
CAUSE OF DEATH?
HARD TO TELL. THERE'S SO MUCH BLOOD.
LOOKS LIKE HE DID THREE ROUNDS WITH THE GARBAGE GRINDER.
HERSHELL LEWIS...USED TO WRITE PULP FICTION FOR FLESH WOUND PRESS.
CENSORSHIP LOBBY'S BEEN TRYING TO GET HIM BANNED FOR YEARS.
ECKHART – YOUR PEOPLE TURN ANYTHING UP?
A FEW STRANDS OF HAIR...IN THE VICTIM'S MOUTH AND UNDER THE FINGERNAILS. ANIMAL HAIR, PROBABLY FROM A PRIMATE.
WE ALSO FOUND THIS – WEDGED UNDER THE RIBCAGE, RIGHT WHERE THE HEART SHOULD'VE BEEN.
THERE'S A NOTE INSIDE.
HEAR NO EVIL
SEE NO EVIL
SPEAK NO EVIL
LOOKS LIKE OUR PERP'S TRYING TO MAKE A POINT, DOESN'T IT?

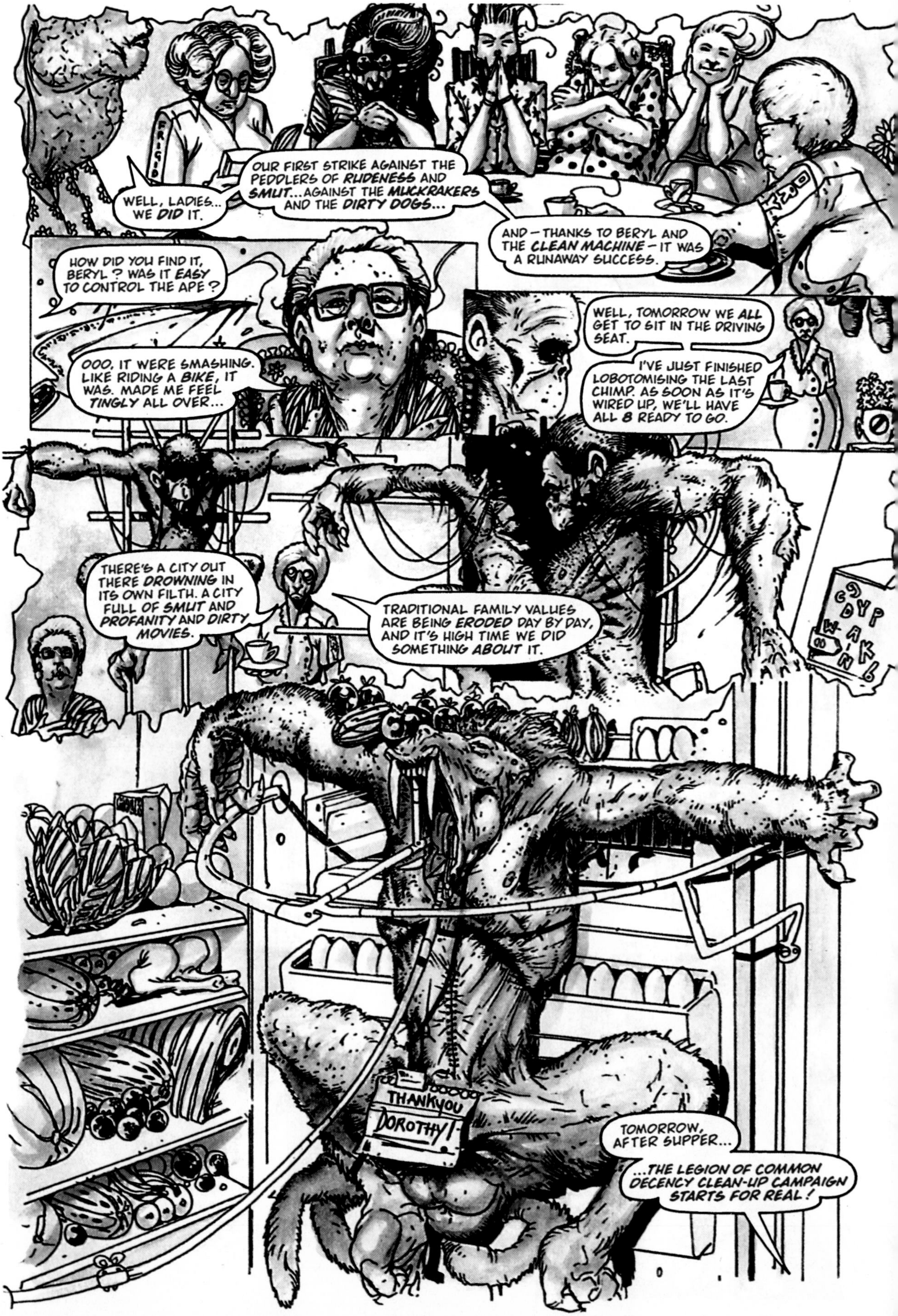
WELL, LADIES... WE DID IT.
OUR FIRST STRIKE AGAINST THE PEDDLERS OF RUDENESS AND SMUT... AGAINST THE MUCKRAKERS AND THE DIRTY DOGS...
AND — THANKS TO BERYL AND THE CLEAN MACHINE — IT WAS A RUNAWAY SUCCESS.
HOW DID YOU FIND IT, BERYL ? WAS IT EASY TO CONTROL THE APE ?
OOO, IT WERE SMASHING. LIKE RIDING A BIKE, IT WAS. MADE ME FEEL TINGLY ALL OVER...
WELL, TOMORROW WE ALL GET TO SIT IN THE DRIVING SEAT.
I'VE JUST FINISHED LOBOTOMISING THE LAST CHIMP. AS SOON AS IT'S WIRED UP, WE'LL HAVE ALL 8 READY TO GO.
THERE'S A CITY OUT THERE DROWNING IN ITS OWN FILTH. A CITY FULL OF SMUT AND PROFANITY AND DIRTY MOVIES.
TRADITIONAL FAMILY VALUES ARE BEING ERODED DAY BY DAY, AND IT'S HIGH TIME WE DID SOMETHING ABOUT IT.
THANKYOU DOROTHY!
TOMORROW, AFTER SUPPER...
...THE LEGION OF COMMON DECENCY CLEAN-UP CAMPAIGN STARTS FOR REAL !

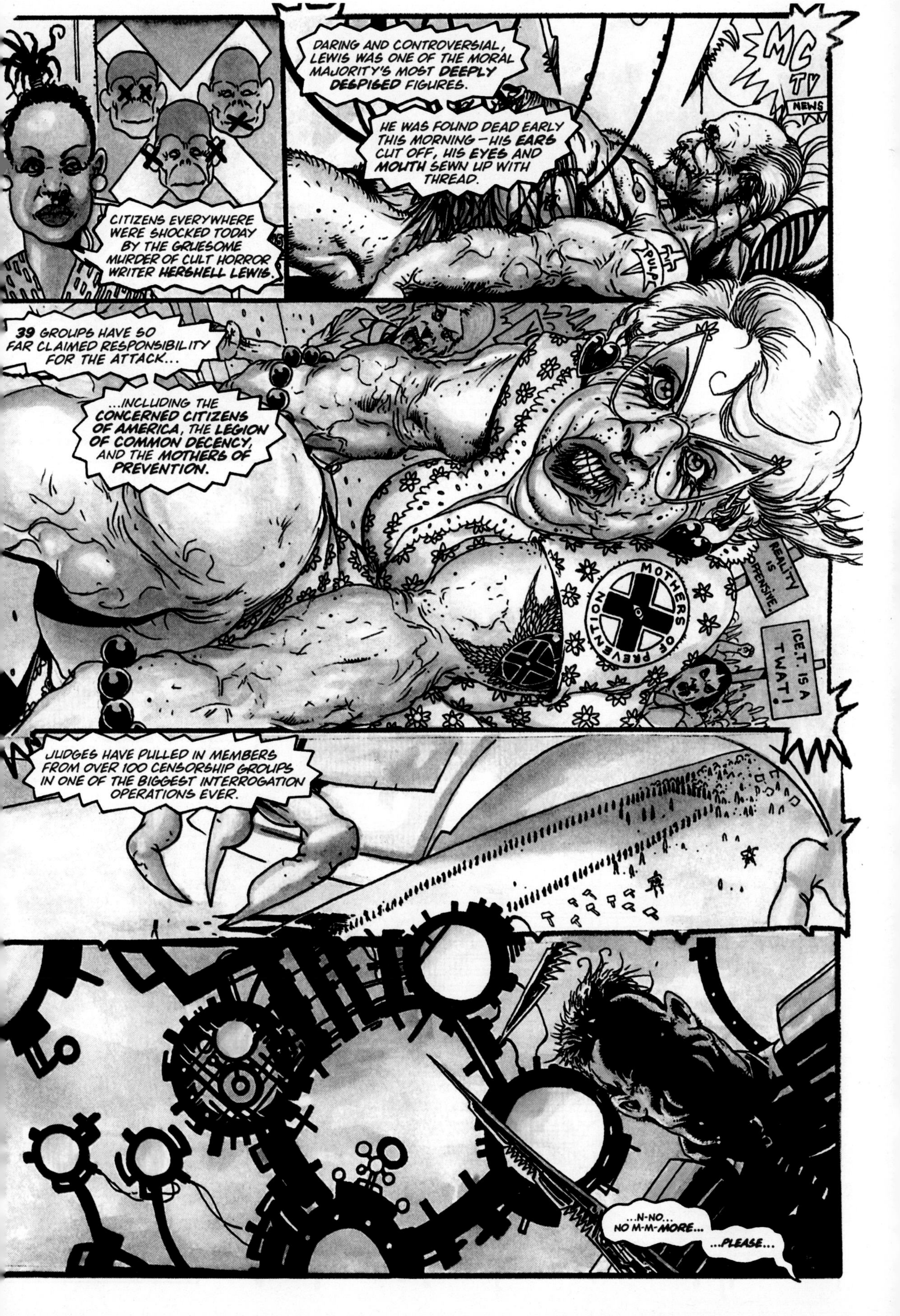
MC TV NEWS
CITIZENS EVERYWHERE WERE SHOCKED TODAY BY THE GRUESOME MURDER OF CULT HORROR WRITER HERSHELL LEWIS.
DARING AND CONTROVERSIAL, LEWIS WAS ONE OF THE MORAL MAJORITY'S MOST DEEPLY DESPISED FIGURES.
HE WAS FOUND DEAD EARLY THIS MORNING — HIS EARS CUT OFF, HIS EYES AND MOUTH SEWN UP WITH THREAD.
PULP
39 GROUPS HAVE SO FAR CLAIMED RESPONSIBILITY FOR THE ATTACK...
...INCLUDING THE CONCERNED CITIZENS OF AMERICA, THE LEGION OF COMMON DECENCY, AND THE MOTHERS OF PREVENTION.
MOTHERS OF PREVENTION
REALITY IS OFFENSIVE.
ICE.T. IS A TWAT!
JUDGES HAVE PULLED IN MEMBERS FROM OVER 100 CENSORSHIP GROUPS IN ONE OF THE BIGGEST INTERROGATION OPERATIONS EVER.
...N-NO... NO M-M-MORE...
...PLEASE...

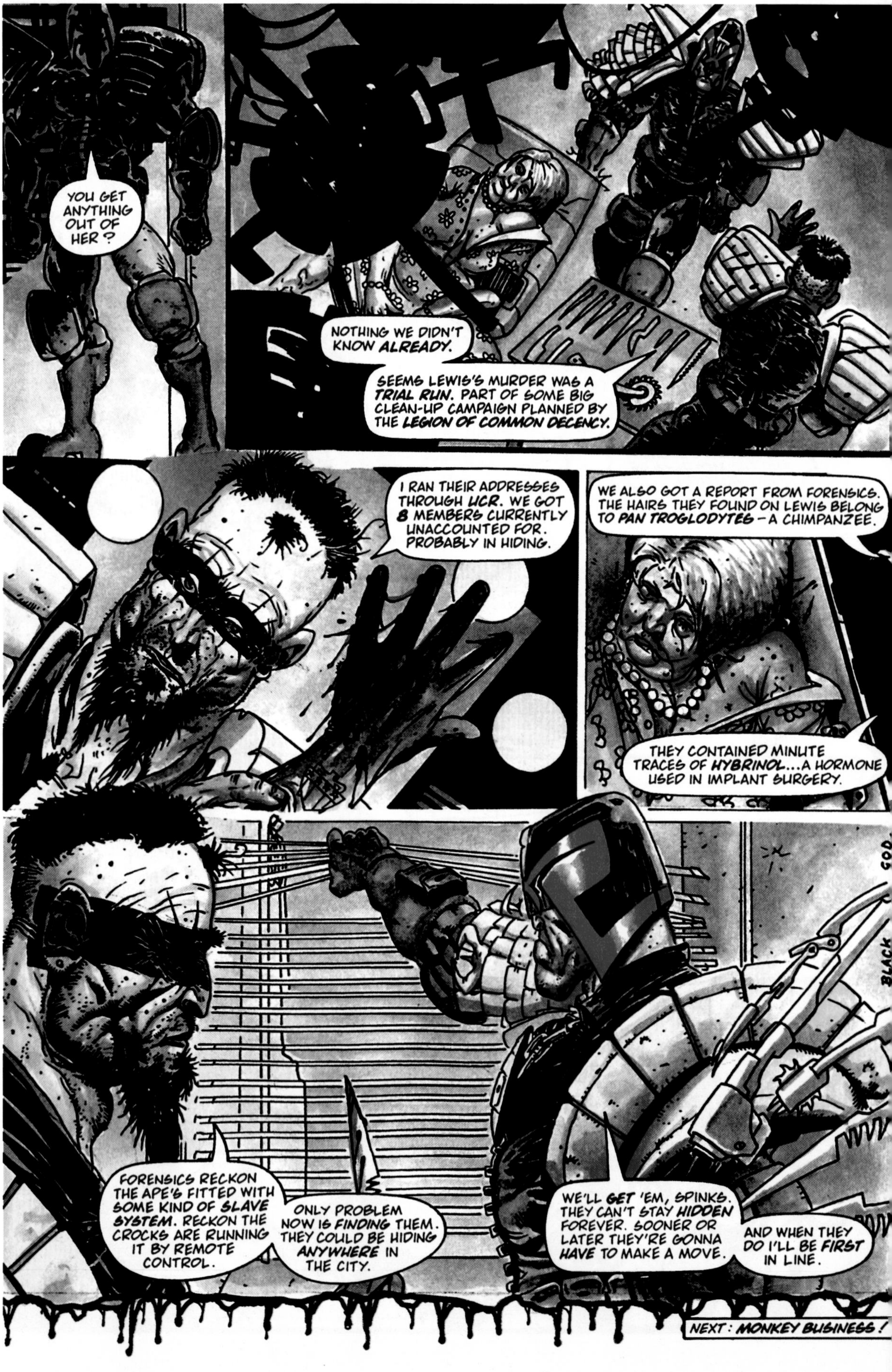

YOU GET ANYTHING OUT OF HER ?
NOTHING WE DIDN'T KNOW ALREADY.
SEEMS LEWIS'S MURDER WAS A TRIAL RUN. PART OF SOME BIG CLEAN-UP CAMPAIGN PLANNED BY THE LEGION OF COMMON DECENCY.
I RAN THEIR ADDRESSES THROUGH UCR. WE GOT 8 MEMBERS CURRENTLY UNACCOUNTED FOR. PROBABLY IN HIDING.
WE ALSO GOT A REPORT FROM FORENSICS. THE HAIRS THEY FOUND ON LEWIS BELONG TO PAN TROGLODYTES – A CHIMPANZEE.
THEY CONTAINED MINUTE TRACES OF HYBRINOL... A HORMONE USED IN IMPLANT SURGERY.
FORENSICS RECKON THE APE'S FITTED WITH SOME KIND OF SLAVE SYSTEM. RECKON THE CROCKS ARE RUNNING IT BY REMOTE CONTROL.
ONLY PROBLEM NOW IS FINDING THEM. THEY COULD BE HIDING ANYWHERE IN THE CITY.
WE'LL GET 'EM, SPINKS. THEY CAN'T STAY HIDDEN FOREVER. SOONER OR LATER THEY'RE GONNA HAVE TO MAKE A MOVE.
AND WHEN THEY DO I'LL BE FIRST IN LINE.
BLACK GOD.
NEXT: MONKEY BUSINESS!

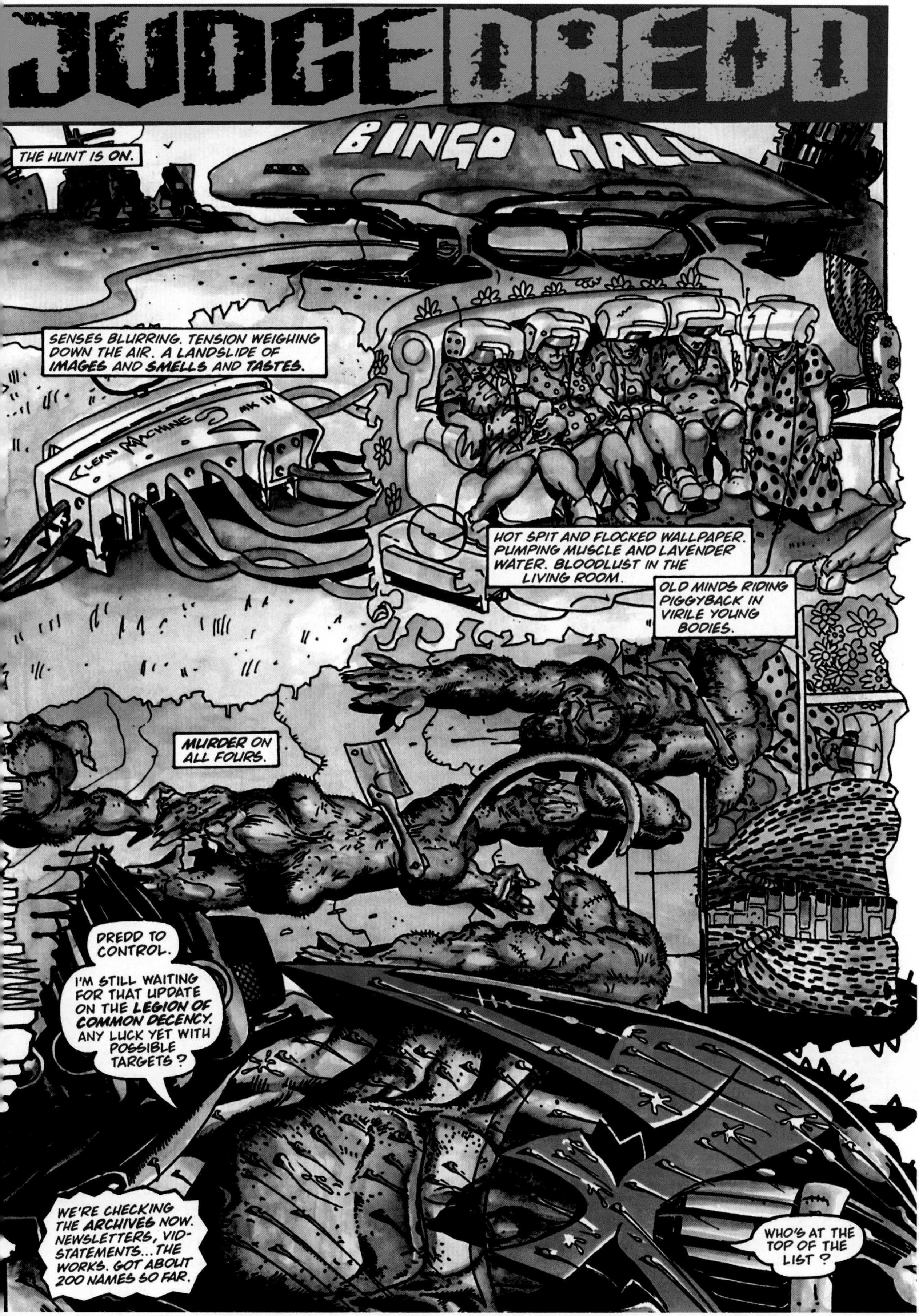
JUDGE DREDD
BINGO HALL
THE HUNT IS ON.
SENSES BLURRING. TENSION WEIGHING DOWN THE AIR. A LANDSLIDE OF IMAGES AND SMELLS AND TASTES.
CLEAN MACHINE MK IV
HOT SPIT AND FLOCKED WALLPAPER. PUMPING MUSCLE AND LAVENDER WATER. BLOODLUST IN THE LIVING ROOM.
OLD MINDS RIDING PIGGYBACK IN VIRILE YOUNG BODIES.
MURDER ON ALL FOURS.
DREDD TO CONTROL.
I'M STILL WAITING FOR THAT UPDATE ON THE LEGION OF COMMON DECENCY. ANY LUCK YET WITH POSSIBLE TARGETS?
WE'RE CHECKING THE ARCHIVES NOW. NEWSLETTERS, VID-STATEMENTS... THE WORKS. GOT ABOUT 200 NAMES SO FAR.
WHO'S AT THE TOP OF THE LIST?

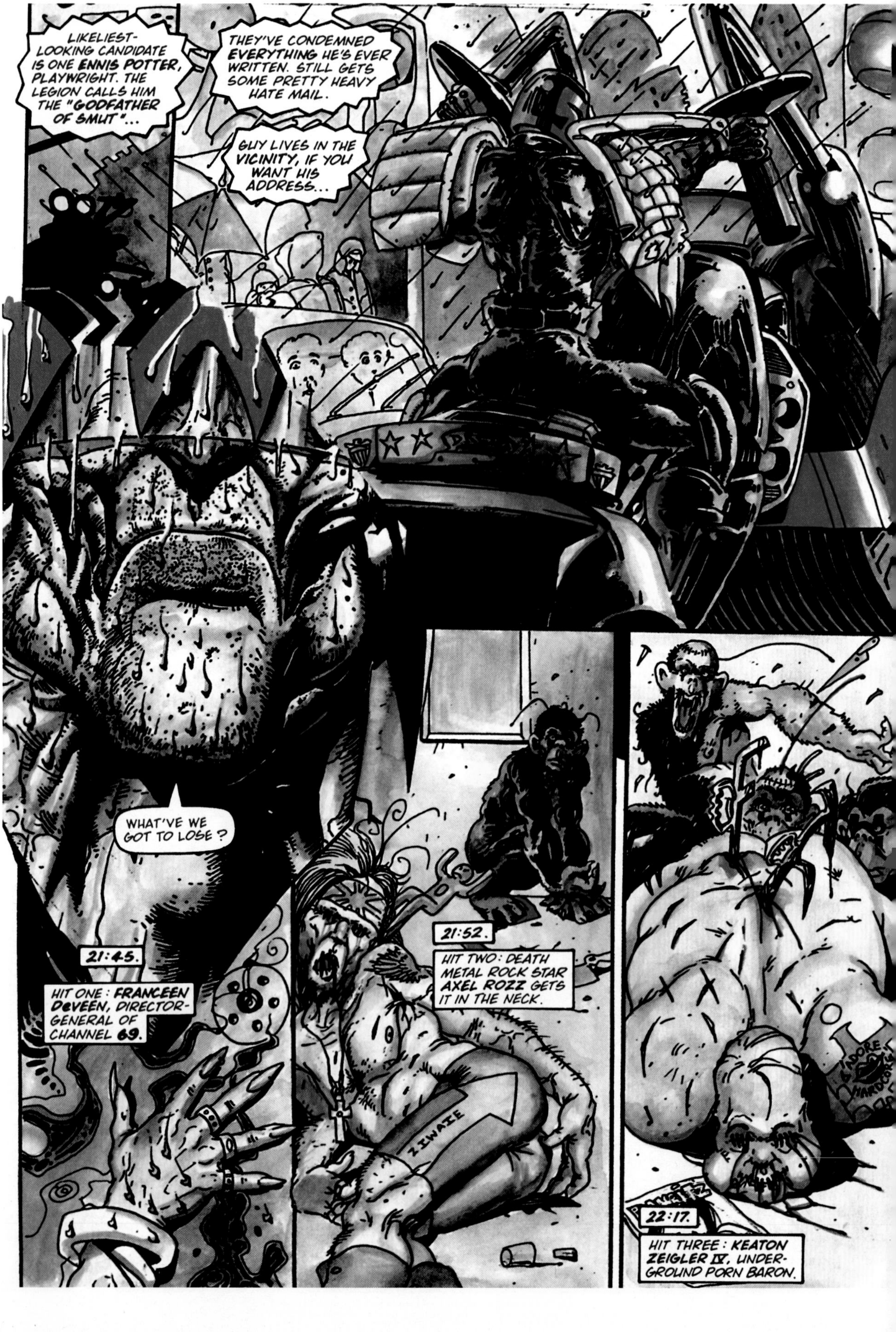
LIKELIEST-LOOKING CANDIDATE IS ONE ENNIS POTTER, PLAYWRIGHT. THE LEGION CALLS HIM THE "GODFATHER OF SMUT"...
THEY'VE CONDEMNED EVERYTHING HE'S EVER WRITTEN. STILL GETS SOME PRETTY HEAVY HATE MAIL.
GUY LIVES IN THE VICINITY, IF YOU WANT HIS ADDRESS...
WHAT'VE WE GOT TO LOSE?
21:45.
HIT ONE: FRANCEEN DeVEEN, DIRECTOR-GENERAL OF CHANNEL 69.
21:52.
HIT TWO: DEATH METAL ROCK STAR AXEL ROZZ GETS IT IN THE NECK.
22:17.
HIT THREE: KEATON ZEIGLER IV, UNDER-GROUND PORN BARON.

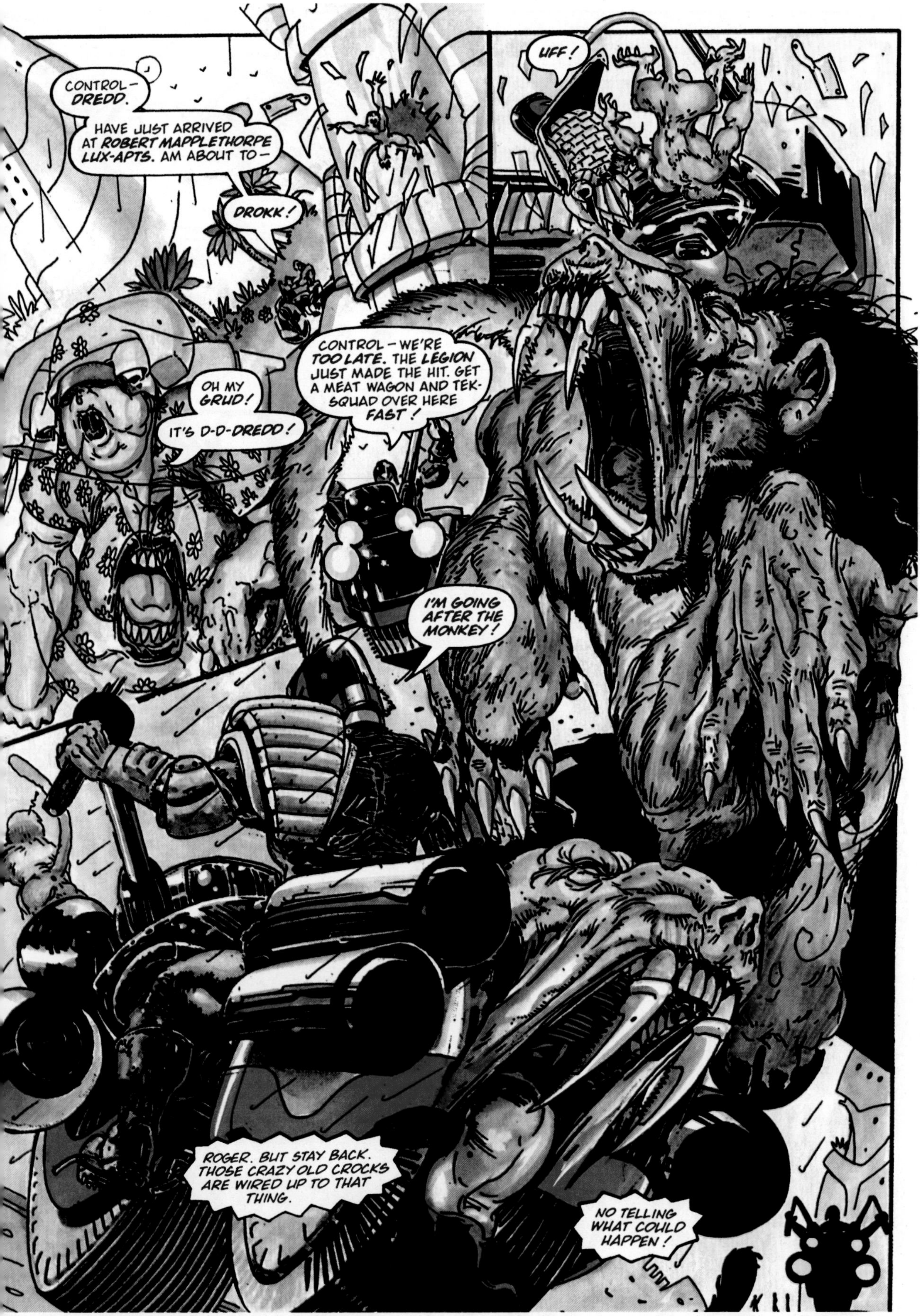
CONTROL-DREDD.
HAVE JUST ARRIVED AT ROBERT MAPPLETHORPE LUX-APTS. AM ABOUT TO—
DROKK!
UFF!
OH MY GRUD!
IT'S D-D-DREDD!
CONTROL—WE'RE TOO LATE. THE LEGION JUST MADE THE HIT. GET A MEAT WAGON AND TEK-SQUAD OVER HERE FAST!
I'M GOING AFTER THE MONKEY!
ROGER. BUT STAY BACK. THOSE CRAZY OLD CROCKS ARE WIRED UP TO THAT THING.
NO TELLING WHAT COULD HAPPEN!

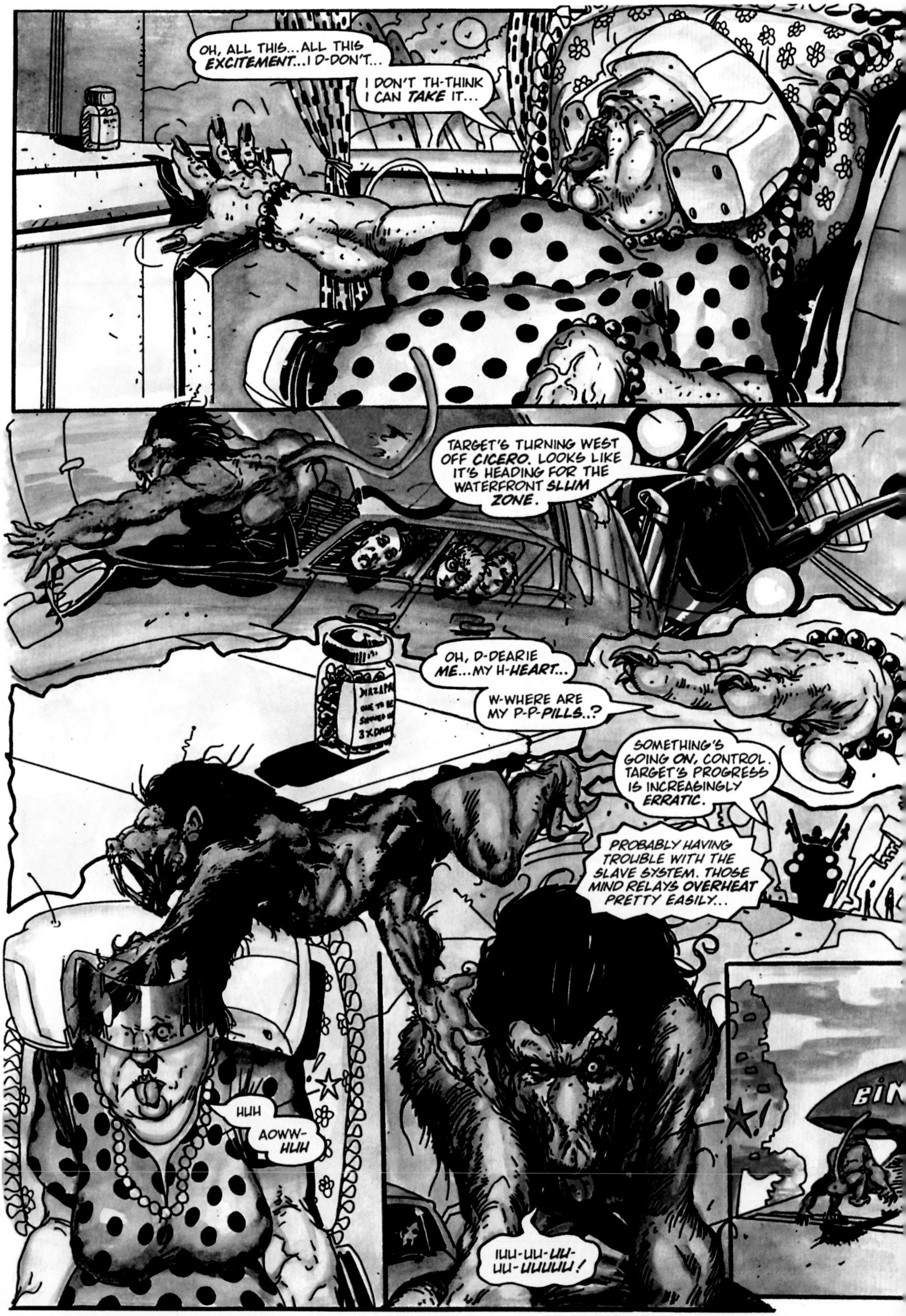
OH, ALL THIS...ALL THIS EXCITEMENT...I D-DON'T...
I DON'T TH-THINK I CAN TAKE IT...
TARGET'S TURNING WEST OFF CICERO. LOOKS LIKE IT'S HEADING FOR THE WATERFRONT SLUM ZONE.
OH, D-DEARIE ME...MY H-HEART...
W-WHERE ARE MY P-P-PILLS..?
SOMETHING'S GOING ON, CONTROL. TARGET'S PROGRESS IS INCREASINGLY ERRATIC.
PROBABLY HAVING TROUBLE WITH THE SLAVE SYSTEM. THOSE MIND RELAYS OVERHEAT PRETTY EASILY...
HUH
AOWW-HUH
UUU-UU-UU-UU-UU-UUUUU!

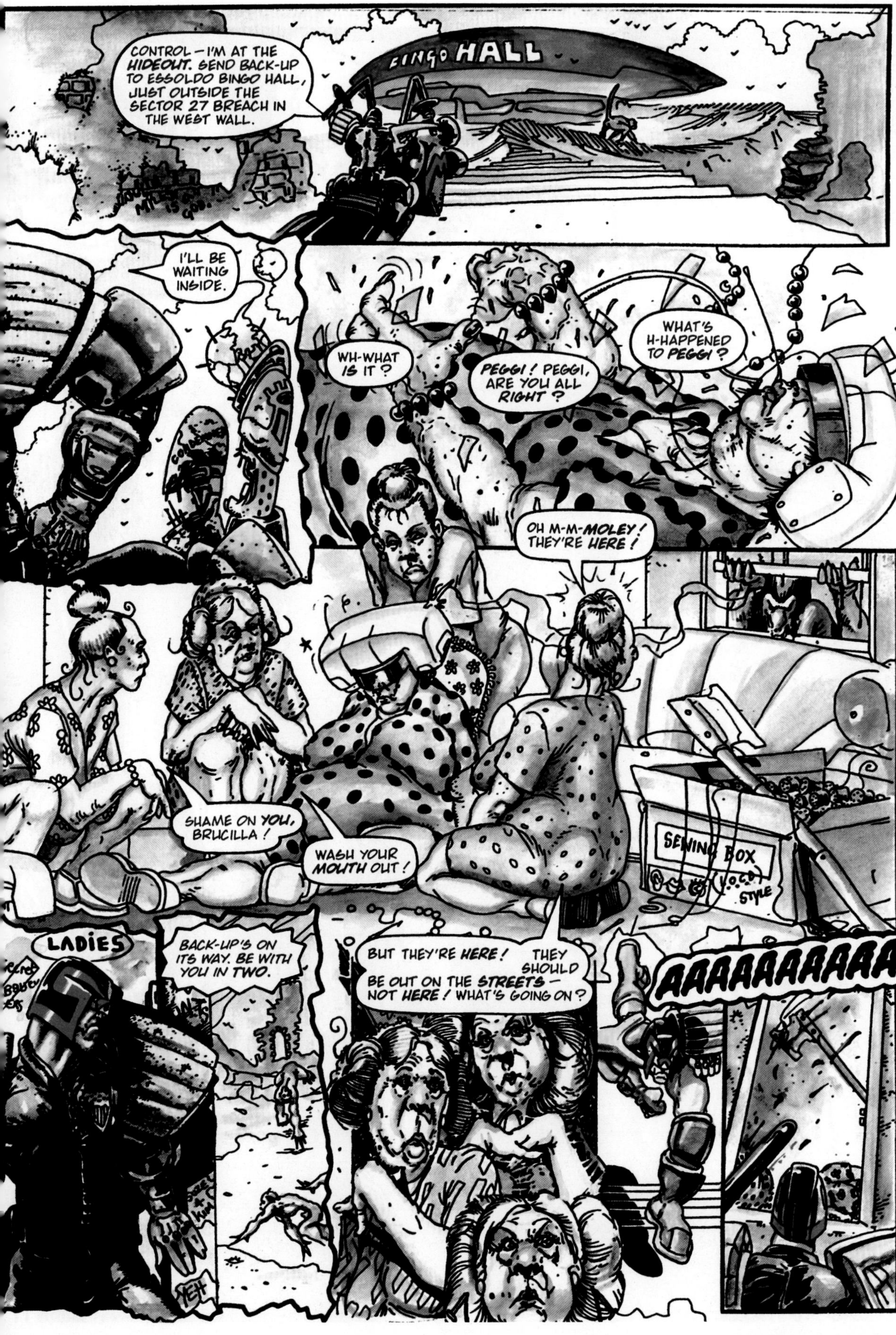
BINGO HALL
CONTROL — I'M AT THE HIDEOUT. SEND BACK-UP TO ESSOLDO BINGO HALL, JUST OUTSIDE THE SECTOR 27 BREACH IN THE WEST WALL.
I'LL BE WAITING INSIDE.
WH-WHAT IS IT?
PEGGI! PEGGI, ARE YOU ALL RIGHT?
WHAT'S H-HAPPENED TO PEGGI?
OH M-M-MOLEY! THEY'RE HERE!
SHAME ON YOU, BRUCILLA!
WASH YOUR MOUTH OUT!
SEWING BOX
LADIES
BACK-UP'S ON ITS WAY. BE WITH YOU IN TWO.
BUT THEY'RE HERE! THEY SHOULD BE OUT ON THE STREETS — NOT HERE! WHAT'S GOING ON?
AAAAAAAAAA

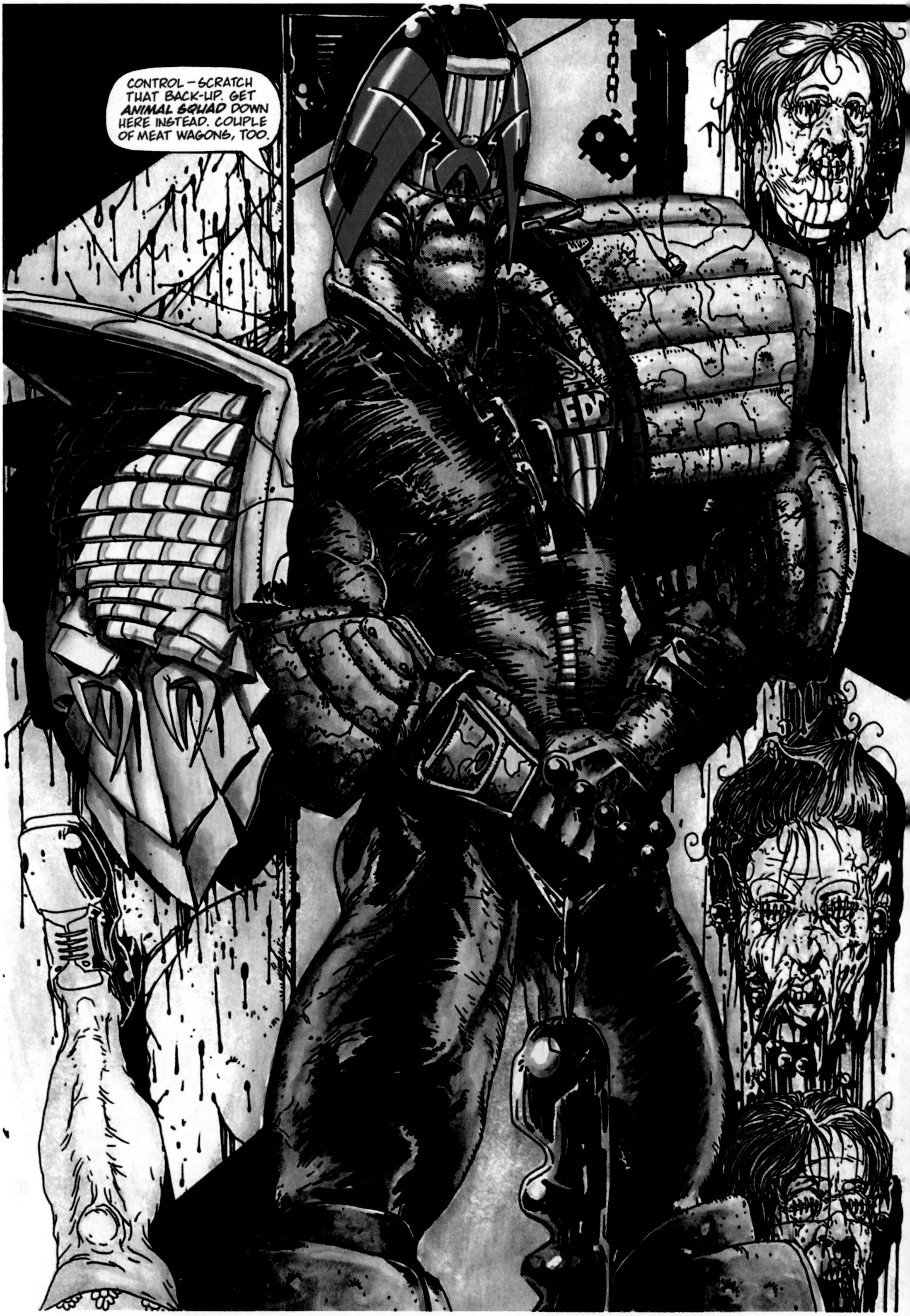
CONTROL—SCRATCH THAT BACK-UP. GET ANIMAL SQUAD DOWN HERE INSTEAD. COUPLE OF MEAT WAGONS, TOO.

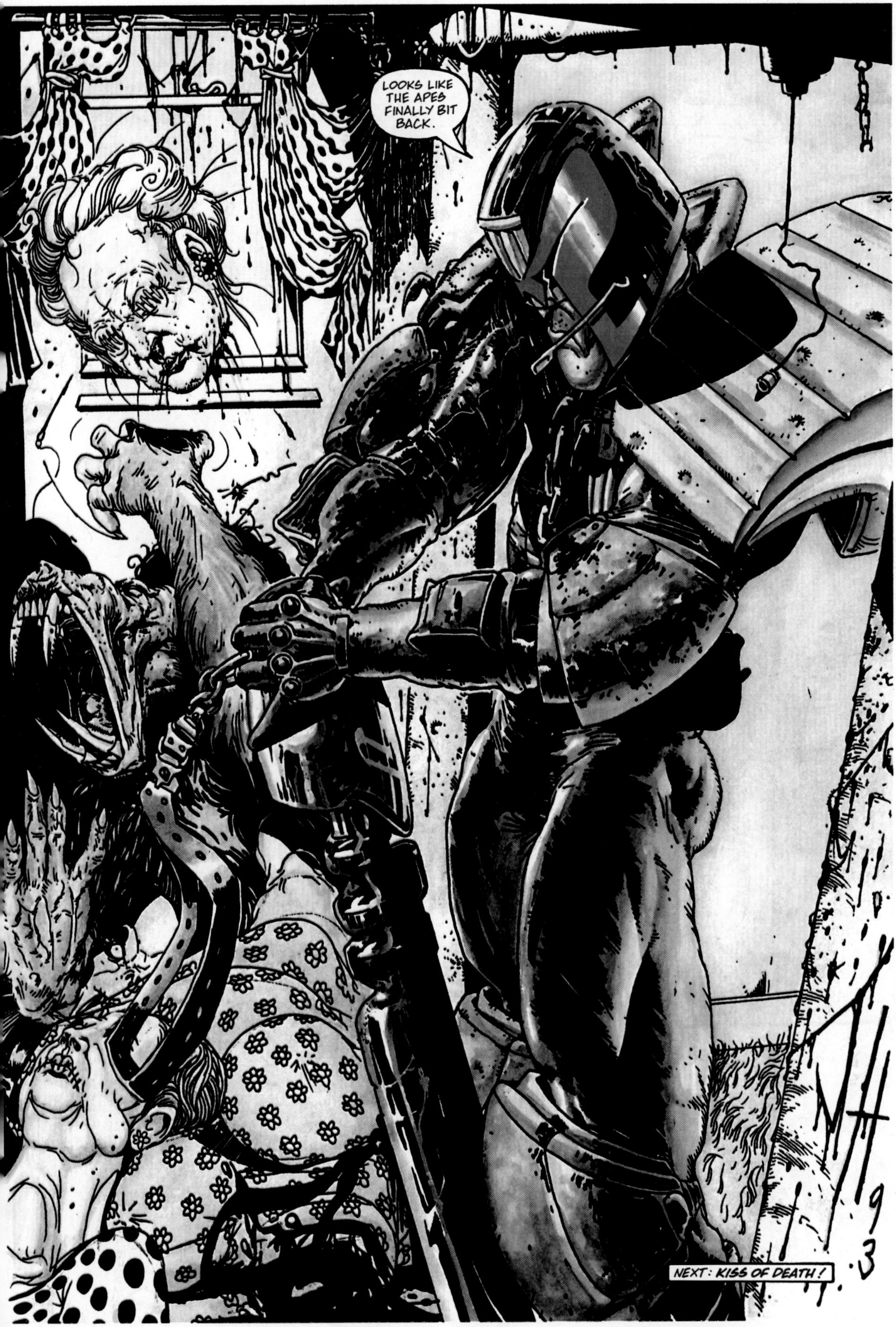
LOOKS LIKE THE APES FINALLY BIT BACK.
NEXT: KISS OF DEATH!
93

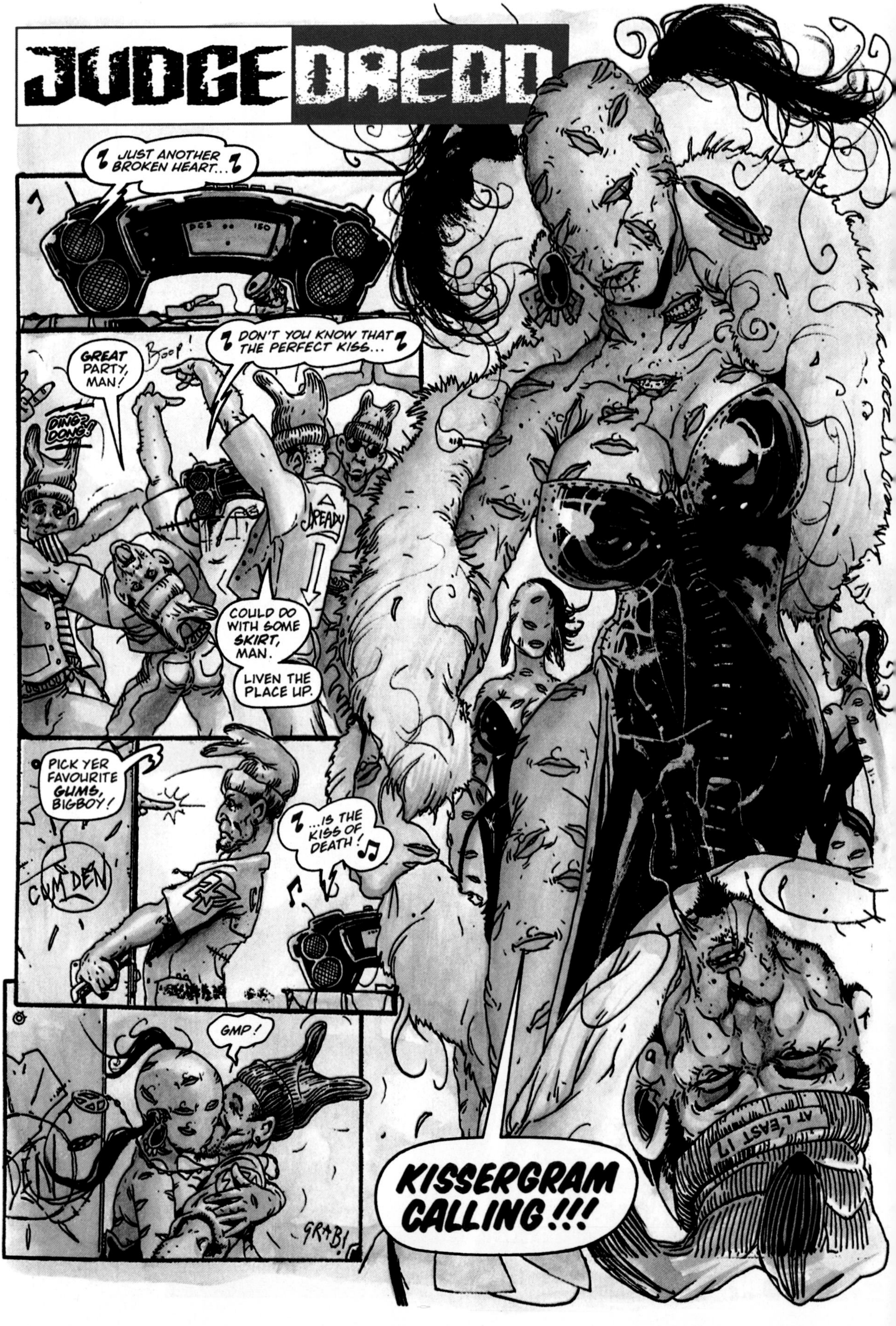
JUDGE DREDD
JUST ANOTHER BROKEN HEART...
GREAT PARTY, MAN!
DON'T YOU KNOW THAT THE PERFECT KISS...
BOOP!
DING DONG!
COULD DO WITH SOME SKIRT, MAN.
LIVEN THE PLACE UP.
PICK YER FAVOURITE GUMS, BIGBOY!
...IS THE KISS OF DEATH!
GMP!
GRAB!
KISSERGRAM CALLING!!!

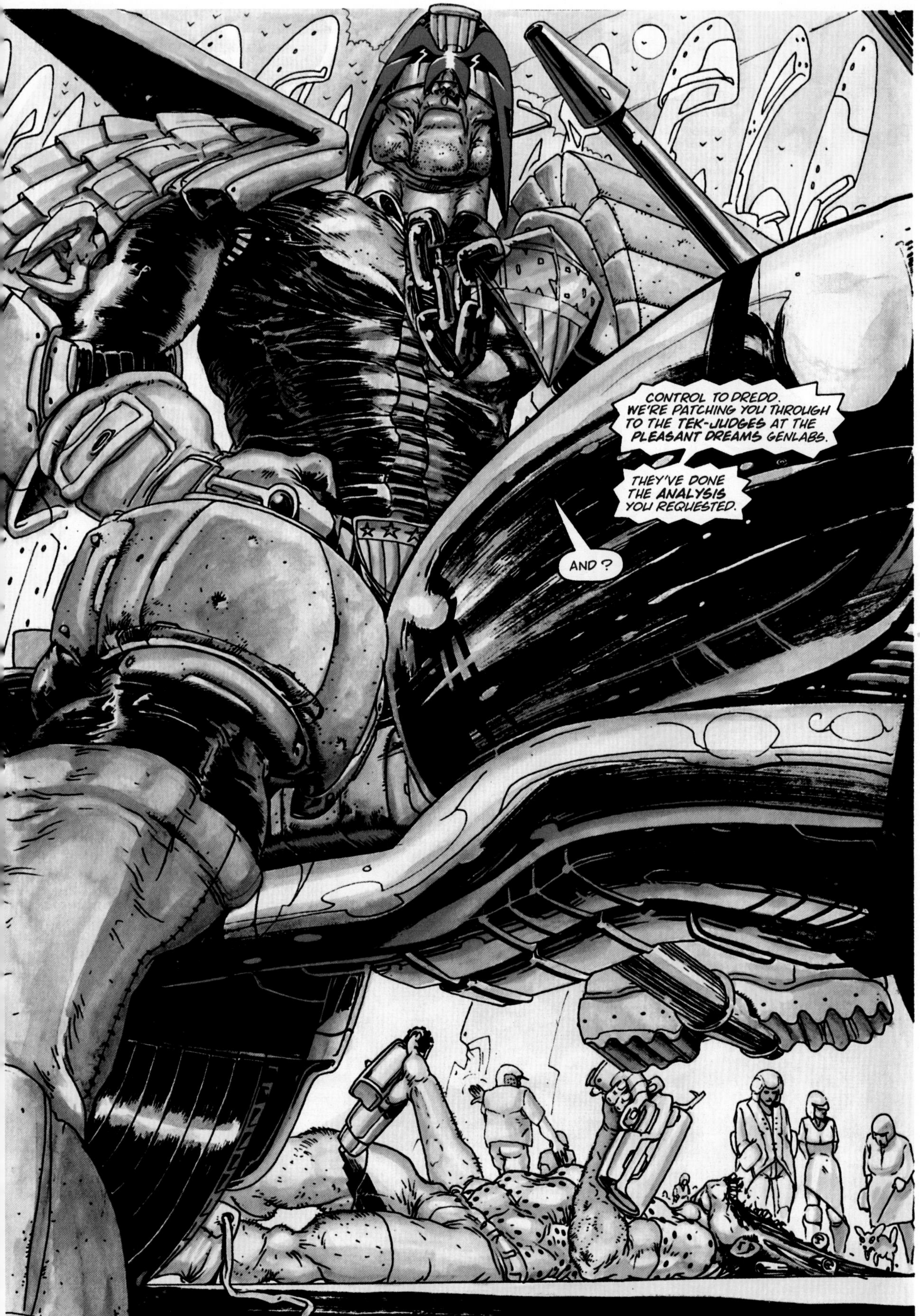
CONTROL TO DREDD. WE'RE PATCHING YOU THROUGH TO THE TEK-JUDGES AT THE PLEASANT DREAMS GENLABS.
THEY'VE DONE THE ANALYSIS YOU REQUESTED.
AND?

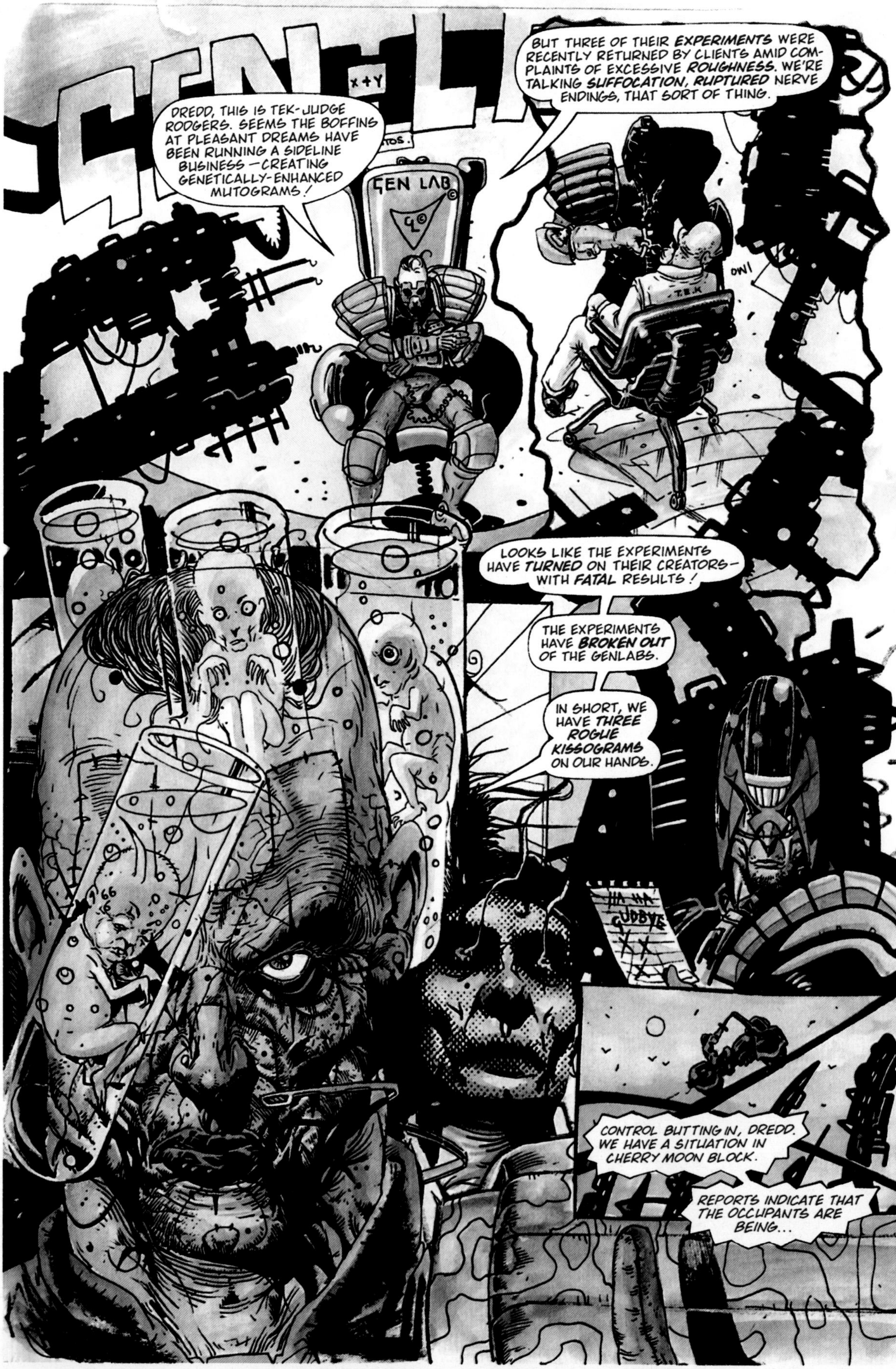
GEN LAB
DREDD, THIS IS TEK-JUDGE RODGERS. SEEMS THE BOFFINS AT PLEASANT DREAMS HAVE BEEN RUNNING A SIDELINE BUSINESS —CREATING GENETICALLY-ENHANCED MUTOGRAMS!
BUT THREE OF THEIR EXPERIMENTS WERE RECENTLY RETURNED BY CLIENTS AMID COMPLAINTS OF EXCESSIVE ROUGHNESS. WE'RE TALKING SUFFOCATION, RUPTURED NERVE ENDINGS, THAT SORT OF THING.
OW!
LOOKS LIKE THE EXPERIMENTS HAVE TURNED ON THEIR CREATORS— WITH FATAL RESULTS!
THE EXPERIMENTS HAVE BROKEN OUT OF THE GENLABS.
IN SHORT, WE HAVE THREE ROGUE KISSOGRAMS ON OUR HANDS.
HA HA GUDBYE XX
CONTROL BUTTING IN, DREDD. WE HAVE A SITUATION IN CHERRY MOON BLOCK.
REPORTS INDICATE THAT THE OCCUPANTS ARE BEING...

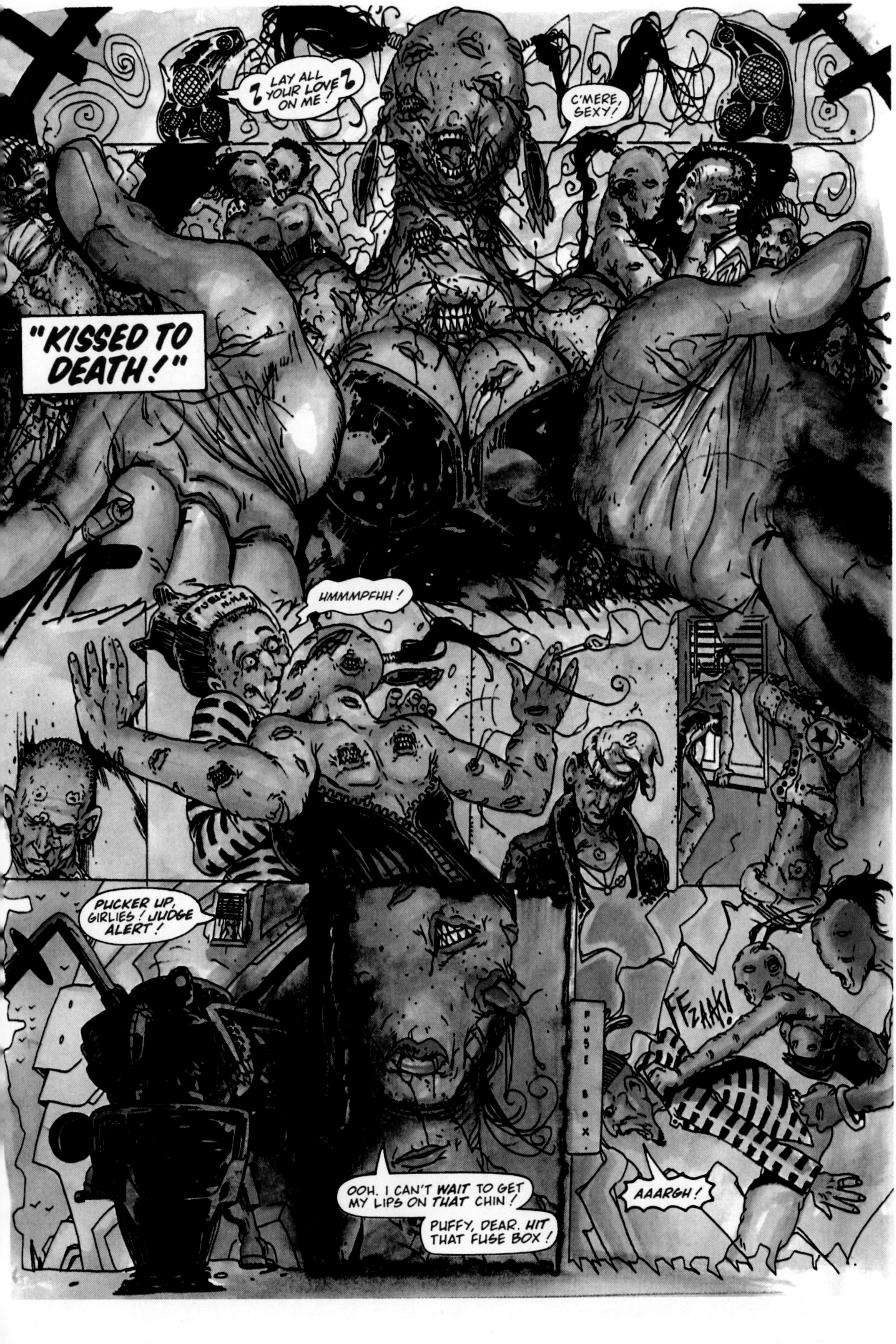
LAY ALL YOUR LOVE ON ME!
C'MERE, SEXY!
"KISSED TO DEATH!"
UMMMPFHH!
PUCKER UP, GIRLIES! JUDGE ALERT!
OOH. I CAN'T WAIT TO GET MY LIPS ON THAT CHIN!
PUFFY, DEAR. HIT THAT FUSE BOX!
FUSE BOX
FFZAAK!
AAARGH!

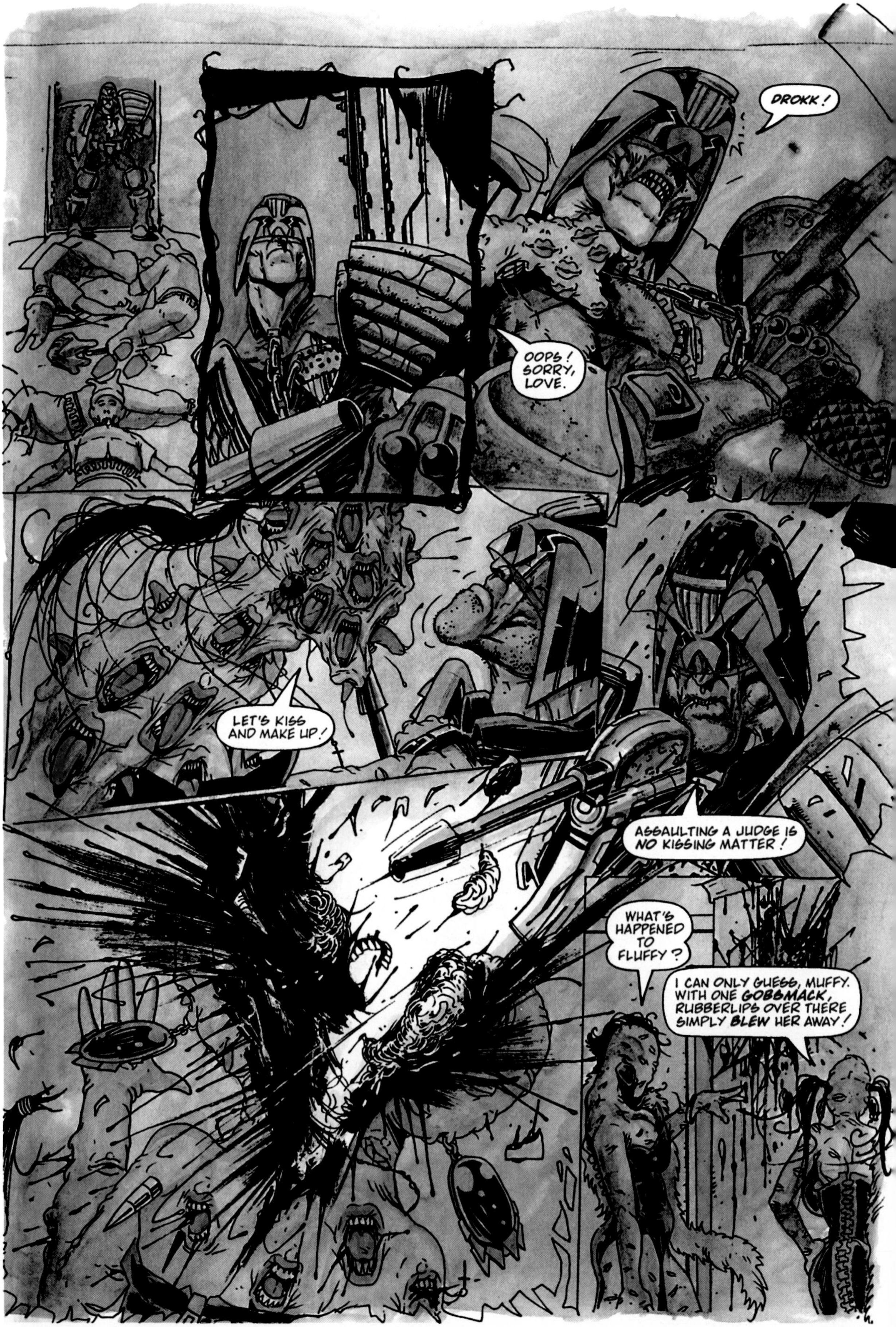
DROKK!
OOPS! SORRY, LOVE.
LET'S KISS AND MAKE UP!
ASSAULTING A JUDGE IS NO KISSING MATTER!
WHAT'S HAPPENED TO FLUFFY?
I CAN ONLY GUESS, MUFFY. WITH ONE GOBSMACK, RUBBERLIPS OVER THERE SIMPLY BLEW HER AWAY!

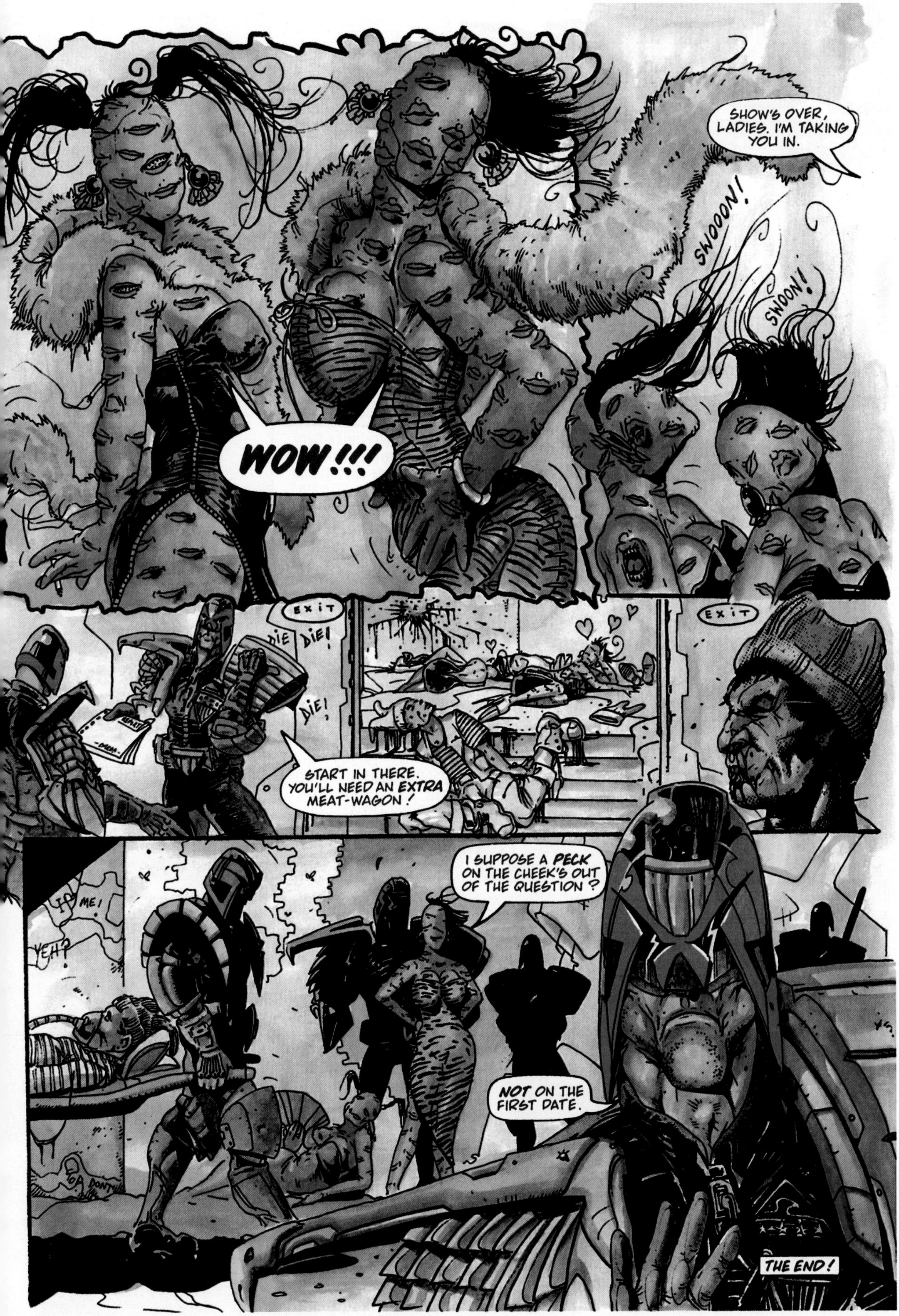
SHOW'S OVER, LADIES. I'M TAKING YOU IN.
WOW!!!
SWOOON!
SWOON!
EXIT
DIE DIE!
DIE!
START IN THERE. YOU'LL NEED AN EXTRA MEAT-WAGON!
EXIT
I SUPPOSE A PECK ON THE CHEEK'S OUT OF THE QUESTION?
NOT ON THE FIRST DATE.
THE END!

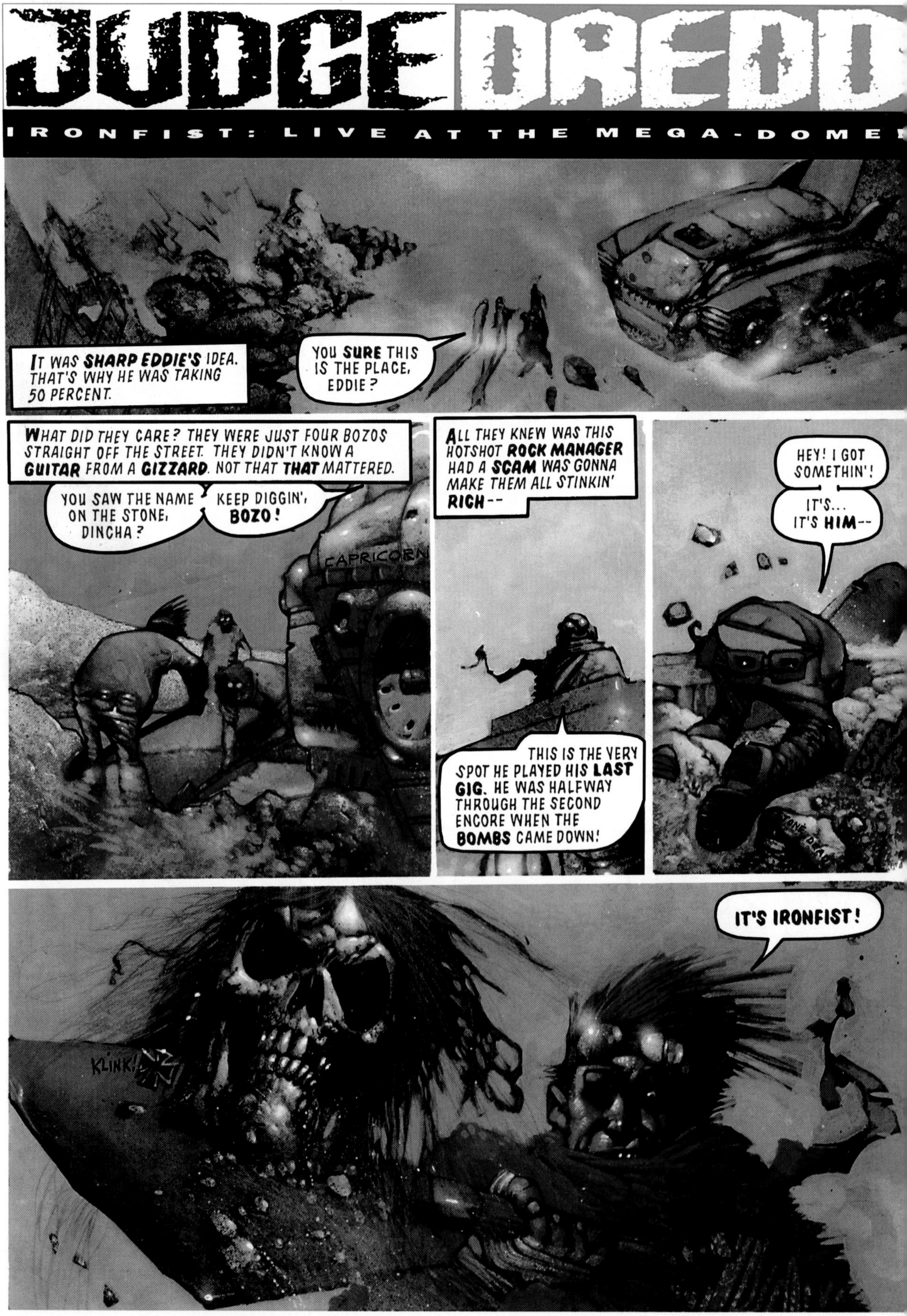
JUDGE DREDD
IRONFIST: LIVE AT THE MEGA-DOME
IT WAS SHARP EDDIE'S IDEA. THAT'S WHY HE WAS TAKING 50 PERCENT.
YOU SURE THIS IS THE PLACE, EDDIE?
WHAT DID THEY CARE? THEY WERE JUST FOUR BOZOS STRAIGHT OFF THE STREET. THEY DIDN'T KNOW A GUITAR FROM A GIZZARD. NOT THAT THAT MATTERED.
YOU SAW THE NAME ON THE STONE, DINCHA?
KEEP DIGGIN', BOZO!
CAPRICORN
ALL THEY KNEW WAS THIS HOTSHOT ROCK MANAGER HAD A SCAM WAS GONNA MAKE THEM ALL STINKIN' RICH--
THIS IS THE VERY SPOT HE PLAYED HIS LAST GIG. HE WAS HALFWAY THROUGH THE SECOND ENCORE WHEN THE BOMBS CAME DOWN!
HEY! I GOT SOMETHIN'!
IT'S... IT'S HIM--
IT'S IRONFIST!
KLINK!

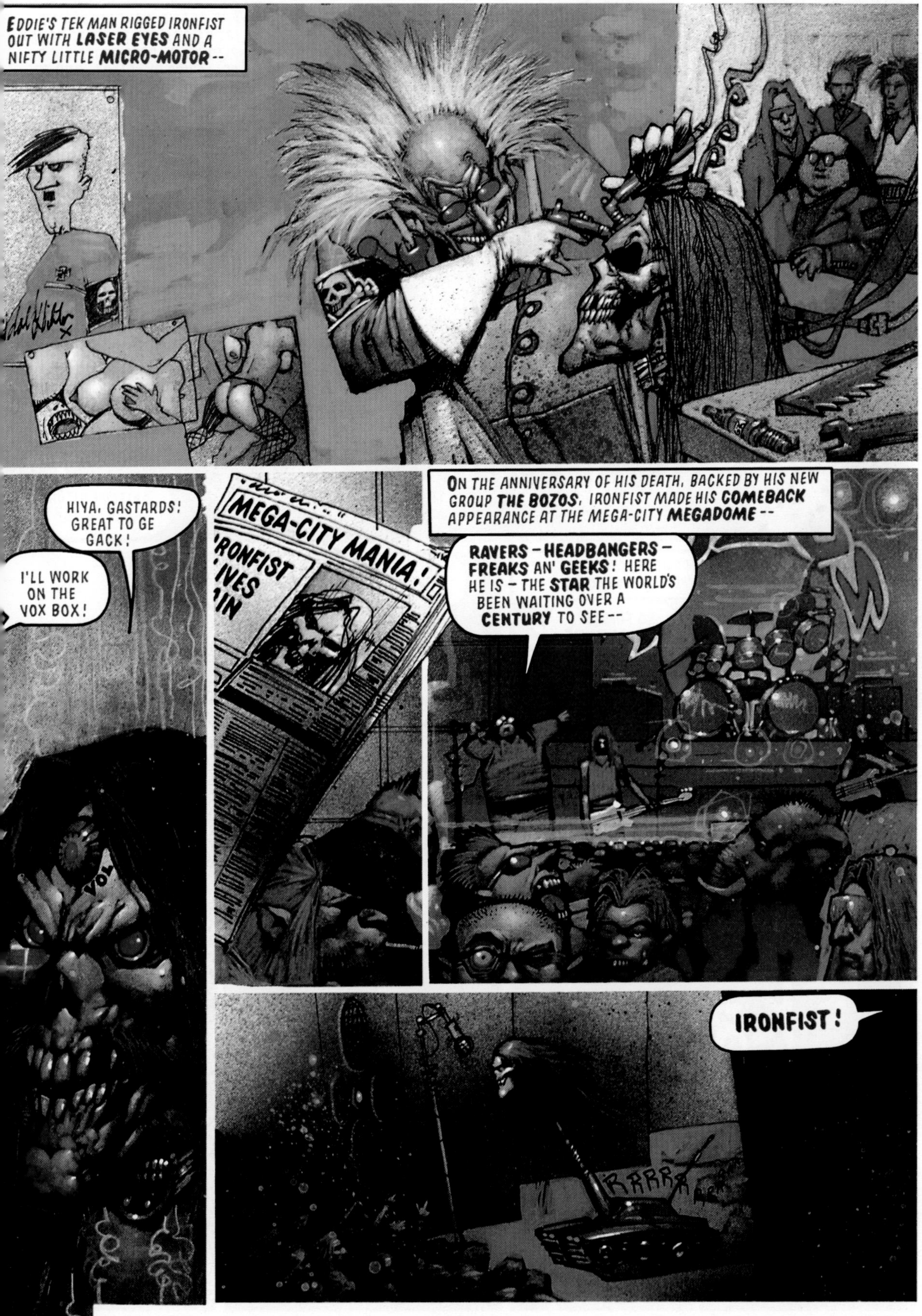
EDDIE'S TEK MAN RIGGED IRONFIST OUT WITH LASER EYES AND A NIFTY LITTLE MICRO-MOTOR --
HIYA, GASTARDS! GREAT TO GE GACK!
I'LL WORK ON THE VOX BOX!
VOL
MEGA-CITY MANIA!
RONFIST IVES AIN
ON THE ANNIVERSARY OF HIS DEATH, BACKED BY HIS NEW GROUP THE BOZOS, IRONFIST MADE HIS COMEBACK APPEARANCE AT THE MEGA-CITY MEGADOME --
RAVERS – HEADBANGERS – FREAKS AN' GEEKS! HERE HE IS – THE STAR THE WORLD'S BEEN WAITING OVER A CENTURY TO SEE --
IRONFIST!
RRRR

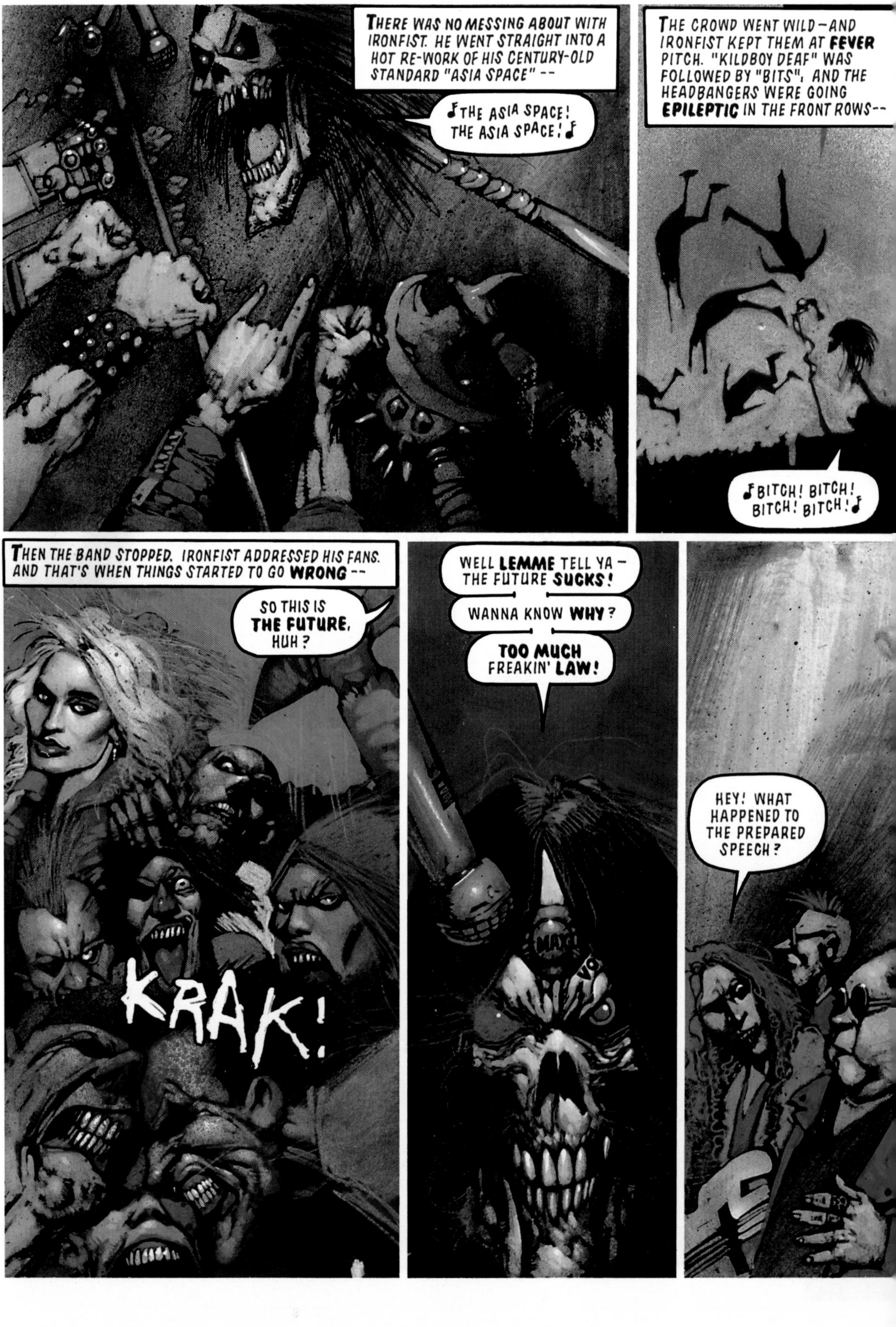

THERE WAS NO MESSING ABOUT WITH IRONFIST. HE WENT STRAIGHT INTO A HOT RE-WORK OF HIS CENTURY-OLD STANDARD "ASIA SPACE" --
♪ THE ASIA SPACE! THE ASIA SPACE! ♪
THE CROWD WENT WILD – AND IRONFIST KEPT THEM AT FEVER PITCH. "KILDBOY DEAF" WAS FOLLOWED BY "BITS", AND THE HEADBANGERS WERE GOING EPILEPTIC IN THE FRONT ROWS --
♪ BITCH! BITCH! BITCH! BITCH! ♪
THEN THE BAND STOPPED. IRONFIST ADDRESSED HIS FANS. AND THAT'S WHEN THINGS STARTED TO GO WRONG --
SO THIS IS THE FUTURE, HUH?
KRAK!
WELL LEMME TELL YA – THE FUTURE SUCKS!
WANNA KNOW WHY?
TOO MUCH FREAKIN' LAW!
HEY! WHAT HAPPENED TO THE PREPARED SPEECH?

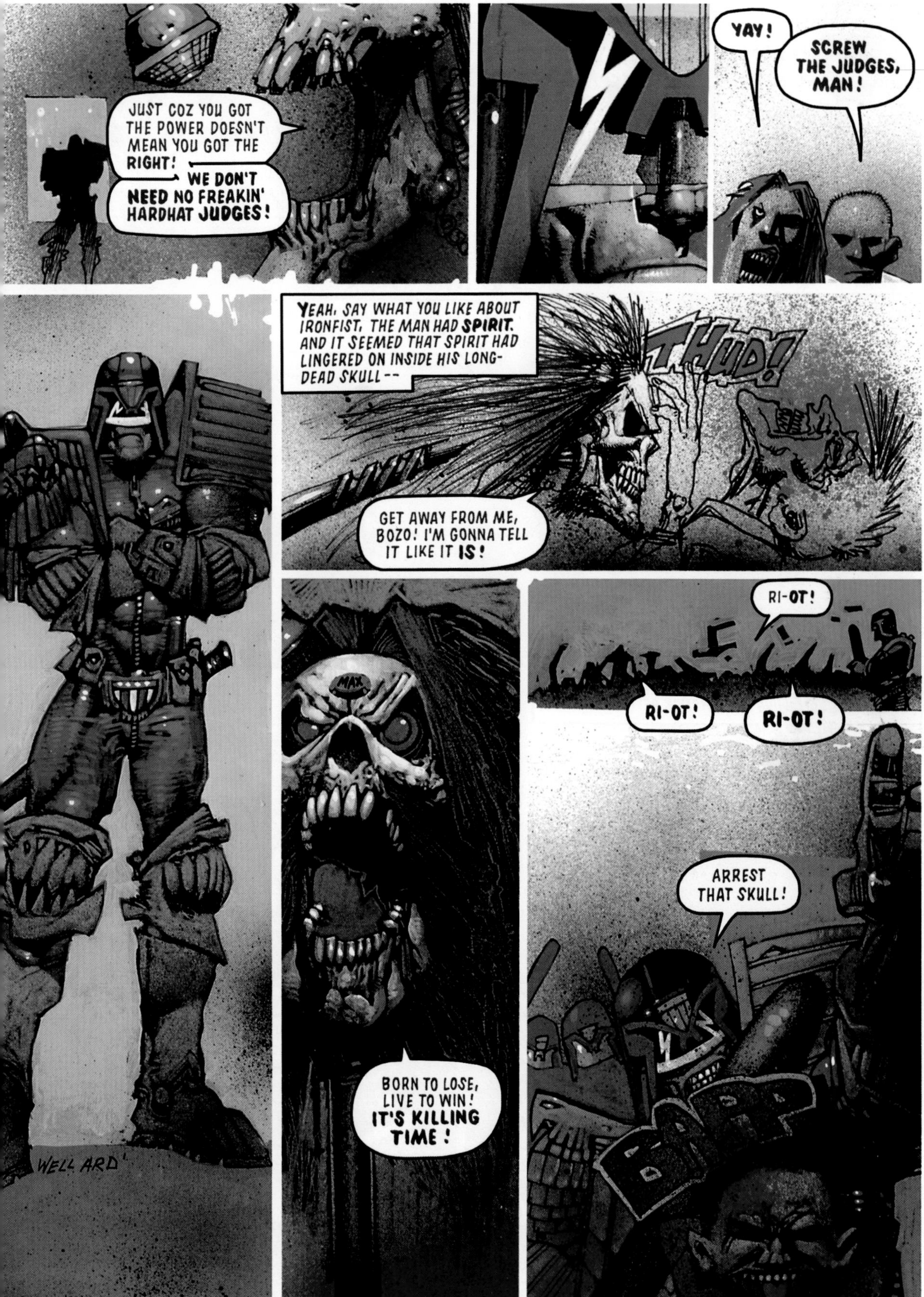
JUST COZ YOU GOT THE POWER DOESN'T MEAN YOU GOT THE RIGHT!
WE DON'T NEED NO FREAKIN' HARDHAT JUDGES!
YAY!
SCREW THE JUDGES, MAN!
YEAH, SAY WHAT YOU LIKE ABOUT IRONFIST, THE MAN HAD SPIRIT. AND IT SEEMED THAT SPIRIT HAD LINGERED ON INSIDE HIS LONG-DEAD SKULL--
THUD!
GET AWAY FROM ME, BOZO! I'M GONNA TELL IT LIKE IT IS!
WELL ARD'
MAX
BORN TO LOSE, LIVE TO WIN! IT'S KILLING TIME!
RI-OT!
RI-OT!
RI-OT!
ARREST THAT SKULL!

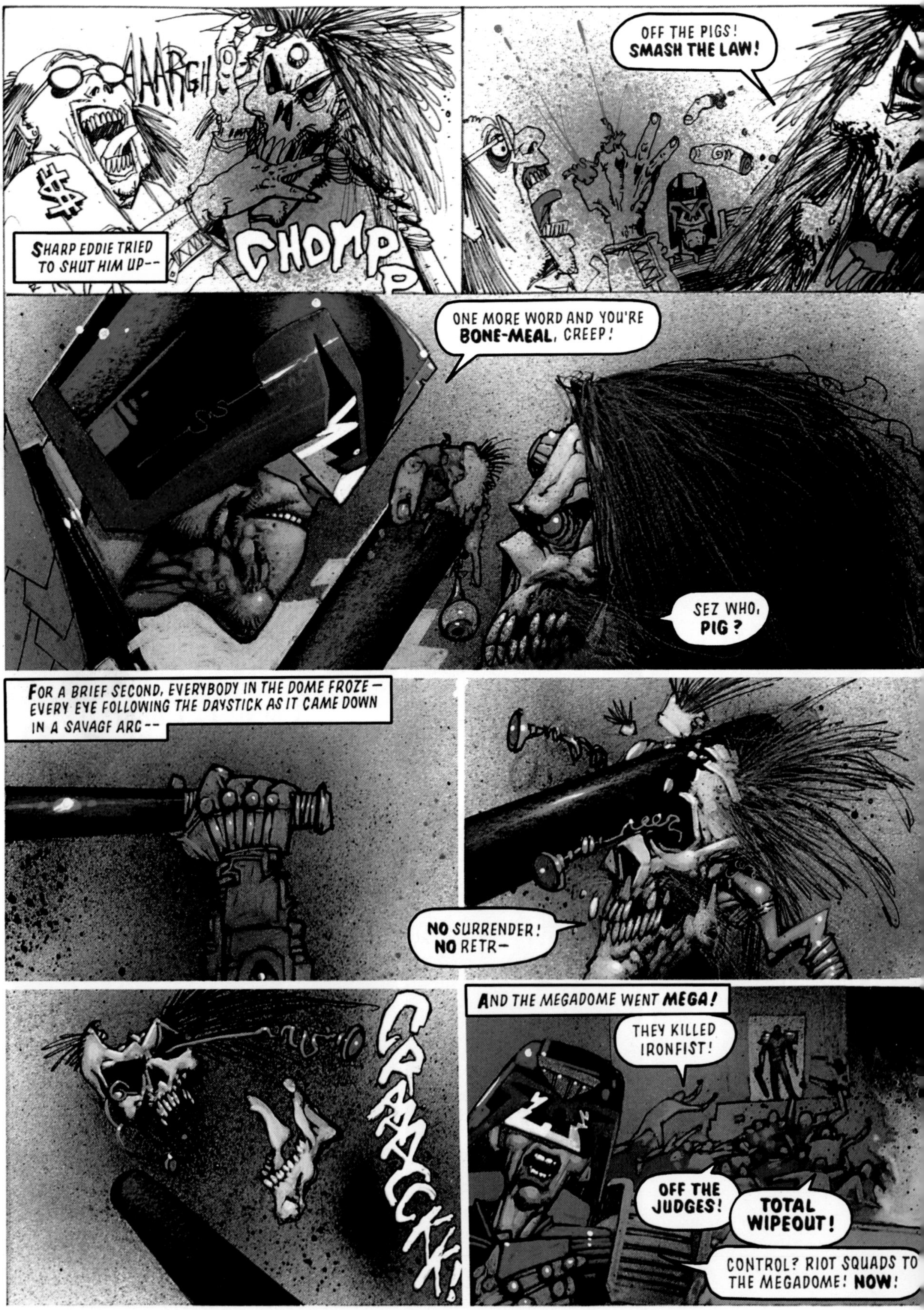
AAARGH!
SHARP EDDIE TRIED TO SHUT HIM UP--
CHOMPP
OFF THE PIGS! SMASH THE LAW!
ONE MORE WORD AND YOU'RE BONE-MEAL, CREEP!
SEZ WHO, PIG?
FOR A BRIEF SECOND, EVERYBODY IN THE DOME FROZE — EVERY EYE FOLLOWING THE DAYSTICK AS IT CAME DOWN IN A SAVAGE ARC--
NO SURRENDER! NO RETR-
CRAACKK!
AND THE MEGADOME WENT MEGA!
THEY KILLED IRONFIST!
OFF THE JUDGES!
TOTAL WIPEOUT!
CONTROL? RIOT SQUADS TO THE MEGADOME! NOW!

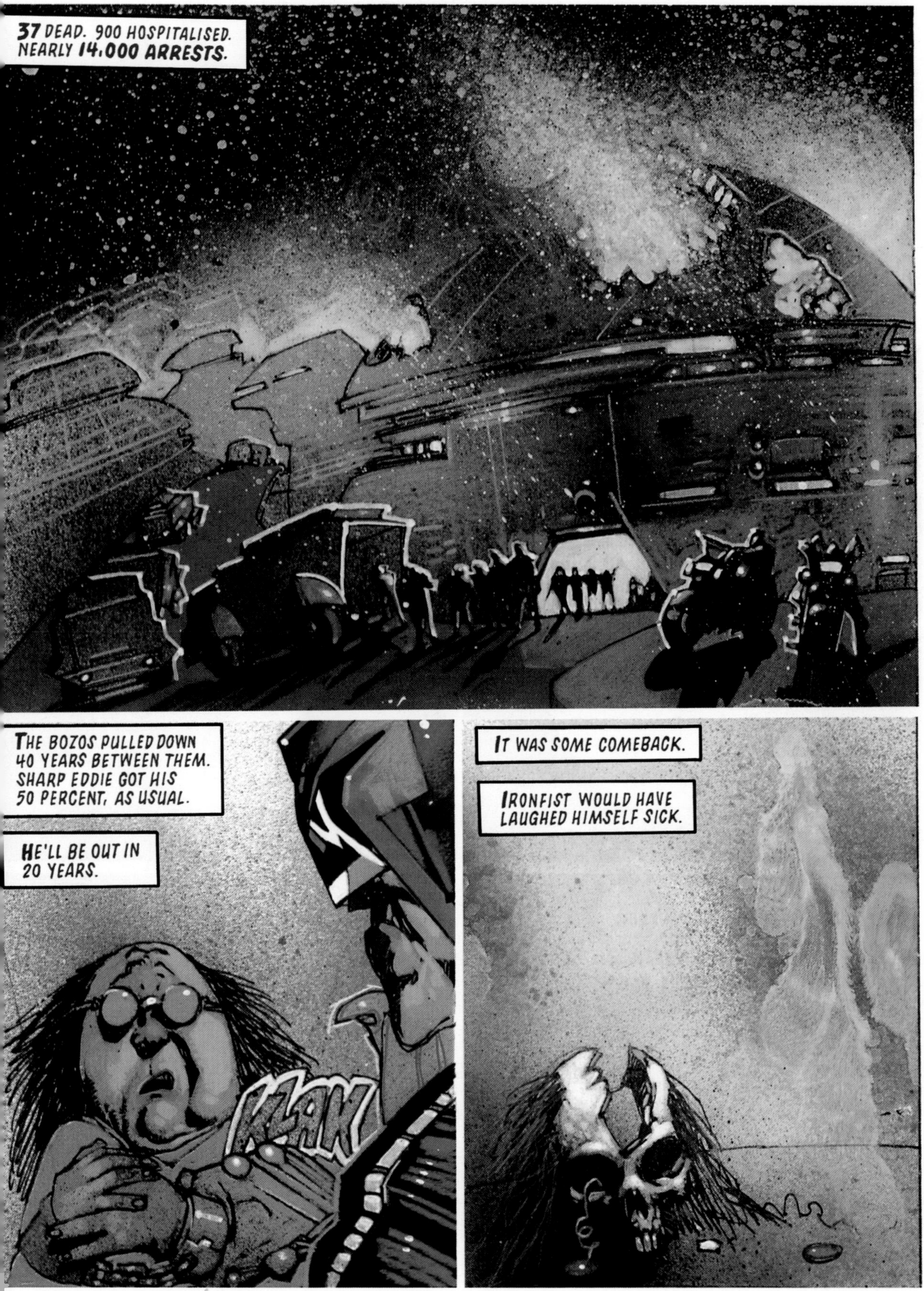
37 DEAD. 900 HOSPITALISED.
NEARLY 14,000 ARRESTS.
THE BOZOS PULLED DOWN 40 YEARS BETWEEN THEM. SHARP EDDIE GOT HIS 50 PERCENT, AS USUAL.
HE'LL BE OUT IN 20 YEARS.
KLAK
IT WAS SOME COMEBACK.
IRONFIST WOULD HAVE LAUGHED HIMSELF SICK.

THE END

JUDGE DREDD

'TWAS THE NIGHT BEFORE CHRISTMAS, AND...

'TWAS THE NIGHT **AFTER** CHRISTMAS...

'TWOULD'VE BEEN THE NIGHT BEFORE CHRISTMAS BUT SIMON WAS **LATE** FINISHING THE ARTWORK, OK? JUST READ THE **DROKKIN'** STORY, CREEPS!

BLIP BLIP

INTRUDER ALERT! COMING IN OVER NORTH WALL!

ATTENTION AIRCRAFT BEARING TANGO ALPHA THREE FOUR FOUR. YOU ARE IN **VIOLATION** OF MEGA-CITY ONE AIRSPACE!

IDENTIFY YOURSELF!

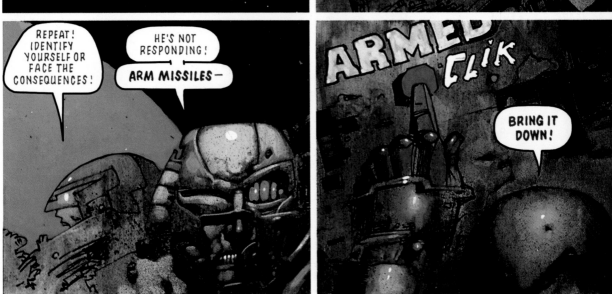

REPEAT! IDENTIFY YOURSELF OR FACE THE CONSEQUENCES!

HE'S NOT RESPONDING!

ARM MISSILES—

ARMED

CLIK

BRING IT DOWN!

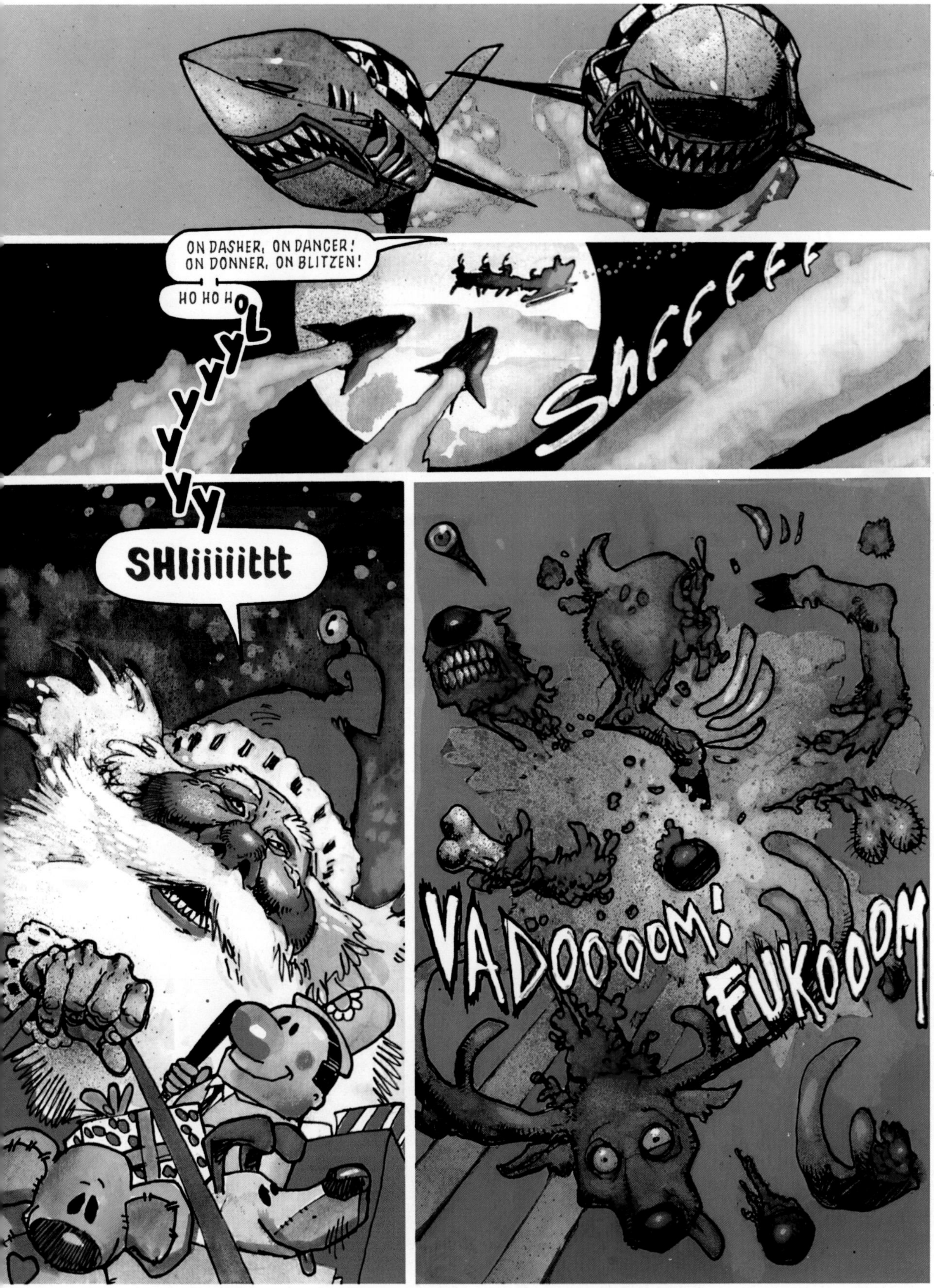
ON DASHER, ON DANCER! ON DONNER, ON BLITZEN!
HO HO HO
SHFFFFF
LYYYYYYy
SHIiiiiittt
VADOOOOM!
FUKOOOM

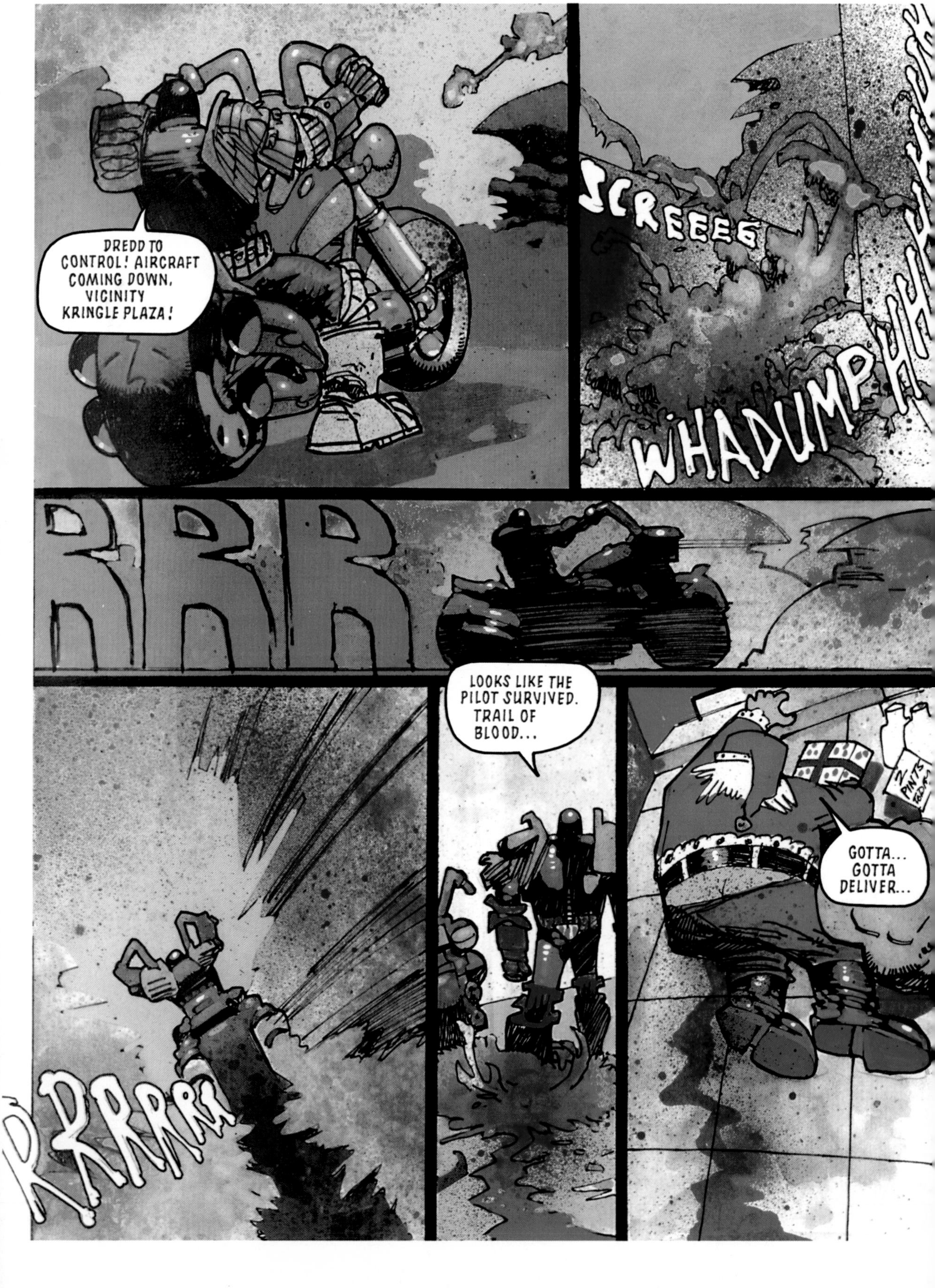
DREDD TO CONTROL! AIRCRAFT COMING DOWN, VICINITY KRINGLE PLAZA!
SCREEEG
WHADUMPHH
RRR
RRRRRR
LOOKS LIKE THE PILOT SURVIVED. TRAIL OF BLOOD...
GOTTA... GOTTA DELIVER...

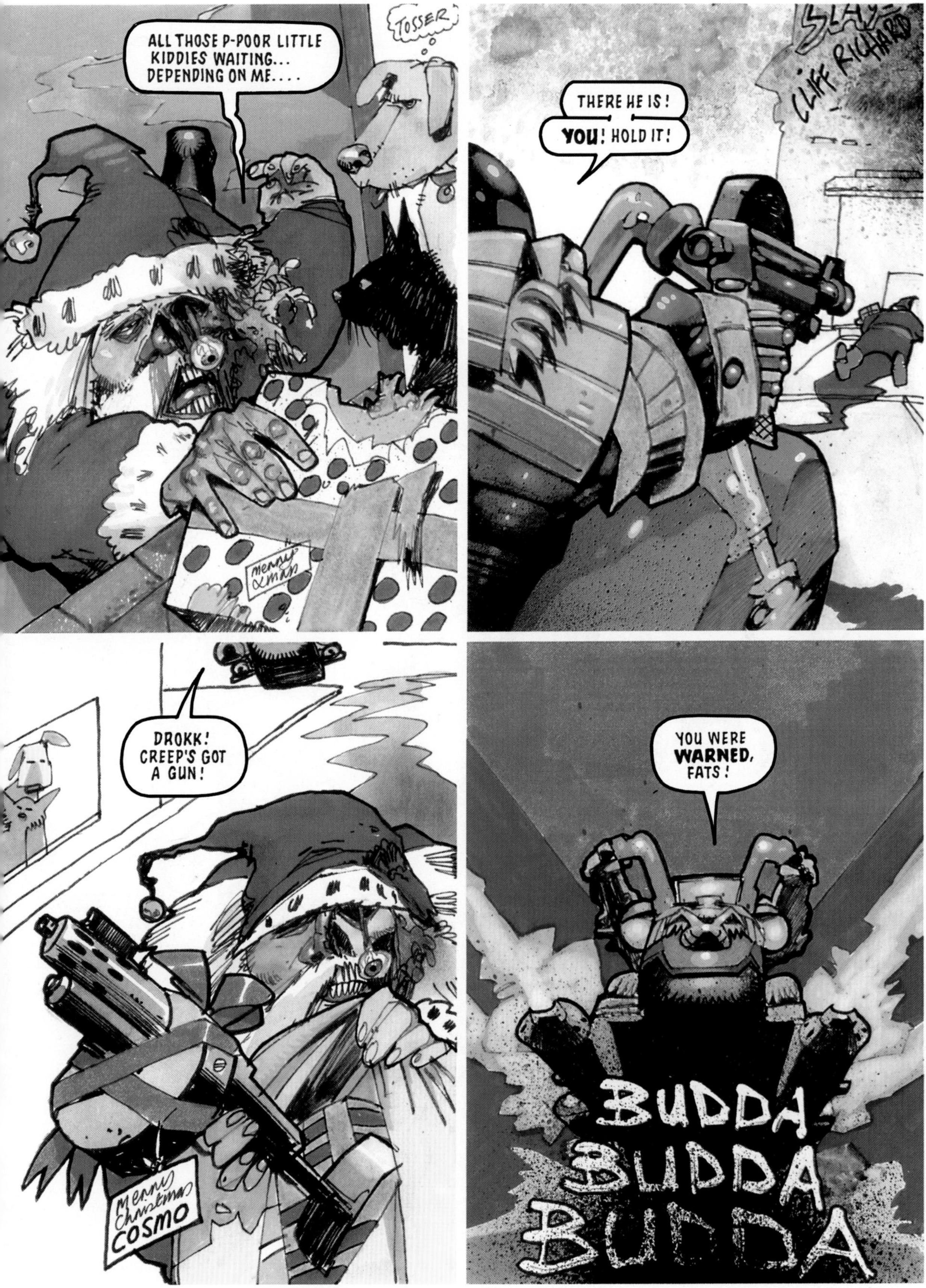
ALL THOSE P-POOR LITTLE KIDDIES WAITING... DEPENDING ON ME....
TOSSER
merry Xmas
CLIFF RICHARD
THERE HE IS!
YOU! HOLD IT!
DROKK! CREEP'S GOT A GUN!
Merry Christmas COSMO
YOU WERE WARNED, FATS!
BUDDA
BUDDA
BUDDA

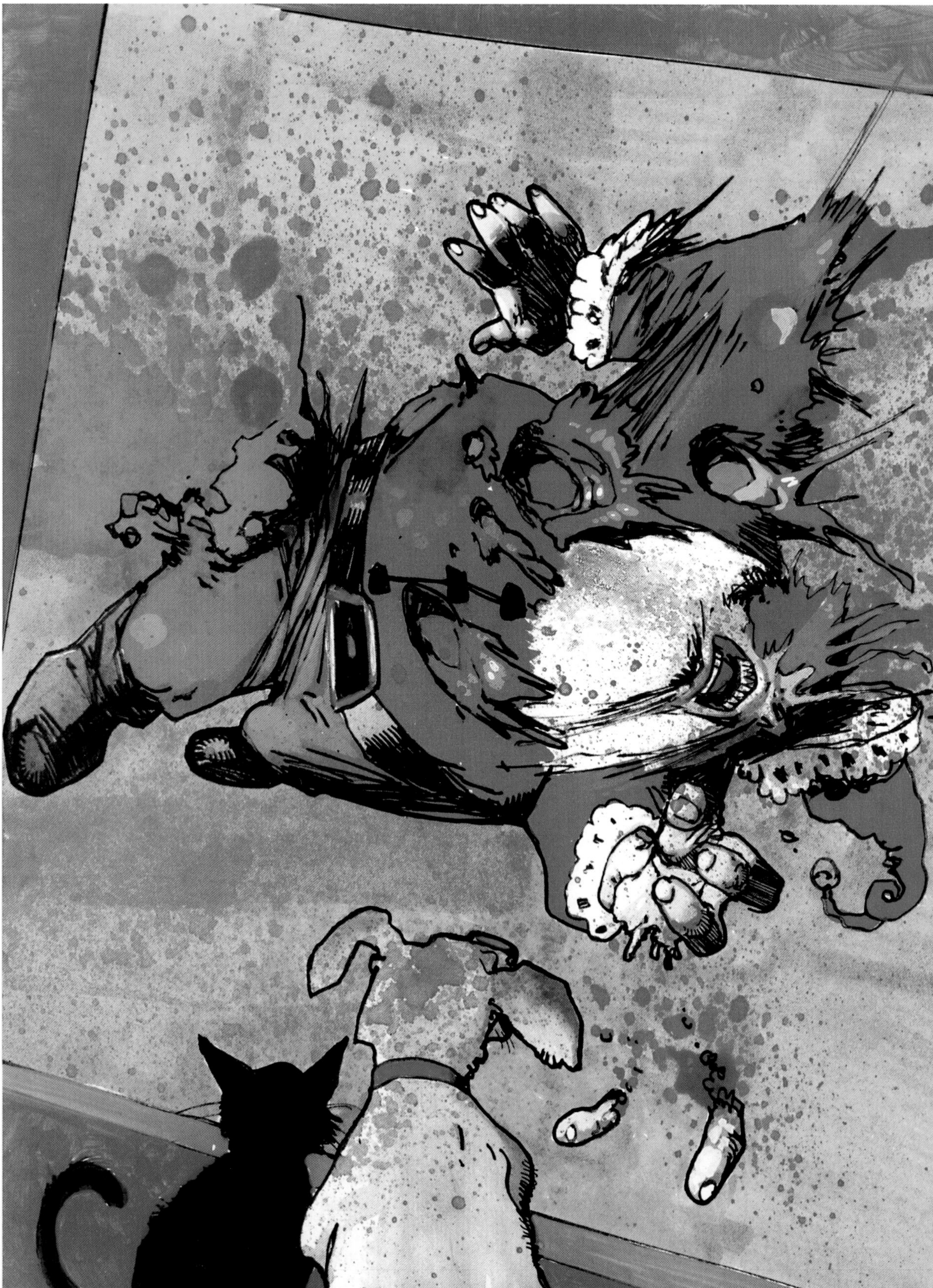

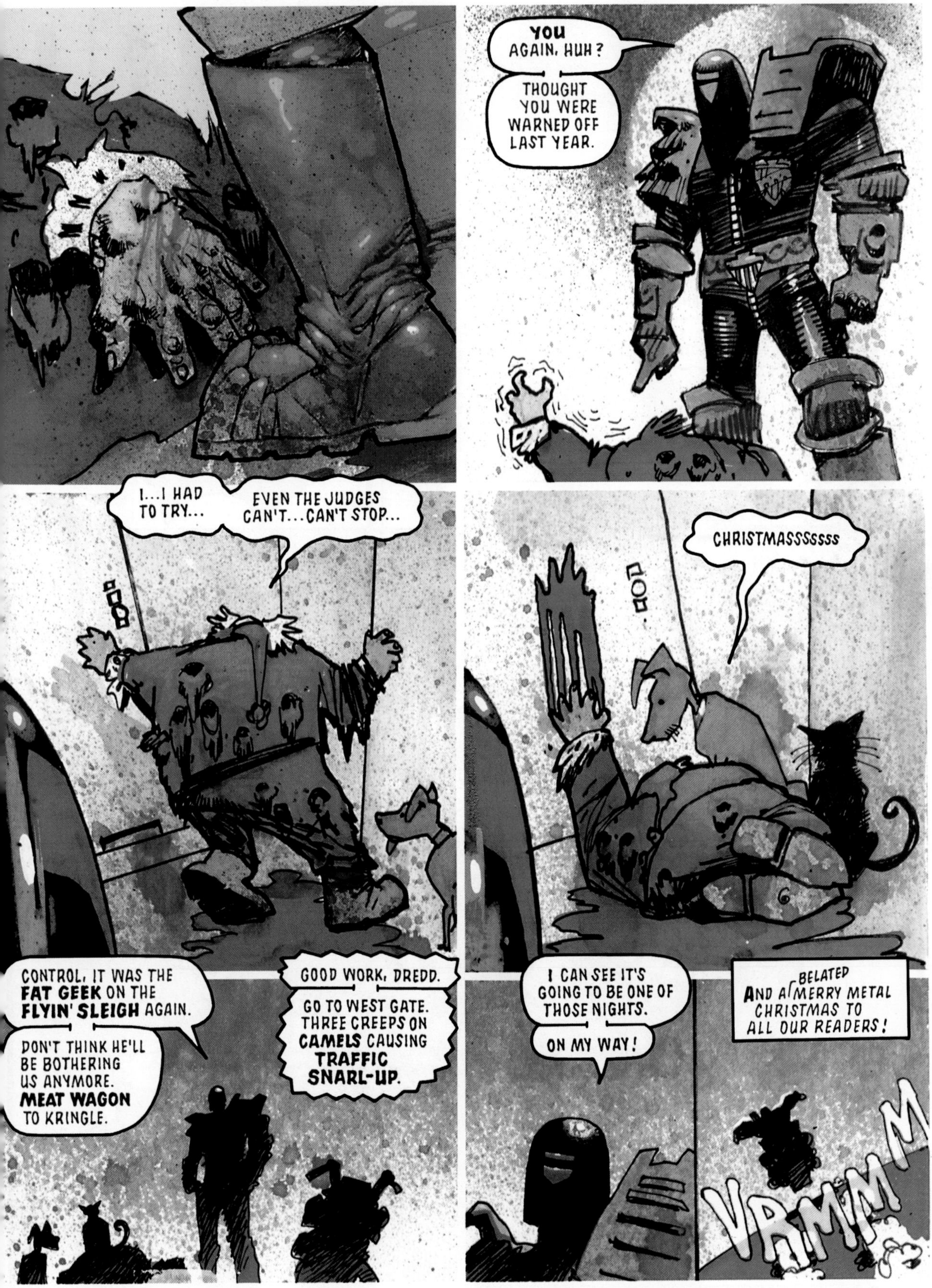
YOU AGAIN, HUH?
THOUGHT YOU WERE WARNED OFF LAST YEAR.
I...I HAD TO TRY...
EVEN THE JUDGES CAN'T...CAN'T STOP...
CHRISTMASSSSSSS
CONTROL, IT WAS THE FAT GEEK ON THE FLYIN' SLEIGH AGAIN.
DON'T THINK HE'LL BE BOTHERING US ANYMORE. MEAT WAGON TO KRINGLE.
GOOD WORK, DREDD.
GO TO WEST GATE. THREE CREEPS ON CAMELS CAUSING TRAFFIC SNARL-UP.
I CAN SEE IT'S GOING TO BE ONE OF THOSE NIGHTS.
ON MY WAY!
AND A BELATED MERRY METAL CHRISTMAS TO ALL OUR READERS!
VRMMM

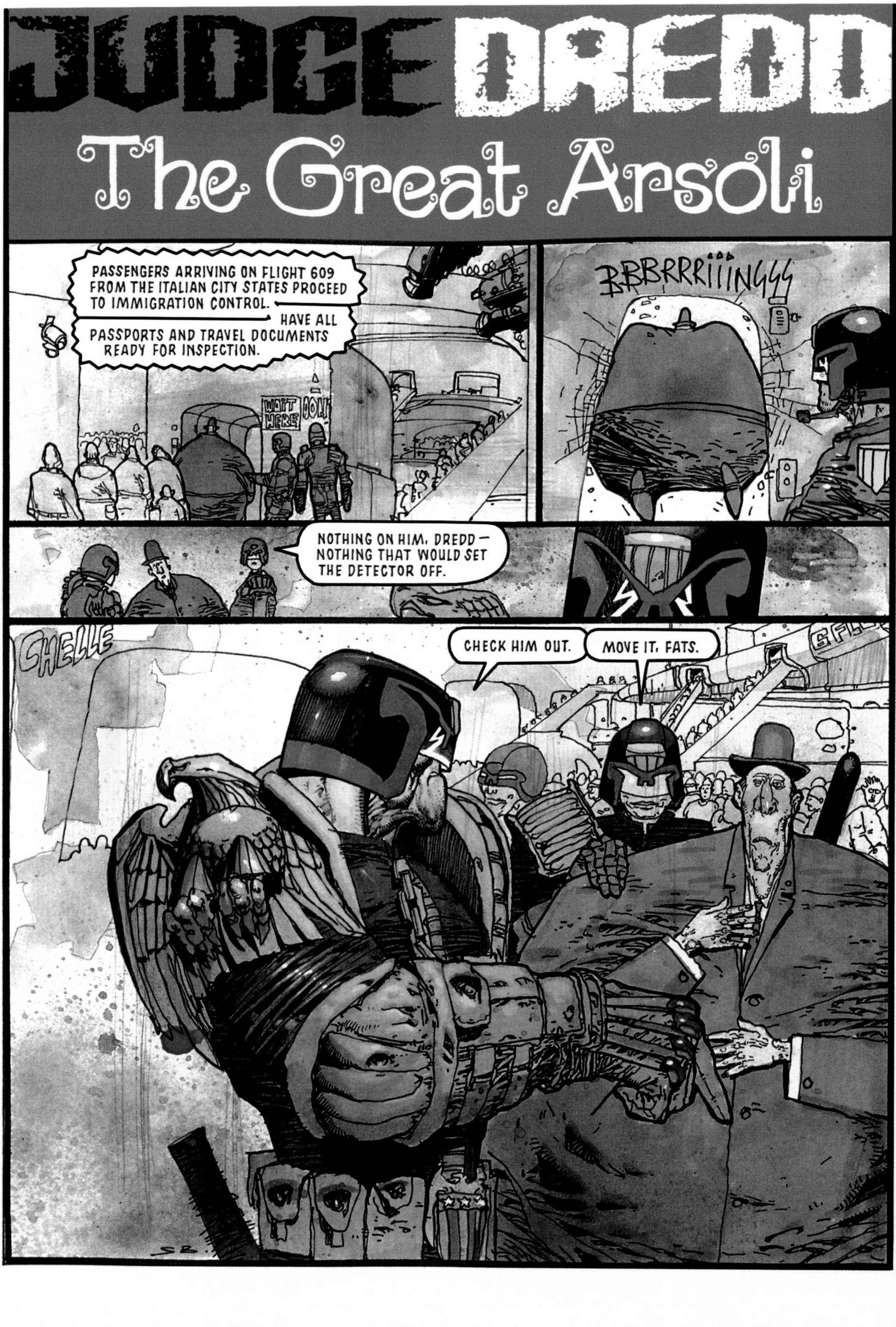
JUDGE DREDD
The Great Arsoli
PASSENGERS ARRIVING ON FLIGHT 609 FROM THE ITALIAN CITY STATES PROCEED TO IMMIGRATION CONTROL.
HAVE ALL PASSPORTS AND TRAVEL DOCUMENTS READY FOR INSPECTION.
WAIT HERE
BBBRRRRIIINGSS
NOTHING ON HIM, DREDD — NOTHING THAT WOULD SET THE DETECTOR OFF.
CHECK HIM OUT.
MOVE IT, FATS.
SB

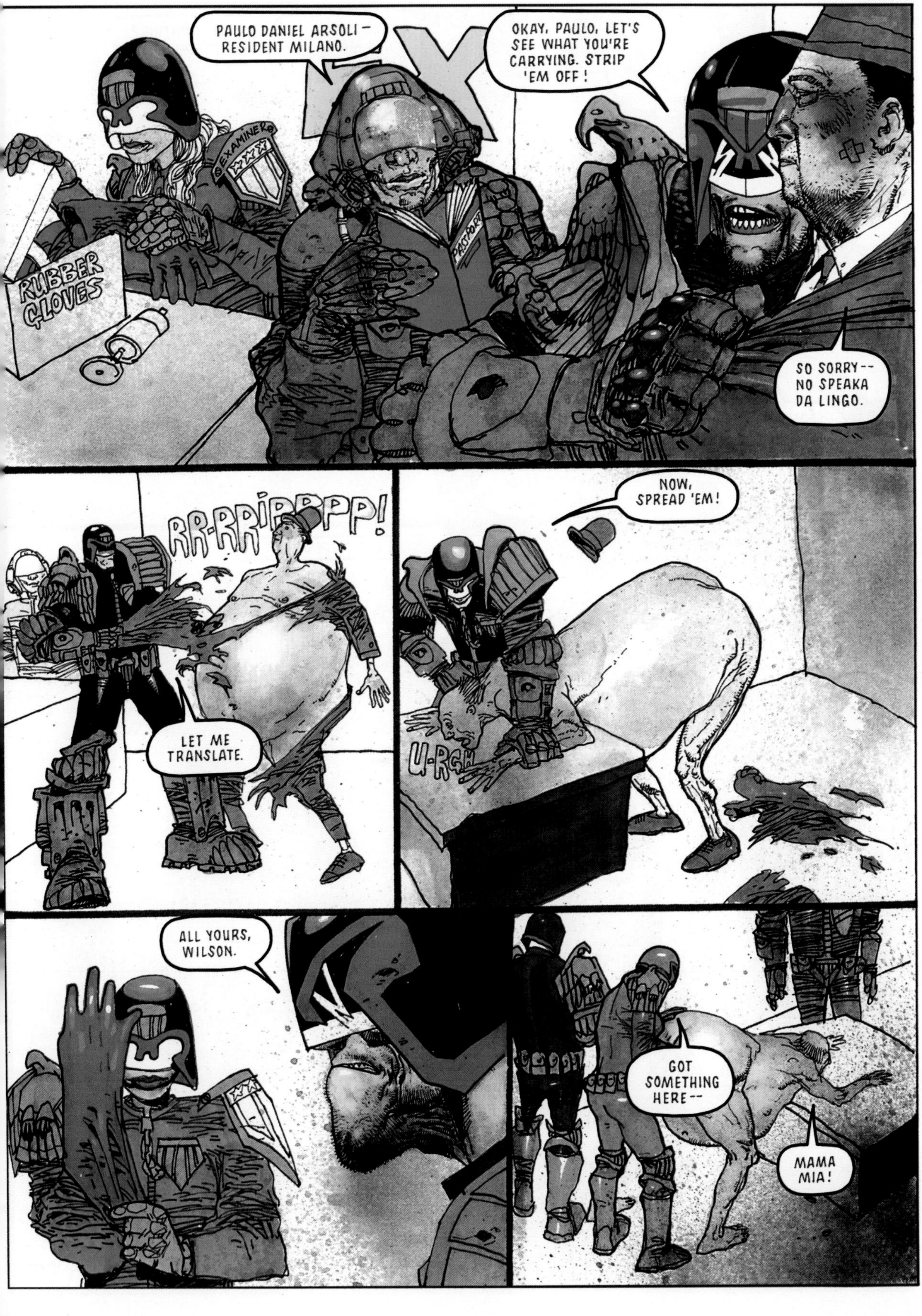
PAULO DANIEL ARSOLI — RESIDENT MILANO.
OKAY, PAULO, LET'S SEE WHAT YOU'RE CARRYING. STRIP 'EM OFF!
RUBBER GLOVES
PASSPORT
EXAMINER
SO SORRY-- NO SPEAKA DA LINGO.
RR-RRIPPPPP!
LET ME TRANSLATE.
NOW, SPREAD 'EM!
U-RGH
ALL YOURS, WILSON.
GOT SOMETHING HERE--
MAMA MIA!

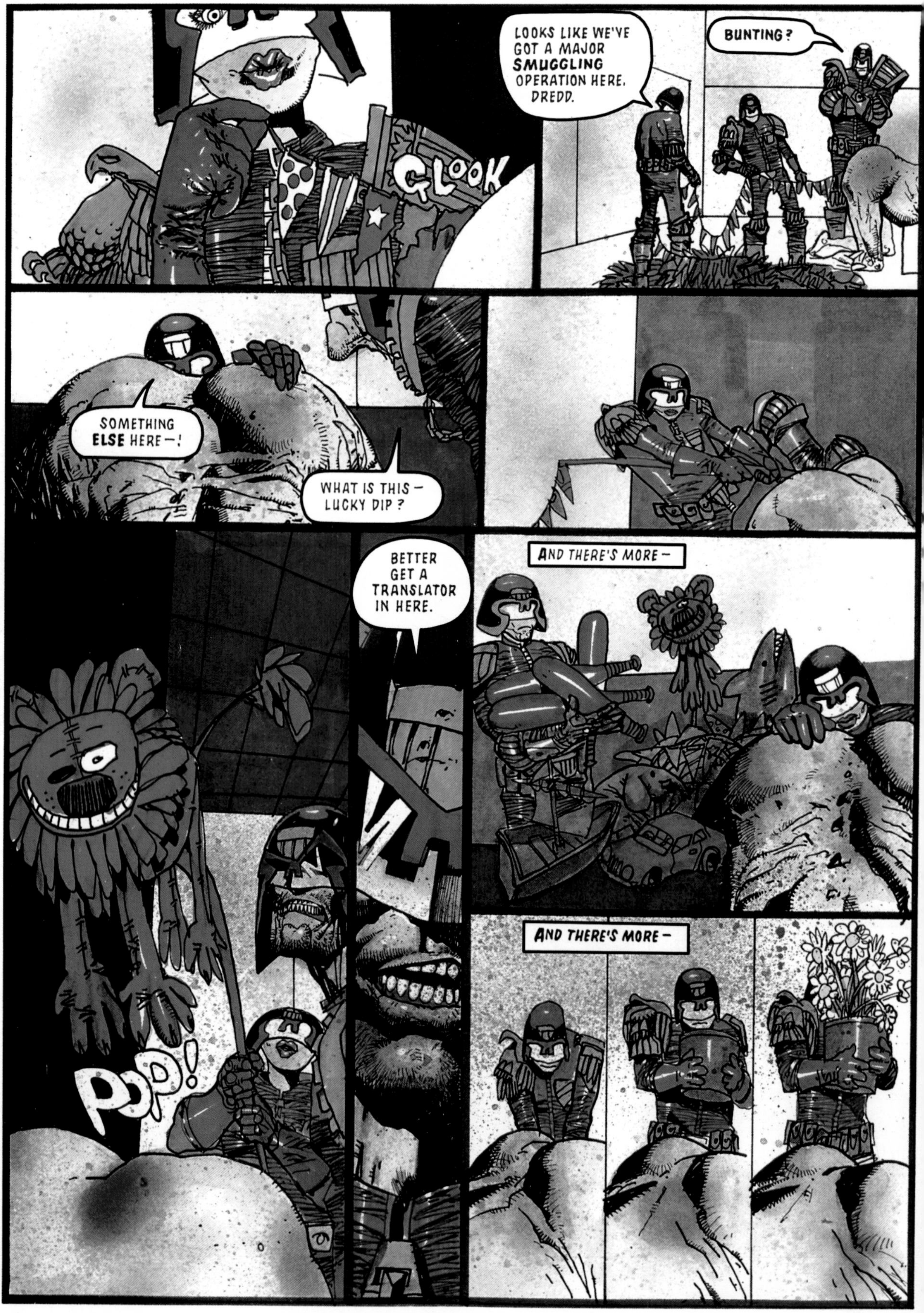
GLOOK
LOOKS LIKE WE'VE GOT A MAJOR SMUGGLING OPERATION HERE, DREDD.
BUNTING?
SOMETHING ELSE HERE—!
WHAT IS THIS— LUCKY DIP?
BETTER GET A TRANSLATOR IN HERE.
AND THERE'S MORE—
POP!
AND THERE'S MORE—

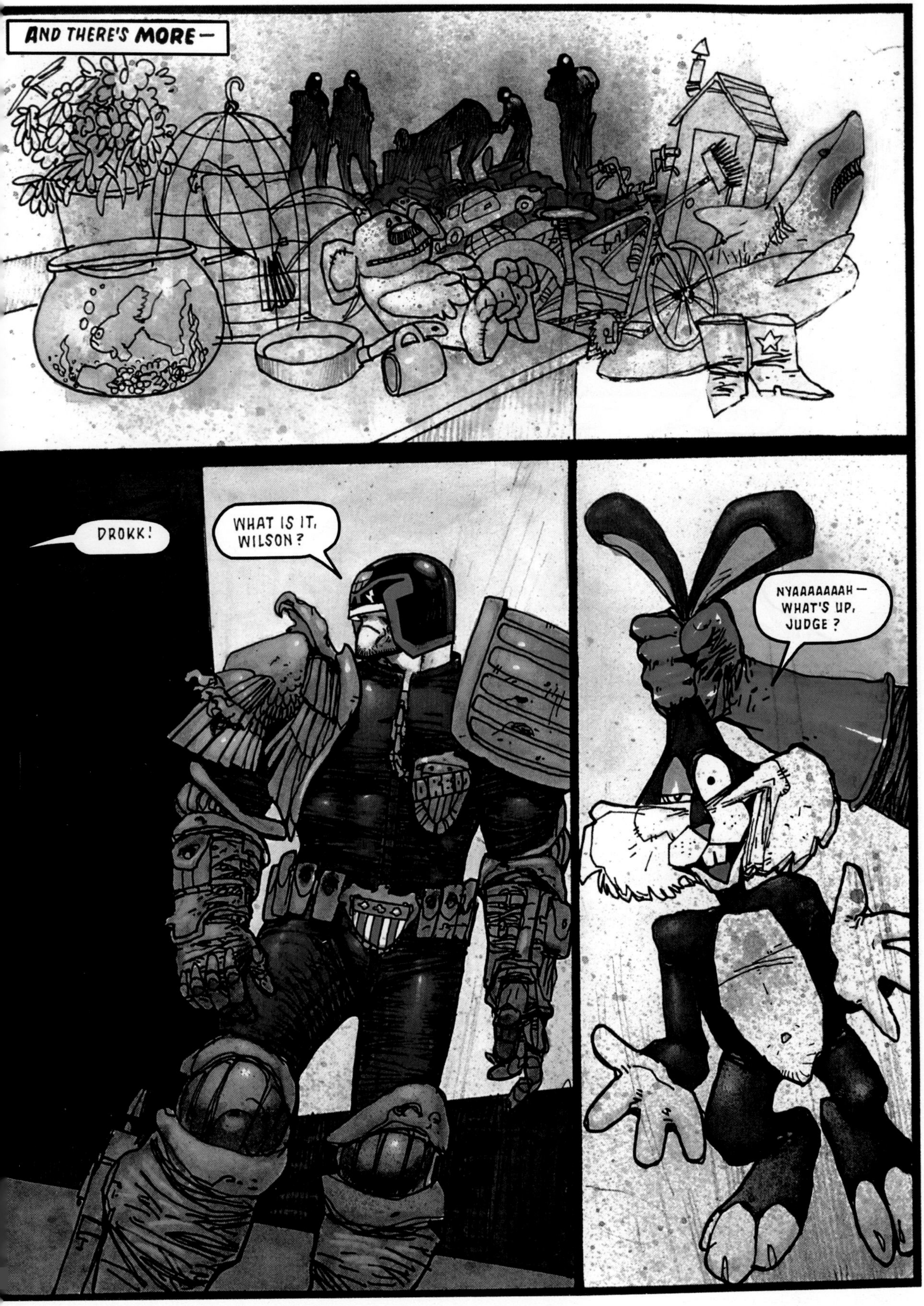
AND THERE'S MORE—
DROKK!
WHAT IS IT, WILSON?
NYAAAAAAAH— WHAT'S UP, JUDGE?

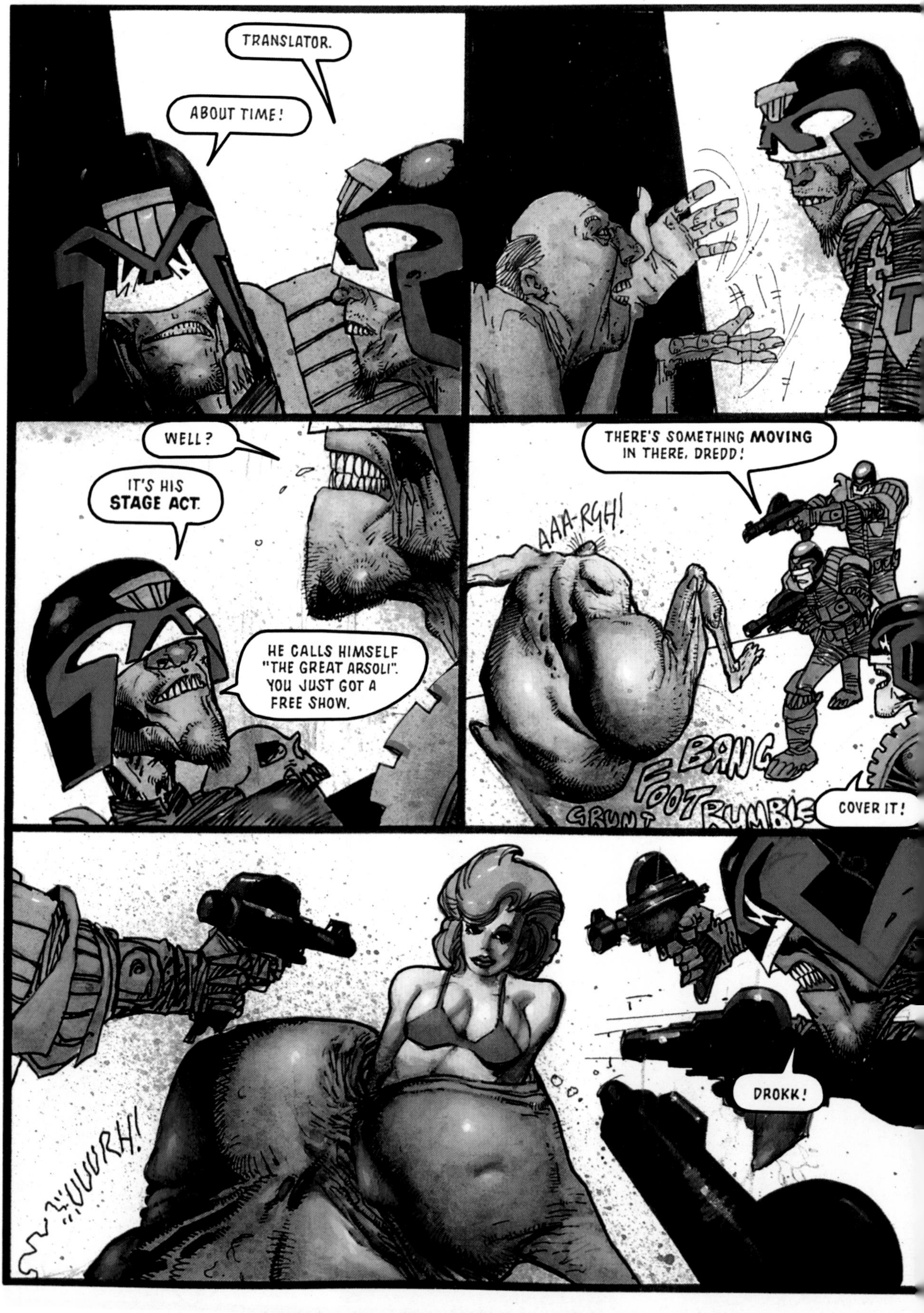
TRANSLATOR.
ABOUT TIME!
WELL?
IT'S HIS STAGE ACT.
HE CALLS HIMSELF "THE GREAT ARSOLI". YOU JUST GOT A FREE SHOW.
THERE'S SOMETHING MOVING IN THERE, DREDD!
AAA-RGH!
BANG
FOOT
RUMBLE
GRUNT
COVER IT!
UUURH!
DROKK!

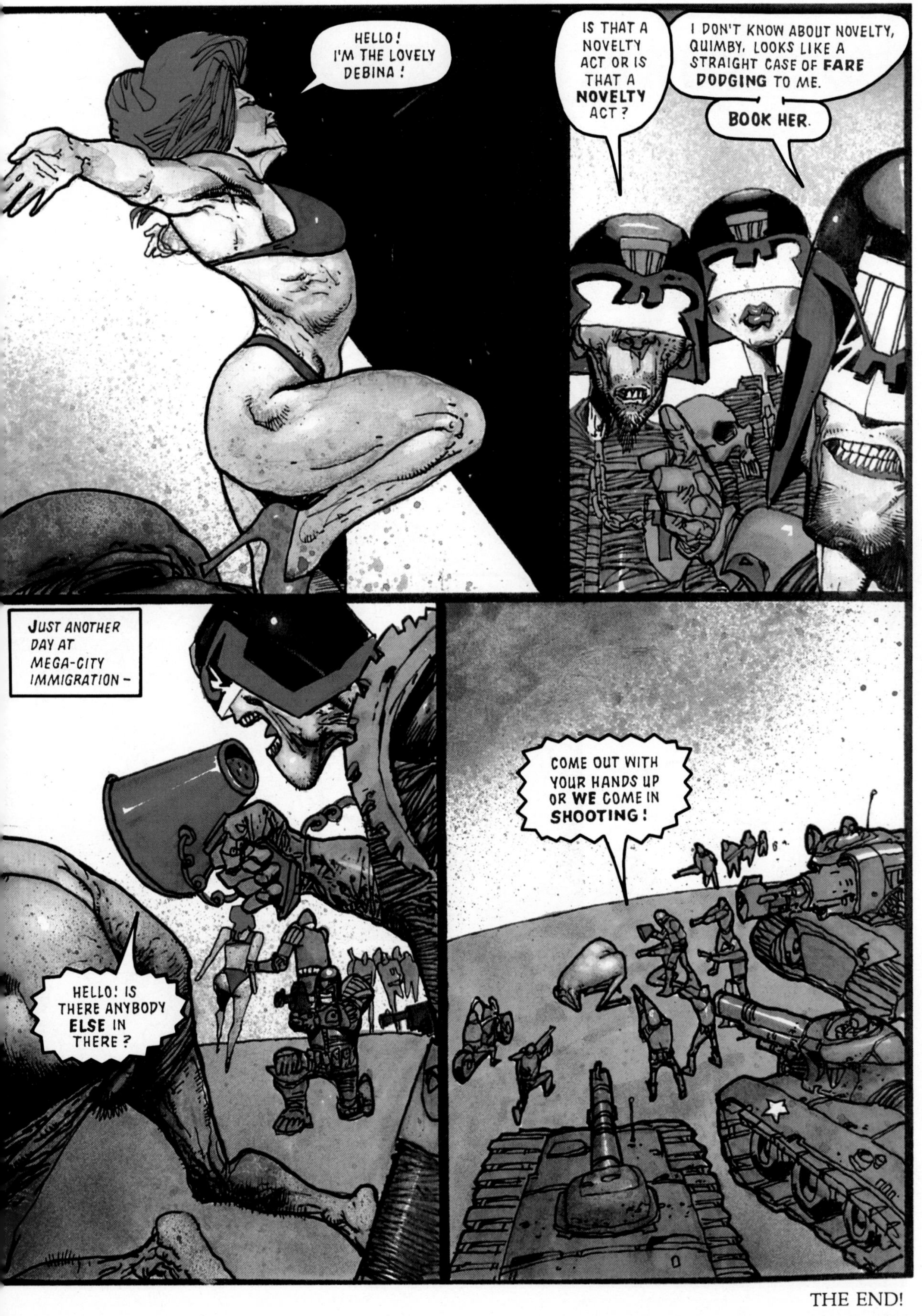
HELLO! I'M THE LOVELY DEBINA!
IS THAT A NOVELTY ACT OR IS THAT A NOVELTY ACT?
I DON'T KNOW ABOUT NOVELTY, QUIMBY. LOOKS LIKE A STRAIGHT CASE OF FARE DODGING TO ME.
BOOK HER.
JUST ANOTHER DAY AT MEGA-CITY IMMIGRATION –
HELLO! IS THERE ANYBODY ELSE IN THERE?
COME OUT WITH YOUR HANDS UP OR WE COME IN SHOOTING!

THE END!

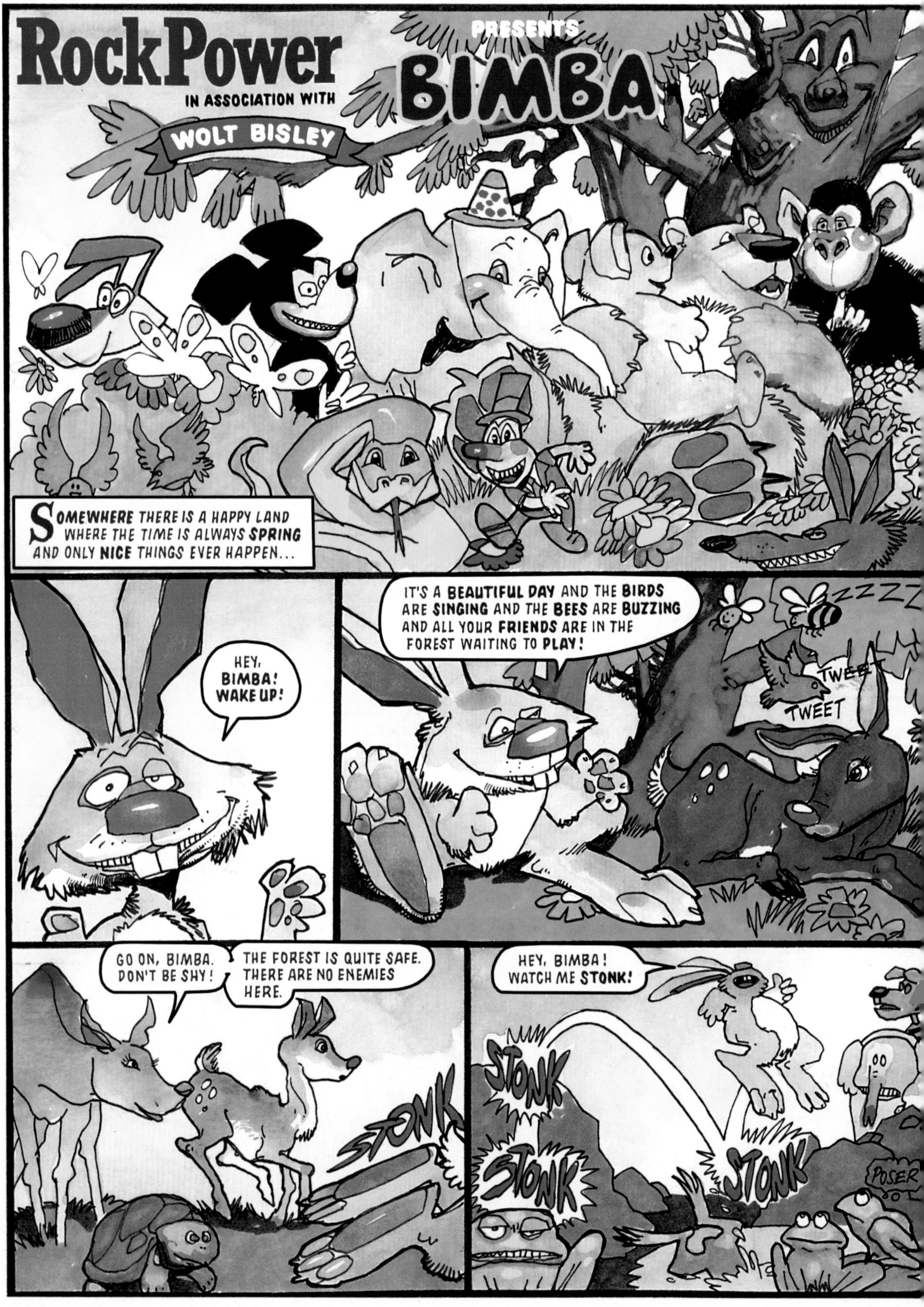
RockPower
PRESENTS
BIMBA
IN ASSOCIATION WITH
WOLT BISLEY
SOMEWHERE THERE IS A HAPPY LAND WHERE THE TIME IS ALWAYS SPRING AND ONLY NICE THINGS EVER HAPPEN...
HEY, BIMBA! WAKE UP!
IT'S A BEAUTIFUL DAY AND THE BIRDS ARE SINGING AND THE BEES ARE BUZZING AND ALL YOUR FRIENDS ARE IN THE FOREST WAITING TO PLAY!
ZZZZ
TWEET
TWEET
GO ON, BIMBA. DON'T BE SHY!
THE FOREST IS QUITE SAFE. THERE ARE NO ENEMIES HERE.
STONK
HEY, BIMBA! WATCH ME STONK!
STONK
STONK
STONK
POSER

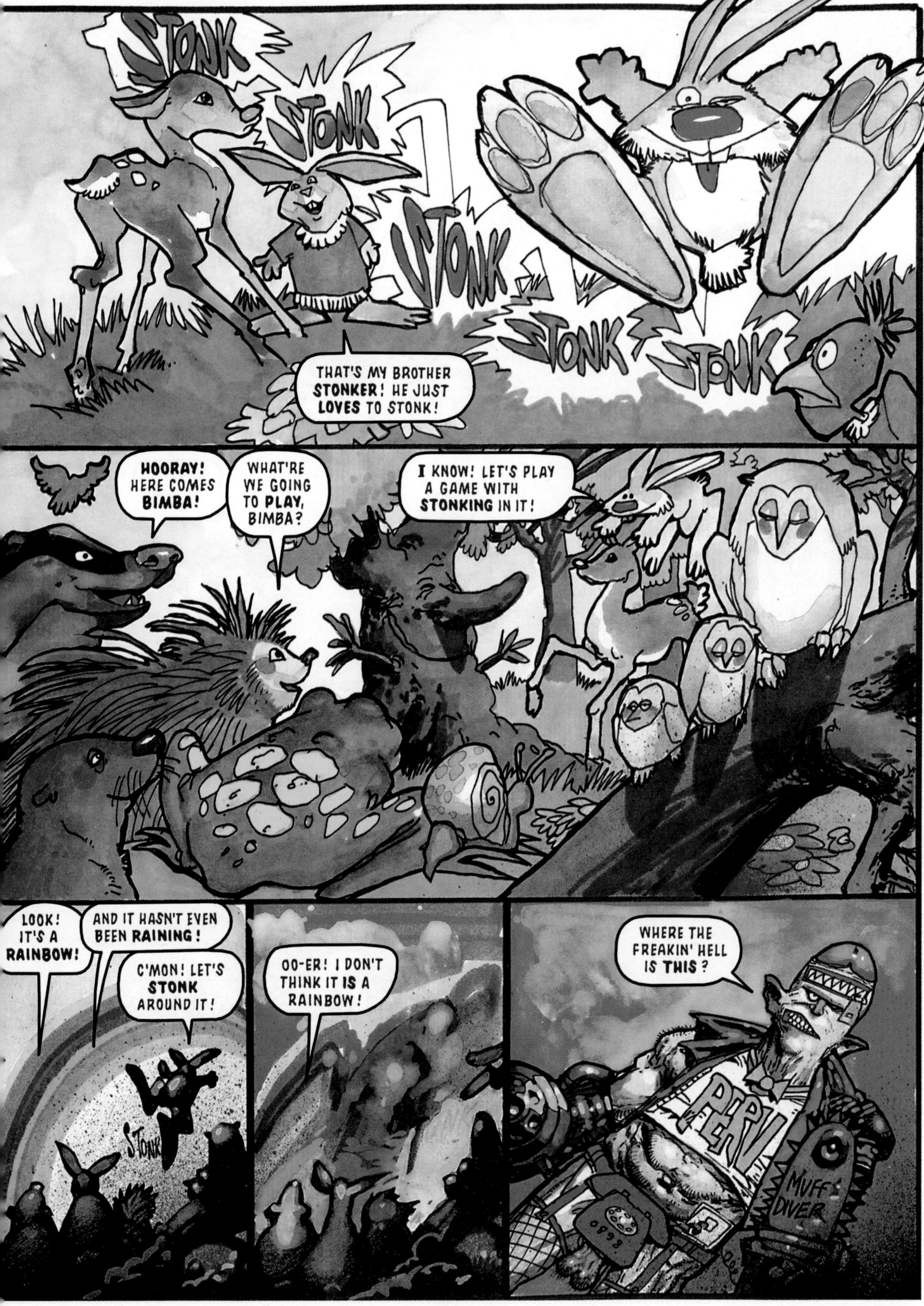
STONK
STONK
STONK
STONK
STONK
THAT'S MY BROTHER STONKER! HE JUST LOVES TO STONK!
HOORAY! HERE COMES BIMBA!
WHAT'RE WE GOING TO PLAY, BIMBA?
I KNOW! LET'S PLAY A GAME WITH STONKING IN IT!
LOOK! IT'S A RAINBOW!
AND IT HASN'T EVEN BEEN RAINING!
C'MON! LET'S STONK AROUND IT!
STONK
OO-ER! I DON'T THINK IT IS A RAINBOW!
WHERE THE FREAKIN' HELL IS THIS?
PERV
MUFF DIVER

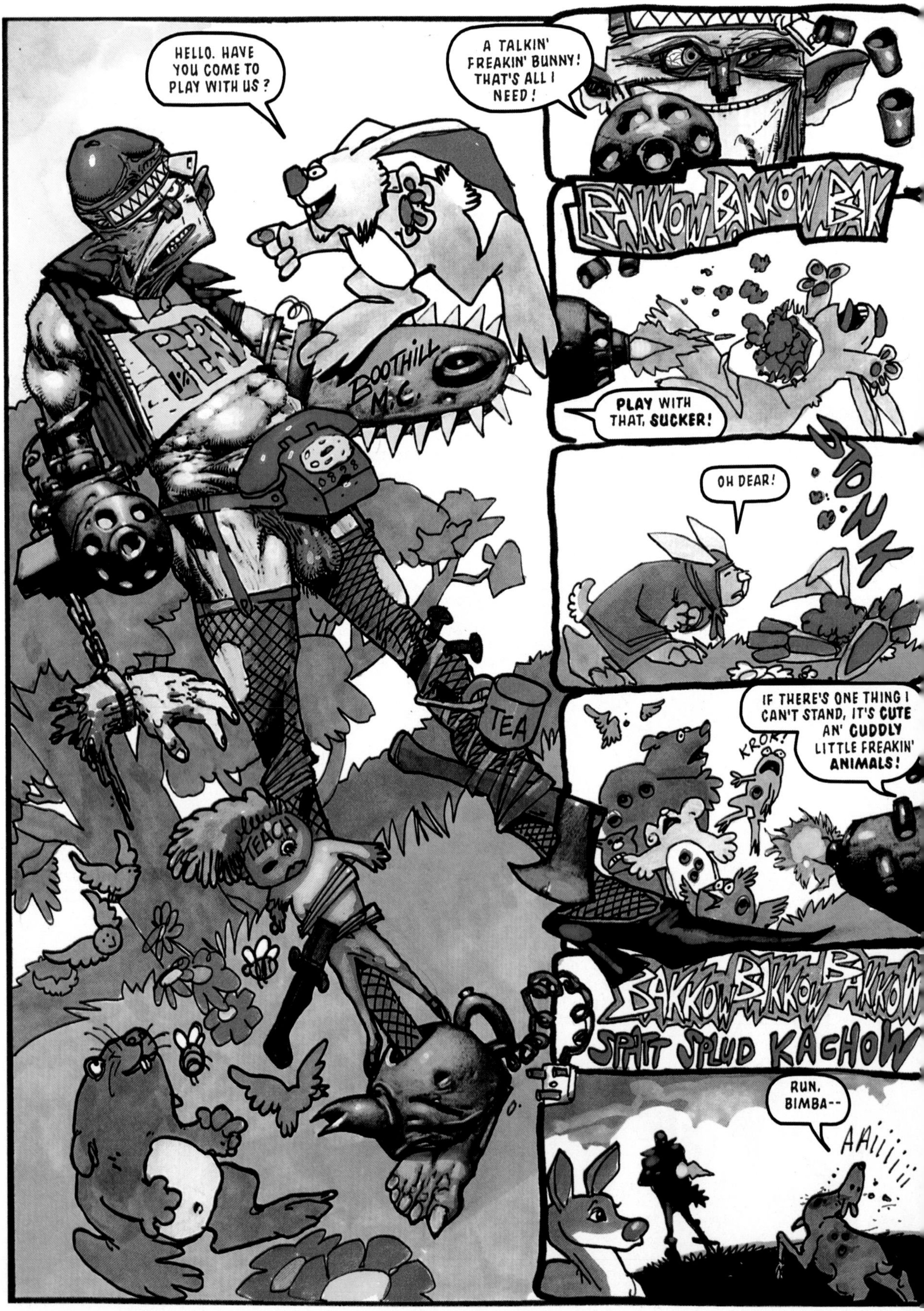
HELLO. HAVE YOU COME TO PLAY WITH US?
A TALKIN' FREAKIN' BUNNY! THAT'S ALL I NEED!
BOOTHILL M.C.
BAKKOW BAKKOW BAK
PLAY WITH THAT, SUCKER!
OH DEAR!
STONK
TEA
IF THERE'S ONE THING I CAN'T STAND, IT'S CUTE AN' CUDDLY LITTLE FREAKIN' ANIMALS!
KROK!
BAKKOW BAKKOW BAKKOW
SPATT SPLUD KACHOW
RUN, BIMBA--
AAIIIII

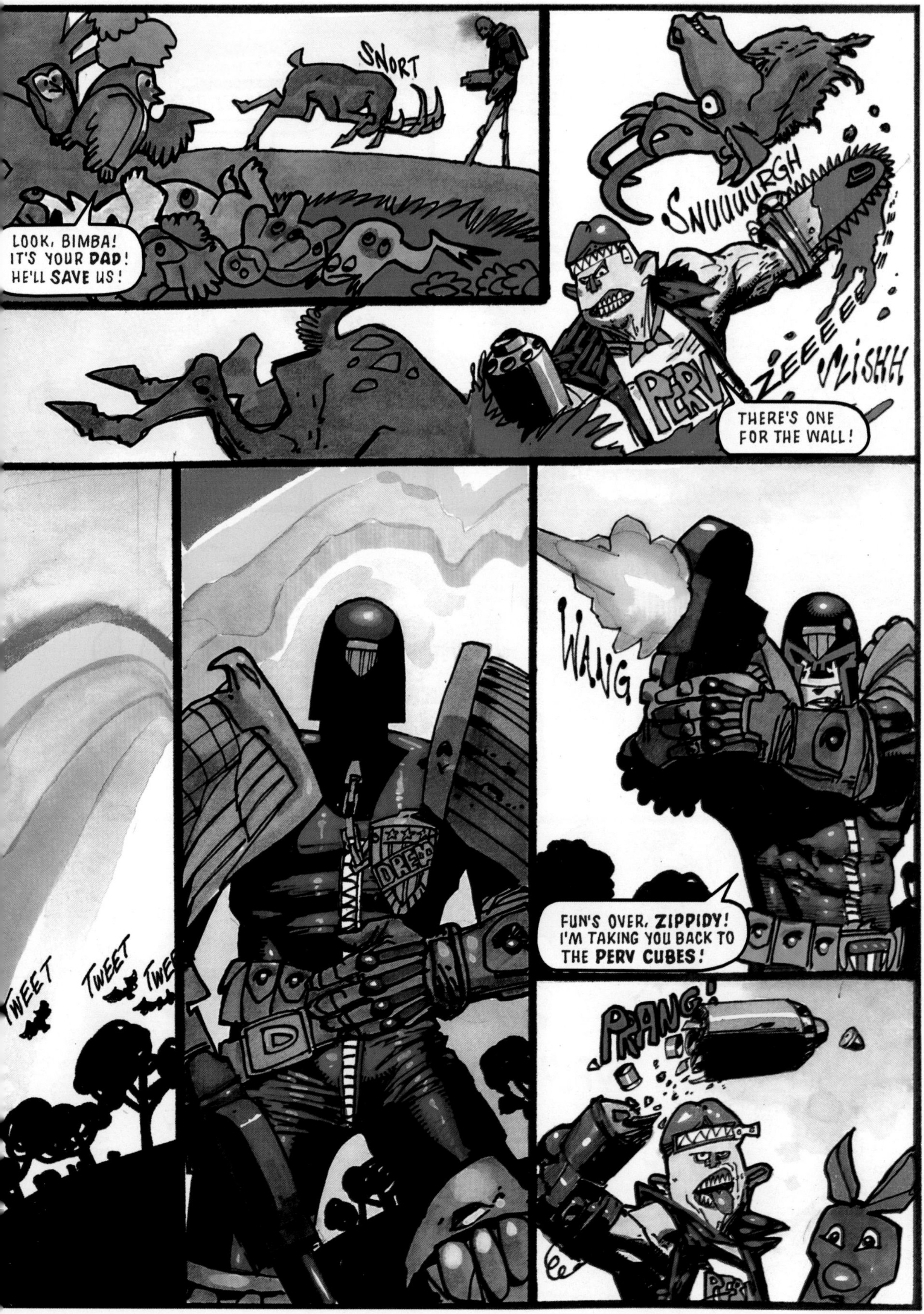
SNORT
LOOK, BIMBA! IT'S YOUR DAD! HE'LL SAVE US!
SNUUUURGH
ZEEEEEE
SLISHH
PERV
THERE'S ONE FOR THE WALL!
TWEET
TWEET
WANG
FUN'S OVER, ZIPPIDY! I'M TAKING YOU BACK TO THE PERV CUBES!
PRANG!

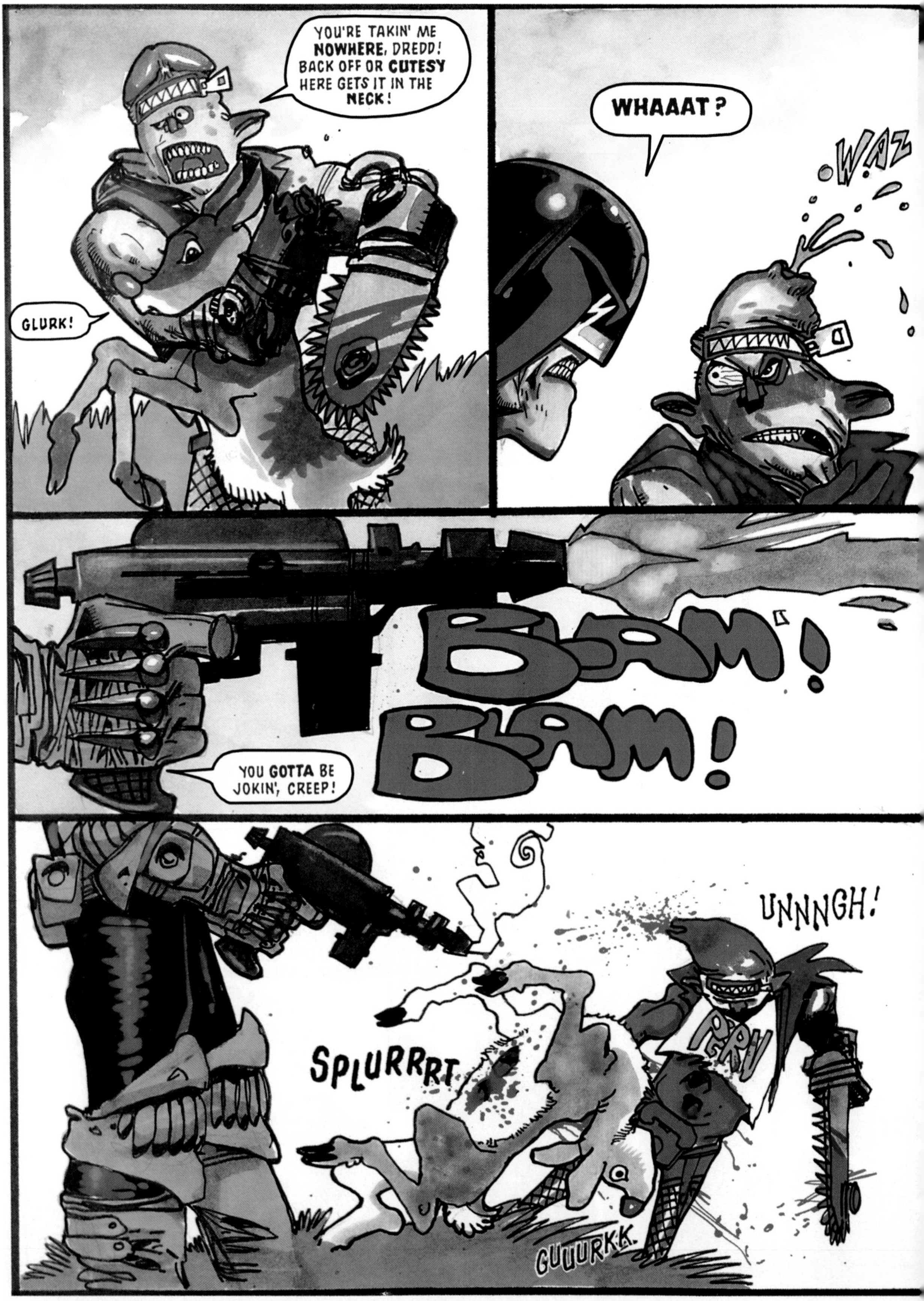
YOU'RE TAKIN' ME NOWHERE, DREDD! BACK OFF OR CUTESY HERE GETS IT IN THE NECK!
GLURK!
WHAAAT?
WAZ
BLAM! BLAM!
YOU GOTTA BE JOKIN', CREEP!
UNNNGH!
PERV
SPLURRRT
GUUURKK.

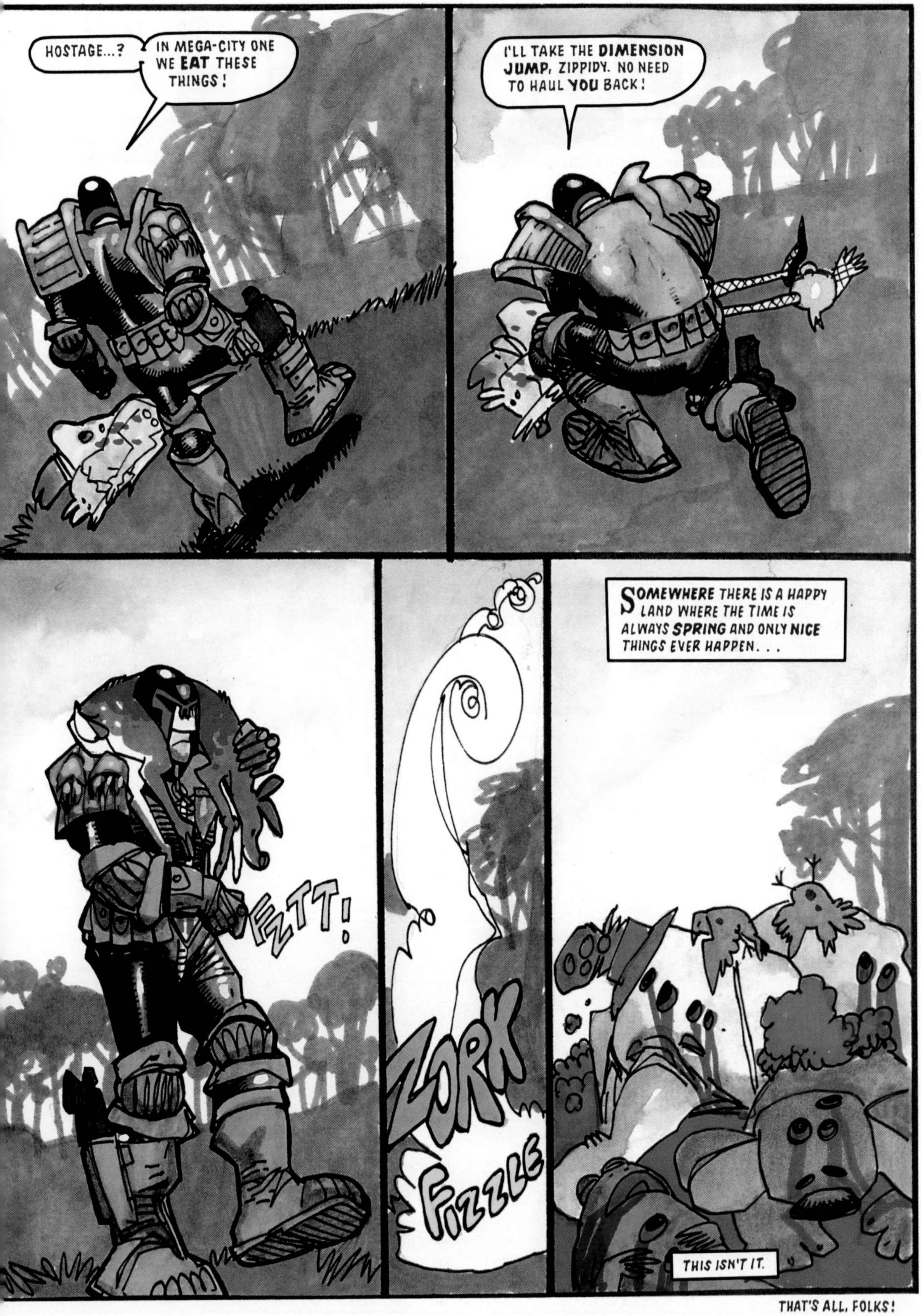

HOSTAGE...?
IN MEGA-CITY ONE WE EAT THESE THINGS!
I'LL TAKE THE DIMENSION JUMP, ZIPPIDY. NO NEED TO HAUL YOU BACK!
FZTT!
ZORK
FIZZLE
SOMEWHERE THERE IS A HAPPY LAND WHERE THE TIME IS ALWAYS SPRING AND ONLY NICE THINGS EVER HAPPEN...
THIS ISN'T IT.

THAT'S ALL, FOLKS!

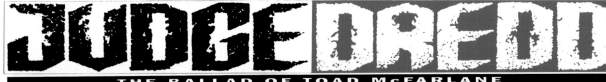

JUDGE DREDD

THE BALLAD OF TOAD McFARLANE
('cept it's not a ballad)

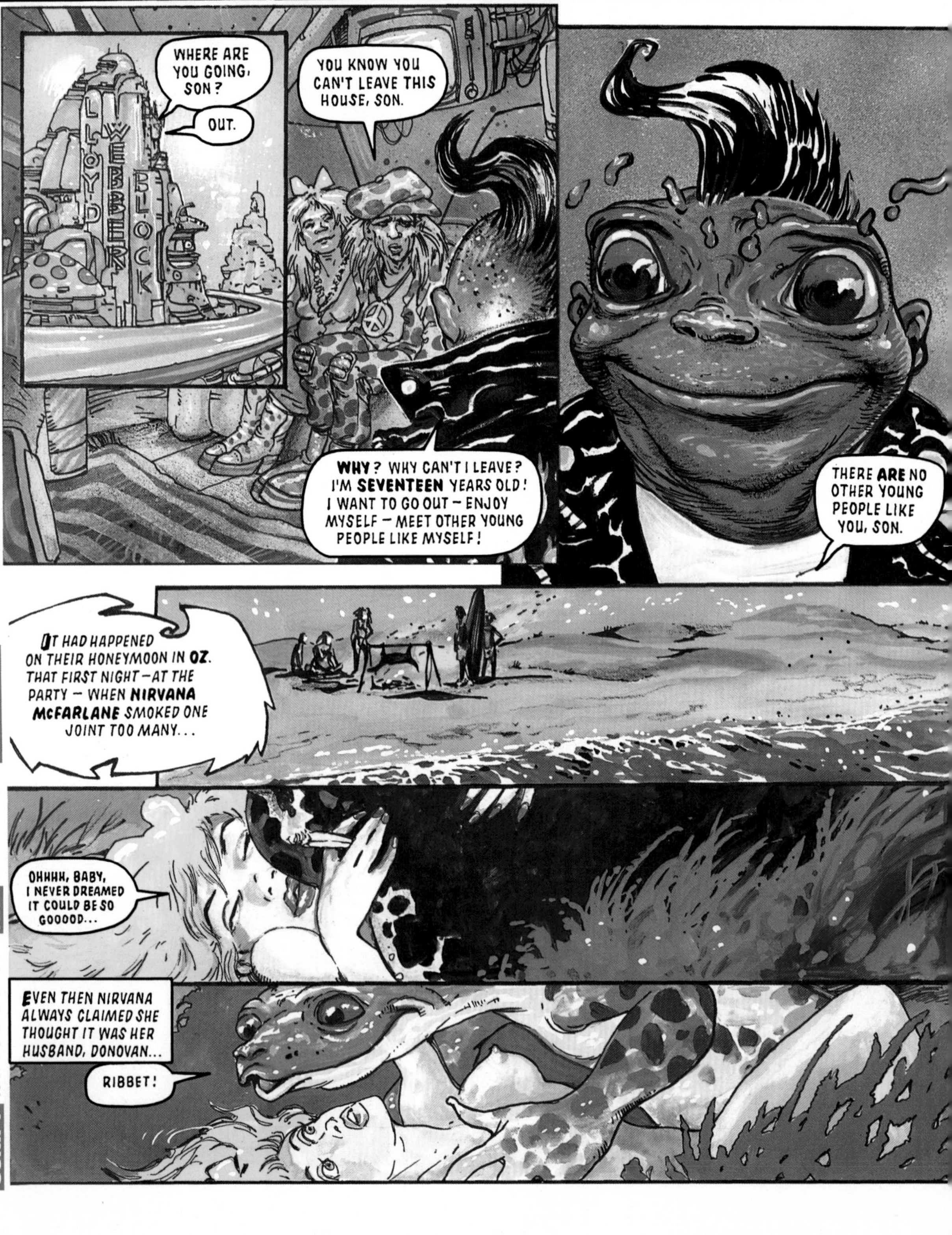

WHERE ARE YOU GOING, SON?
OUT.
LLOYD WEBBER BLOCK
YOU KNOW YOU CAN'T LEAVE THIS HOUSE, SON.
WHY? WHY CAN'T I LEAVE? I'M SEVENTEEN YEARS OLD! I WANT TO GO OUT – ENJOY MYSELF – MEET OTHER YOUNG PEOPLE LIKE MYSELF!
THERE ARE NO OTHER YOUNG PEOPLE LIKE YOU, SON.
IT HAD HAPPENED ON THEIR HONEYMOON IN OZ. THAT FIRST NIGHT – AT THE PARTY – WHEN NIRVANA McFARLANE SMOKED ONE JOINT TOO MANY...
OHHHH, BABY, I NEVER DREAMED IT COULD BE SO GOOOOD...
EVEN THEN NIRVANA ALWAYS CLAIMED SHE THOUGHT IT WAS HER HUSBAND, DONOVAN...
RIBBET!

SCRIPT JOHN WAGNER & ALAN GRANT ART BRENDAN McCARTHY LETTERING TOM FRAME

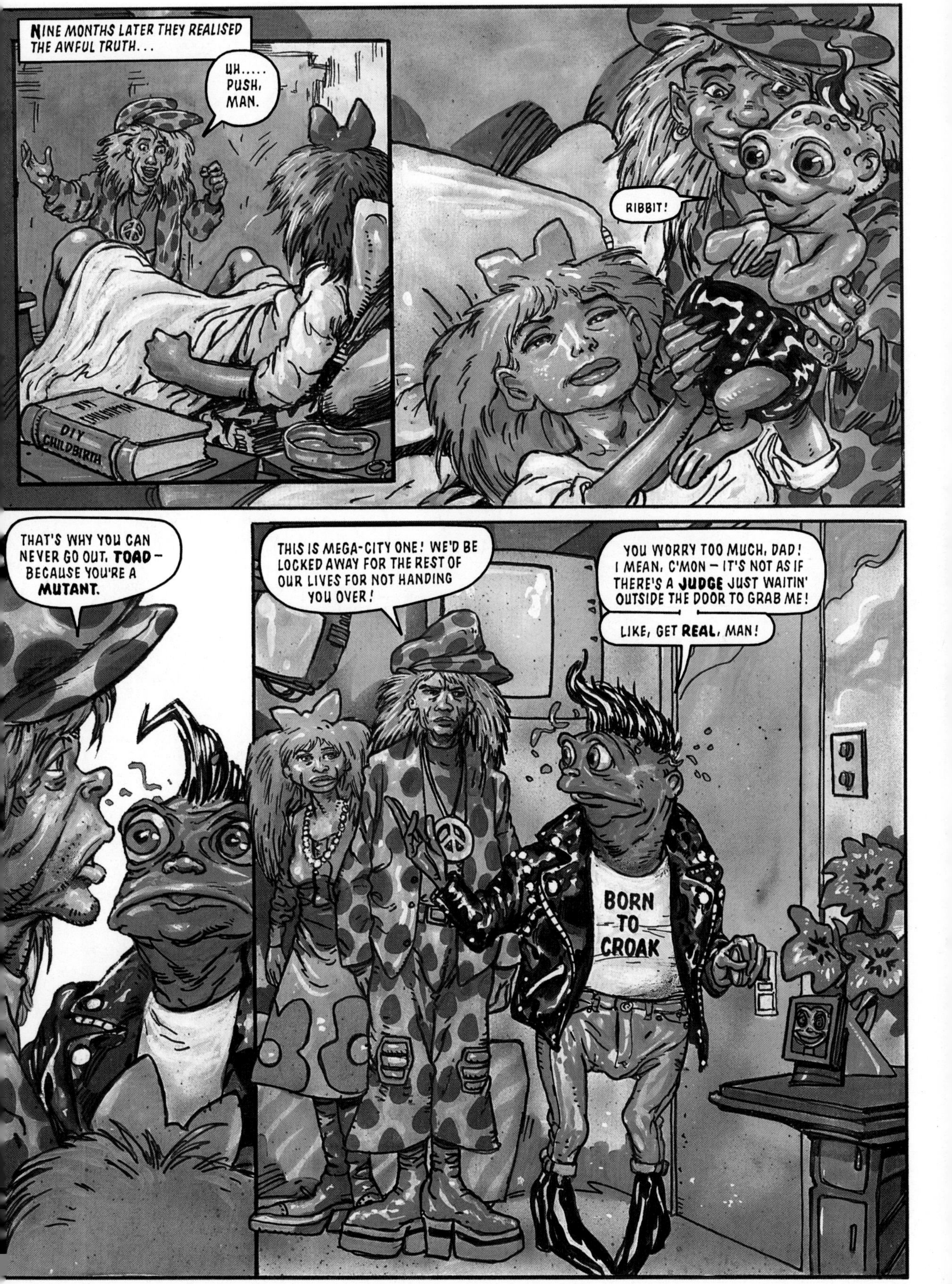
NINE MONTHS LATER THEY REALISED THE AWFUL TRUTH...
UH..... PUSH, MAN.
DIY CHILDBIRTH
RIBBIT!
THAT'S WHY YOU CAN NEVER GO OUT, TOAD — BECAUSE YOU'RE A MUTANT.
THIS IS MEGA-CITY ONE! WE'D BE LOCKED AWAY FOR THE REST OF OUR LIVES FOR NOT HANDING YOU OVER!
YOU WORRY TOO MUCH, DAD! I MEAN, C'MON — IT'S NOT AS IF THERE'S A JUDGE JUST WAITIN' OUTSIDE THE DOOR TO GRAB ME!
LIKE, GET REAL, MAN!
BORN TO CROAK

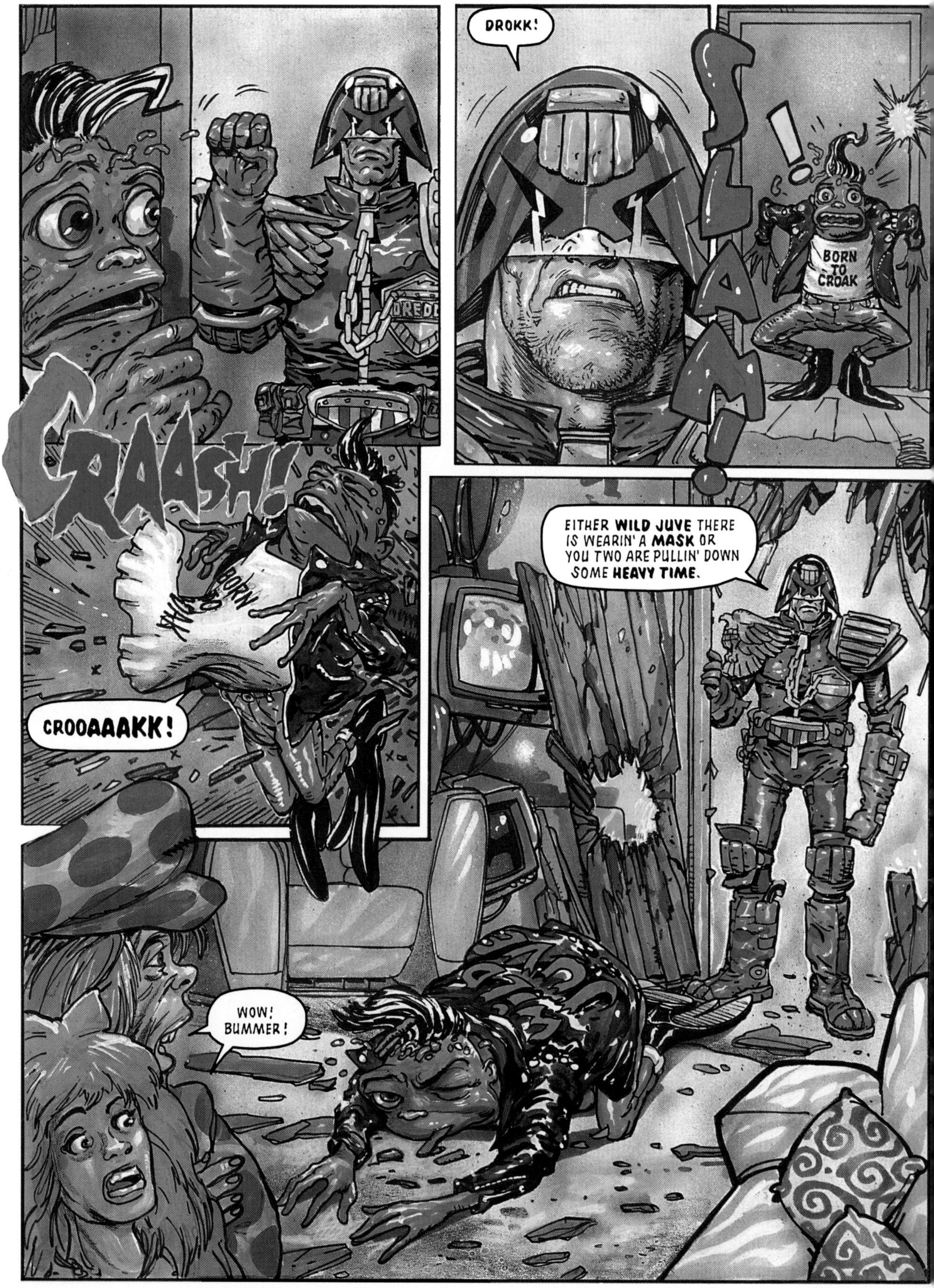
DROKK!
SLAM!
BORN TO CROAK
CRAASH!
CROOAAAKK!
EITHER WILD JUVE THERE IS WEARIN' A MASK OR YOU TWO ARE PULLIN' DOWN SOME HEAVY TIME.
WOW! BUMMER!

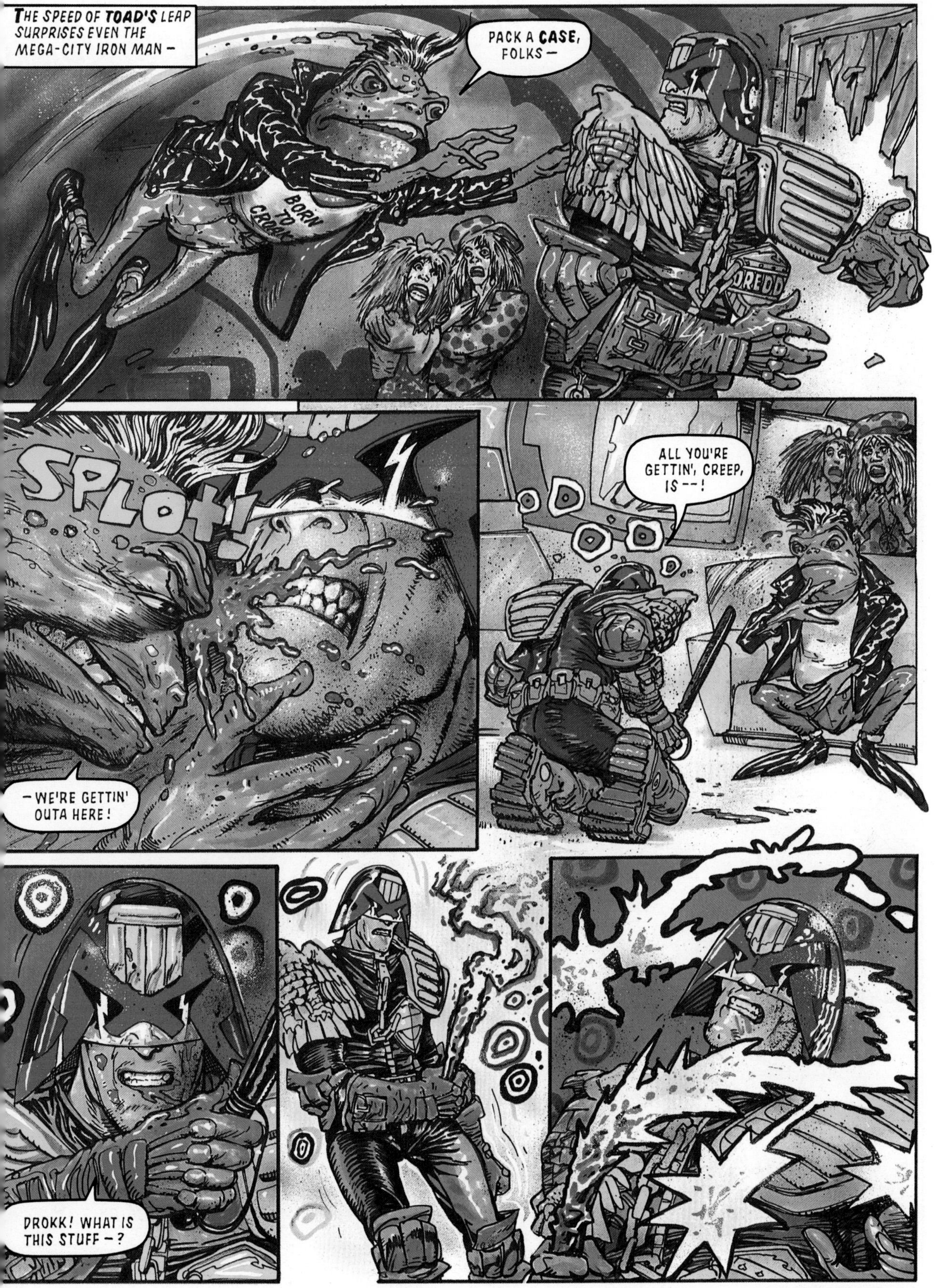

THE SPEED OF TOAD'S LEAP SURPRISES EVEN THE MEGA-CITY IRON MAN —
PACK A CASE, FOLKS —
BORN TO CROAK
DREDD
SPLOT!!
— WE'RE GETTIN' OUTA HERE!
ALL YOU'RE GETTIN', CREEP, IS --!
DROKK! WHAT IS THIS STUFF —?

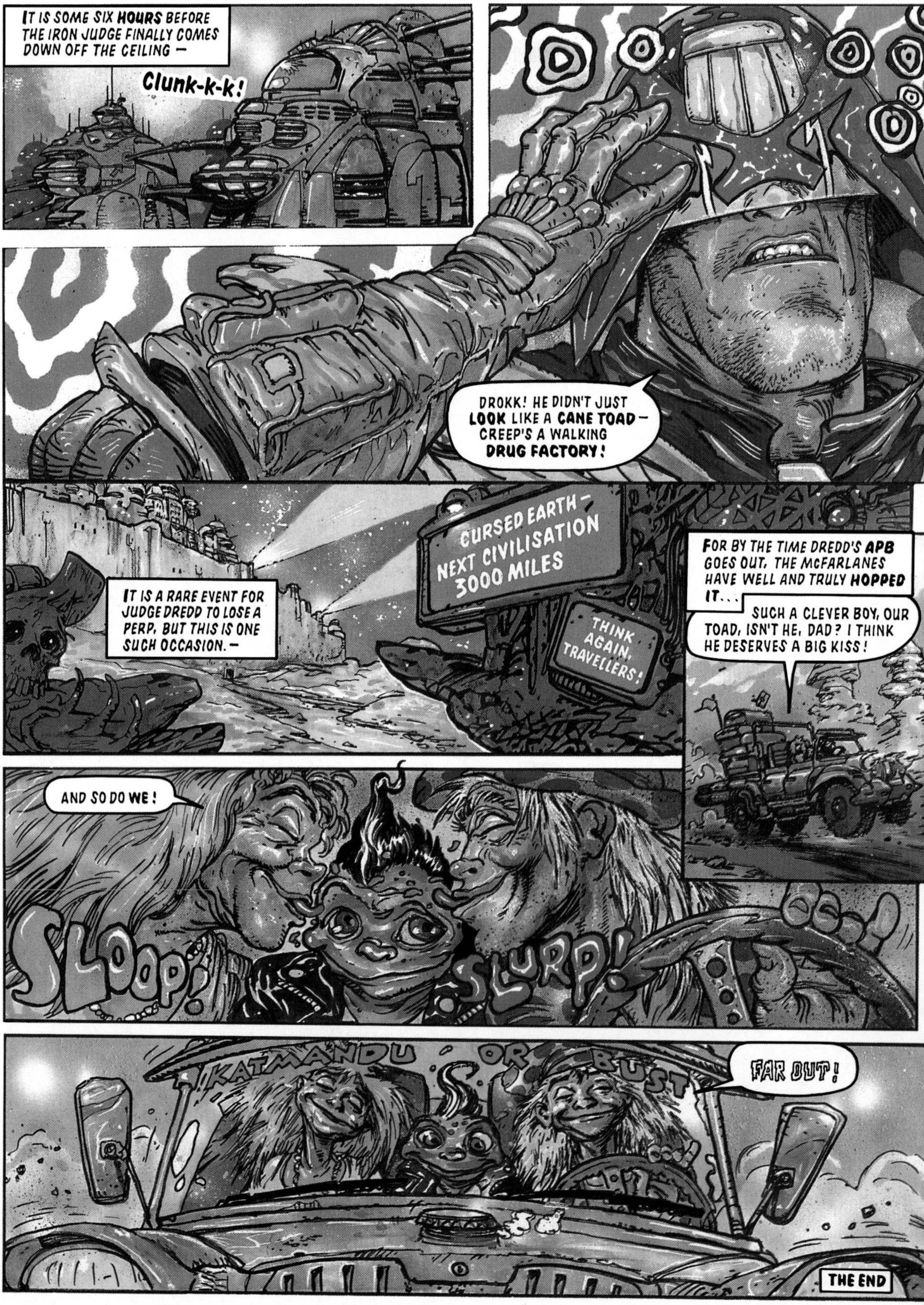
IT IS SOME SIX HOURS BEFORE THE IRON JUDGE FINALLY COMES DOWN OFF THE CEILING —
Clunk-k-k!
DROKK! HE DIDN'T JUST LOOK LIKE A CANE TOAD — CREEP'S A WALKING DRUG FACTORY!
IT IS A RARE EVENT FOR JUDGE DREDD TO LOSE A PERP, BUT THIS IS ONE SUCH OCCASION. —
CURSED EARTH — NEXT CIVILISATION 3000 MILES
THINK AGAIN, TRAVELLERS!
FOR BY THE TIME DREDD'S APB GOES OUT, THE McFARLANES HAVE WELL AND TRULY HOPPED IT...
SUCH A CLEVER BOY, OUR TOAD, ISN'T HE, DAD? I THINK HE DESERVES A BIG KISS!
AND SO DO WE!
SLOOP!
SLURP!
KATMANDU OR BUST
FAR OUT!
THE END

A VIOLENT LIMB

If I was a pompous twat I'd say "ironically, I write to you from Greece, one of the nine countries *Heavy Metal Dredd* was printed in." But I particularly remember the Greek version because the speech balloons and panels in Greek looked a bit special on the page.

Heavy Metal Dredd was first printed in international glossy music mag *Rock Power*, which successfully spanned the globe. As a result, so did Dredd. He had unprecedented exposure, then a final outing in the UK within the pages of *Judge Dredd Megazine*. My first story debuted *Meg* issue 19 — we're going back a while.

Simon Bisley was just landing from a punishing work load on *Sláine, The Horned God*, followed by Batman vs. Dredd tale *Judgement on Gotham*. David Bishop was editing the *Meg* at the time but it was Steve McManus who gave me the call to arms: "Heavy Metal Dredd, no limits, a separate and aggressive Dredd world that gets the point across." Check the first Biz story in this collection to see what he meant!

I love Biz; the man and the artist. There's no difference between the two for me, so let's talk about his art. When Simon first started out I was working on *Nemesis Book 7, 'The Two Torquemadas.'* I was rocked when I first saw his black & white *ABC Warriors* artwork. Then KO'd by *Sláine, The Horned God*. I'll admit I was secretly gutted but became an immediate fan of Simon's, and still am.

It's no coincidence that I'm collaborating with Clint Langley on the cover for this book, because he felt exactly the same way. To add to my pain I visited Simon's house for a couple of days and saw the original artwork for *The Horned God*. On my way home I remember thinking

"so, how do you design kitchens again?" However, in typical Biz style, he helped me back up. He wanted a very twisted A2 study of Batman — in return he gave me a few pointers on colour work. As did Glenn Fabry, which I still use on one shots to this day.

But at the time I needed a colourist, so I found Keith Page, who did a fine job. With John Wagner, Alan Grant and John Smith in the mix, that was the squad. Jim Alexander and Alison Potter also contributed as script writers. Lettered by the late, great Tom Frame.

As I've said, this was not meant for the Dredd universe and these great writers went out on a limb. A violent limb at that, a bit like shaking their muscles loose after a good fight. You be the judge. It was unselfconscious work with funny, unpredictable and brutal scripts. When it was finally published in *JD Megazine*, David Bishop fielded a year's worth of complaints. Man, the UK readers were pissed off! Eventually, Dave called a halt to the proceedings, which became known on the letters page as 'the violence debate.' He dubbed it an over-flipped coin. He was right.

I don't know what today's fans will think. A few boos from the gallery? Good. Enjoy this book — Rebellion and Jon Oliver are doing a great job archiving the work in *2000 AD* and the *Meg*. They must be, otherwise I guess I wouldn't be writing this.

Senior Street Judge Dredd. Pick Up Your Teeth Dredd. Heavy Metal Dredd.

Peace

John Hicklenton

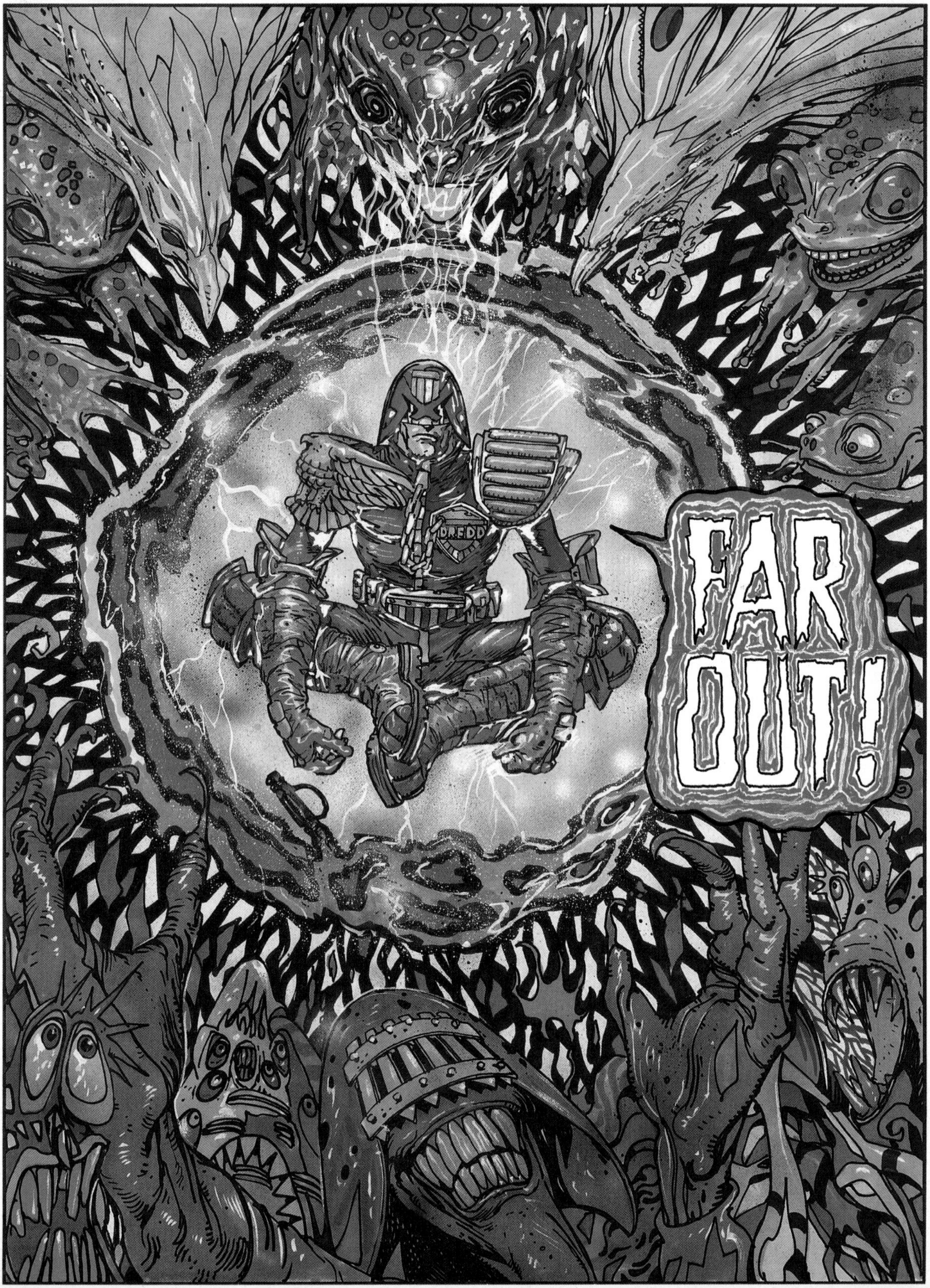
FAR OUT!

JIM ALEXANDER

Jim Alexander penned *Calhab Justice* for the *Megazine* as well as working on various *Judge Dredd* strips.

DAVID BISHOP

David Bishop edited *2000 AD* from Christmas 1995 until the summer of 2000, before leaving to become a full-time writer. He's had nearly 20 novels published, a radio play broadcast by the BBC and had scripted serials for *2000 AD*, *Judge Dredd Megazine* and the *Phantom*. He won a first prize at the 2007 Page International Screenwriting Awards in Los Angeles for his short film script *Danny's Toys*, and recently attained an MA in screenwriting with distinction at Screen Academy Scotland. You can read David's blog at www.viciousimagery.blogspot.com

ALAN GRANT

With over 300 *2000 AD* stories to his name – not to mention over 250 Daily Star *Judge Dredd* strips – **Alan Grant's** prolific creative record speaks for itself. Outside the Galaxy's Greatest Comic, Grant is well-known to *Batman* fans following a lengthy run on various incarnations of the title. More recently he has adapted Robert Louis Stevenson's classic novels *Kidnapped* and *Doctor Jekyll and Mr Hyde* in Graphic Novel format with artist Cam Kennedy. His television work includes scripts for the BBC series *Ace Lightning and the Carnival of Doom* and he is currently writing a feature length animation for a German company.

JOHN SMITH

John Smith is unquestionably a *2000 AD* hero, with a host of creative credits to his name, including *A Love Like Blood*, *Devlin Waugh*, *Firekind*, *Holocaust 12*, *Indigo Prime*, *Pussyfoot 5*, *Revere*, *Slaughterbowl* and *Tyranny Rex*. Smith has also written *Future Shocks*, *Heavy Metal Dredd*, *Judge Dredd*, *Judge Karyn*, *Pulp Sci-Fi*, *Robo-Hunter*, *Rogue Trooper*, *Tales from Beyond Science*, *Tales of Mega-City One* and *Vector 13*. Smith's work beyond the Galaxy's Greatest Comic includes the long-running *New Statesmen* series and *Straitgate* in Crisis, DC/Vertigo's *Hellblazer* and *Scarab*, and Harris Comics' *Vampirella* and *Pantha*. Upcoming series for *2000 AD* include contemporary science-fiction thriller *Dead Eyes* and the urban hoodie horror story *Cradlegrave*, while for *The Megazine* the 'Ship of Fools' sets sail – a madcap *Devlin Waugh* story illustrated by Peter Doherty which sees the culmination of Devlin's twenty-three year long search for his debauched brother Freddy.

JOHN WAGNER

John Wagner has been scripting for *2000 AD* for more years than he cares to remember. His creations include *Judge Dredd*, *Strontium Dog*, *Ace Trucking*, *Al's Baby*, *Button Man* and *Mean Machine*. Outside of *2000 AD* his credits include *Star Wars*, *Lobo*, *The Punisher* and the critically acclaimed *A History of Violence*.

SIMON BISLEY

Simon Bisley occupies an almost unique place in *2000 AD* history as one of the first UK artists to popularise the fully painted style pioneered by Argentinian artist Alberto Brecchia. His highly dynamic artwork made his two major series in the Galaxy's Greatest Comic — *A.B.C. Warriors: The Black Hole* and *Sláine: The Horned God* — very popular, as they remain to date. He also illustrated *Heavy Metal Dredd* in the *Megazine*, an ultra-graphic, adults-only take on the lawman, before going on to paint the hugely successful first *Batman/Judge Dredd* crossover story *Judgement on Gotham*. Bisley has provided countless pin-ups and short pieces across an astonishing variety of comics, from legendary fantasy anthology *Heavy Metal* to anarchic DC superhero series *Lobo*, and has an even more extensive CV in Europe, where his painted style enjoys enormous success.

JOHN HICKLENTON

John Hicklenton has illustrated a wide range of strips across both *2000 AD* and the *Megazine*, including *Heavy Metal Dredd, Judge Dredd, Mean Machine, Nemesis the Warlock, Pandora, Rogue Trooper, Strange Cases* and *Tharg's Future Shocks*. His work can also be seen in *Crisis!* and *Deadline*. Most recently he has provided the art for *Blood of Satanus III* in *Judge Dredd Megazine* and has worked with Pat Mills on *Zombie World*.

BRENDAN McCARTHY

Brendan McCarthy was a key early artist for *2000 AD*, and designed *Zenith* with Grant Morrison, and many of the perennially popular *ABC Warriors* with Pat Mills (and others). He also illustrated *Judge Dredd, Strontium Dog*, and *Tharg's Future Shocks*.
McCarthy's non-*2000 AD* work includes *Skin* in *Crisis, Strange Days, Paradox!*, *Freakwave* in *Vanguard Illustrated* and work for *Revolver*.

COLIN MACNEIL

Since joining *2000 AD* in 1986 **Colin MacNeil** has worked on many strips, including *Chopper* — Song of the Surfer and the infamous death of Johnny Alpha in *Strontium Dog* — The Final Solution. He went on to collaborate with John Wagner on the award winning *Judge Dredd* — America for the *Judge Dredd Megazine*. He has also worked on *Shimura, Maelstrom* and *Fiends of the Eastern Front* — Stalingrad. Most recently working on *Judge Dredd* —Total War, Cadet, Mutants in Mega-City One and Emphatically Evil: The Life and Crimes of P J Maybe. He also provided the atmospheric artwork on *Bloodquest* for Games Workshop. He also enjoys creating large abstract paintings. He says it's art therapy!

DEAN ORMSTON

Dean Ormston's otherworldly pencils first graced the *Megazine*, where he contributed to the epic *Judge Dredd* 'Judgement Day' saga, and pencilled the popular 'Raptaur'. He is the co-creator of antique oddities *Harke and Burr*, and has also pencilled *Heavy Metal Dredd, Judge Death, Missionary Man, Strange Cases*, and *Tales of Telguuth*. Ormston's other non-*2000 AD* work includes *The Crow, The Invisibles, The Monarchy* and *Sandman*. He also worked on character designs for the animated CGI series *Reboot*.